WAR, REVOLUTION & SOCIETY IN THE RIO DE LA PLATA 1808–1810

WAR, REVOLUTION & SOCIETY IN THE RIO DE LA PLATA 1808–1810

Thomas Kinder's narrative of a journey to Madeira, Montevideo and Buenos Aires

El veinte y cinco de Mayo Plaza de la Victoria en Buenos-Ayres.

Edited and with an introduction by
MALYN NEWITT

Signal

This edition first published in 2010 by
Signal Books Limited
36 Minster Road
Oxford
OX4 1LY
www.signalbooks.co.uk

A catalogue record for this book is available from the British Library.

ISBN 978–1–904955–69–6 paper

Cover design and typesetting: Baseline Arts Ltd, Oxford
Cover image: Unmounted fan-leaf, with a view of the Plaza de la Victoria in Buenos Aires, from the British Museum.
Printed in India

Contents

Acknowledgements

〜

I would like to thank the John Carter Brown Library for awarding me a Fellowship in 2007 to work on the manuscript of Thomas Kinder's travels in the Río de la Plata, and for permission to publish the text. I received a great deal of help and encouragement from the staff of the Library and from the other Fellows, for which I am very grateful.

I have benefited greatly at all stages from the advice of Norman Fiering, the former Director of the John Carter Brown Library, and from the support and scholarly comment of Professor Elizabeth Mancke.

My thanks also to Joan Newitt who drew the maps.

Maps

〜

Illustrations

〜

Glossary

Albacore	Yellow fin tuna
Arribeños	Inlanders. Troops recruited from inland
Arroba	A measure of weight equivalent to 25 lbs or 11.5 kilos
Audiencia	The highest court of justice with some administrative functions
Balandra	A one-masted sailing boat
Banda Oriental	Literally 'eastern shore'. The name given to the lands on the left bank of the Río de la Plata which today form Uruguay
Barraca	A hut or shack. Also used for a shantytown
Blandengues	Their full name *Cuerpo de Blandengues de la Frontera de Buenos Aires*. Irregular cavalry originally organised in 1780 as a force to protect the Indian frontier.
Boneta	The Atlantic bonito.
Cabildo Abierto	An open meeting of leading citizens
Chapas	The longer part of cattle horn flattened out for combs
Comercio libre	The name given to the economic policy applied by the government of Carlos IV to the American colonies which allowed them to trade with each other and with all the major ports in Spain and which liberalised some aspects of trade with Brazil
Consulado	Merchant guild (often translated as Chamber of Commerce) established by royal charter
Criollo	Creole. 'Every person born in the country, without exception as to his Parentage' (Kinder)

Cuddy	A nautical term which usually refers to a small cabin or the cook's galley. Used in this account for the common dining area of the passengers and the ship's officers.
Dulces	Sweets. 'Light pastry, barley sugar &c' (Kinder)
Estancia	Cattle ranch
Fiscales	Prosecuting attorneys attached to the Audiencia
Flota	Literally fleet. The term was used for the official trading fleets from Spain to the Indies
Guanaco	A llama
Juna	Indian fig, or Cactus-Apuntia
Junta	Committee or board
Los Niños Expósitos	Literally the Foundling Children. The name of the official printing house in Buenos Aires
Nutria	Coypu (*myocaster*)
Oidor(es)	Judge(s) of the Audiencia
Onza	A gold coin also known as *doblón de a ocho*. It had a weight of 27.0643 grammes and was notionally divided in 8 *escudos*
Pampero	A violent wind coming off the pampas
Patricios	The *Legión Patricia* was made up of soldiers recruited from Creoles in Buenos Aires.
Peninsulares	Spaniards born in Spain
Peso	The term used in South America for the Spanish silver dollar of 8 *reales*
Piastre	Another name for the *peso*
Pilotto	The game known as Pelota (*pilote* in Basque)
Porteño	Inhabitant of Buenos Aires
Quadra	One square or block of the grid of streets on which Buenos Aires was laid out
Quintal	A measure of weight equivalent to 100 lbs or 46 kilos in Spain

Real	Sometimes written *rial*. A unit of currency. There were eight *reales* to the *peso* or dollar
Reconquista	Reconquest. The term conventionally used for Liniers's campaign to force Beresford's army of occupation to surrender
Reducciónes	Reductions. The name given to the Jesuit missions in Paraguay and Brazil
Resguardo	Literally 'protection'. The Resguardo was a military unit dedicated to policing the Río de la Plata against smugglers. Kinder describes the Comandante del Resguardo as 'surveyor of the Customs'
Síndico	Or *Procurador general,* chosen annually to represent the 'needs and grievances of the community before the Cabildo
Sorrellio	Or *Zorrillo,* a skunk

Chronology

Dates relating to Thomas Kinder's voyage are prefaced with (K)

1806   18 January Baird captures Cape Colony

14 April Expedition of Popham and Beresford leaves for Río de la Plata

8 June Expedition reaches mouth of Río de la Plata

25 June Beresford lands at Quilmes

26 June Combat at Reduction

27 June Beresford crosses the Chuela and receives surrender of Buenos Aires

10 July Contents of treasury captured by British at Luján

1 August Beresford defeats Pueyrredón at Perdriel

12 August Beresford surrenders to Liniers

29 August Backhouse sails from the Cape with 2,000 men.

9 October Auchmuty sails from Britain

13 October Backhouse reaches Río de la Plata

29 October Backhouse captures Maldonado and Goretti island

12 November Craufurd sails for South America

1807   5 January Auchmuty reaches Río de la Plata

16 January Auchmuty and Backhouse land below Montevideo

19–20 January Battles outside Montevideo

20 January-3 February Siege and capture of Montevideo

10 February Arrest and deposition of Sobremonte

5 March Pack occupies Colônia do Sacramento

10 May Arrival of Whitelocke

14 June Arrival of Craufurd

28 June-5 July British attack on Buenos Aires

6 July Whitelocke signs treaty to withdraw from Río de la Plata

7 July Treaty of Tilsit

29 November Portuguese royal family leave for Brazil

24 December Beresford secures control of Madeira

31 December Madeira annexed as a British colony

1808 28 January Whitelocke's court martial

23 March Abdication of Carlos IV

24 March Verdict of Whitelocke's court martial

(K) 15 April Leaves Portsmouth on *Northumberland*

24 April Portuguese Governor of Madeira reinstated

(K) 1 May *Northumberland* reaches Madeira

2 May Insurrection in Madrid

16 May Appointment of Liniers as viceroy

6 June Joseph Bonaparte declared king of Spain

(K) 9 June Leaves Madeira

(K) 23 July Reaches Brazil

17 August Liniers informs all Intendants of events in Spain

(K) 8–25 September Resident in Montevideo

25 September Central Junta established in Spain

(K) 29 September Received by Liniers

1809 1 January Attempted coup against Liniers

2 July Arrival of Cisneros at Montevideo

27 July Junta set up in La Paz

25 October Suppression of La Paz revolt by Goyeneche

6 November Cisneros's new trade regulations announced

1810 29 January Central Junta in Spain dissolves itself

5 February Siege of Cádiz begins

(K) March Kinder leaves Buenos Aires

17 May News reaches Buenos Aires of suppression of Central Junta in Seville

21 May Summoning of Cabildo Abierto

25 May Junta elected in Buenos Aires to replace viceroy

Introduction

THE EVENTS LEADING TO THE INDEPENDENCE of the states of the Río de la Plata have been so often described, and their every detail researched in such depth, that it would seem to be impossible for there to be a fresh contemporary account of events that has escaped the attention of all historians. However, it does not appear that any historian has yet made use of Thomas Kinder's account of his stay in Montevideo and Buenos Aires between 1808 and 1810. Indeed, the only other eye-witness version of these events written in English are the letters of Alex McKinnon to George Canning, and McKinnon only arrived in the Río de la Plata in June 1809. This book, therefore, presents an important, and hitherto unpublished, account of the events immediately following the British invasions of 1806–07, including detailed eye-witness reports of the crucial events that took place between September 1808 and May 1810.

During this time Thomas Kinder met many of the most important figures in the Río de la Plata including Ruiz Huidobro, General Elío, the viceroys Santiago de Liniers and Balthazar Cisneros, and the notorious contraband trader Tomás Antonio Romero as well as many lesser characters. He was present when the first official British mission arrived after the new alliance had been made with Spain in 1808 and he describes the events which led to Elío's rebellion against the authority of the viceroy. He was witness to the attempted coup by the Cabildo of Buenos Aires on 1 January 1809 and to the arrival of Balthazar Cisneros as viceroy. He took trouble to become well informed about the events of the failed British attacks on Buenos Aires and on the position of British contraband traders in the region. His account also contains important detail about the society and economy of the cities of the Río de la Plata as well as a great deal of information about the Royal Navy and East India Company ships. A large section of the narrative describes Madeira at the time of Beresford's governorship of the island. As Beresford had commanded the first British attack on Buenos Aires and had governed the city for six weeks before being appointed to occupy and govern Madeira, Kinder's manuscript is an important source for any prospective biographer of the Marshal. Finally, Kinder appended a letter from Alexander Greaves which gives one of the most detailed first-hand accounts of the revolutionary events of May 1810.

Thomas Kinder

The name Thomas Kinder is, unfortunately, rather common and it is not always easy to decide which of the colourful events concerning men of that name can be attributed to the author of this narrative. The author was almost certainly one of the Kinders of St Albans as the records of Trinity College Oxford list him as the 'son of K of St Albans Herts gent'[1], but was he a member of the Kinder family of brewers whose rise into the ranks of the gentry can be documented in detail and who had the habit of calling their male children Thomas? A Thomas Kinder, who started out as a 'common brewer', is on record as buying the Three Horseshoes Inn in St Albans in 1737 and his son, also called Thomas, started the family brewery in 1776, which flourished until it was sold in 1868.[2] He married Elizabeth Cole who was heiress to the manor of Beaumont and set himself up as a country gentleman. His son was also Mayor of St Albans and churchwarden of Sandridge for 41 years.[3] In 1828 this Thomas Kinder, or possibly his son, was involved in a bizarre incident which achieved national notoriety. After church one Sunday, a cousin, also confusingly

1. J.Foster, *Alumni Oxoniensis* 1715–1886, 4 vols, Parkers (Oxford, 1888).
2. Allan Whitaker, *Brewers in Hertfordshire*, University of Hertfordshire Press (Hatfield, 2006) pp.22–4.
3. John Edwin Cussans, *History of Hertfordshire*, 3 vols, Chatto and Windus (London, 1870–1881), reprinted E.P. Publishing (East Ardsley, 1972) vol 3, p.295.

called Thomas Kinder and described as a respectable gentleman, went walking across some land owned by Thomas Kinder the brewer. Suddenly he fell into a pit twelve feet deep. It was only when he was missed at home that a search party was mounted and his feeble cries were heard from underground. A ladder was brought and he was duly rescued. It turned out that the pit had been dug to catch poachers and the incident became part of a national campaign against the laying of traps on private land. Reports of it appeared in almost every newspaper in Britain.[4]

Thomas Kinder the brewer bought the house known as Sandridgebury in the village of Sandridge near St Albans in 1820. He married well in 1839, his wife being Caroline Chevallier the daughter of the Reverend John Chevallier of Aspall Hall in Suffolk. John Chevallier subsequently remarried and had a daughter Frances who was the mother of Earl Kitchener. This Thomas Kinder was, therefore, the half-uncle by marriage of Kitchener of Khartoum!

And there are others, including two mayors of St Albans and the Thomas Kinder who became master of the mint in Hong Kong and Japan.

When he died on 6 June 1846 our Thomas Kinder was described as being in his sixty-fourth year. This indicates a possible birth date between 1781 and 1783. There were at least three Thomas Kinders born in those years but it is most likely that the future author of the diary was the Thomas Kinder, son of Thomas and Elizabeth Kinder, baptised on 5 August 1781 in the church of St Peter in St Albans.[5] He attended Trinity College Oxford where he matriculated in 1798 at the age of 17 and took his BA in 1802.[6] A classical Oxford education is indicated by his attempt to converse with the Portuguese in Madeira using Latin! He was, therefore, 26 years old when he went on his voyage. Kinder and Co Merchants first appear in a London Directory in 1808 as occupying premises at 18 New City Chambers Bishopsgate. As Thomas Kinder was at that time in South

4. See among many other accounts *The Times*, 15 November 1828 and 19 November 1828.
5. Hertfordshire Archives and Local Studies (HALS), Register of baptisms at St Peter's church St Albans DP 93/1/1–5.
6. *Jackson's Oxford Journal*, 6 March 1802; we later hear of him as one of the stewards at the Anniversary Meeting of Trinity College Members *Morning Chronicle*, 29 April 1819.

America and subsequently described himself as 'Thomas Kinder jun', it suggests that he had entered a family business with an elder Thomas Kinder. The firm appears at the same address in directories in 1811 and by 1817 had premises at 1 Sambrook Court, Basinghall Street. In 1820 Thomas Kinder jun & Co are at 2 Sambrook Court and in 1826 at 72 Basinghall Street where they remain until 1838 when they no longer appear in the Directories. Thomas died on 6 June 1846 at Clifton Place West Sussex Square. He and his wife, Fanny, had seven children—'chiefly daughters' as Fanny wrote to Lord Brougham in 1833.[7]

Kinder never explains why he undertook this journey in 1808 but internal evidence in the narrative suggests that his voyage as far as the Río de la Plata was not planned and his original intention had been to go to Rio de Janeiro. Having been a month in the Brazilian capital he seized the opportunity of an English warship being sent to the Río de la Plata with dispatches in August 1808.

> Judging that it offered me a most favorable opportunity of either collecting interesting information, or entering into commercial engagements, I obtained the permission both of the Admiral & of Cap[tain] Mackenzie, to take my passage in that vessel ... [I] cannot suffer so good an opportunity of visiting the Spanish Colonies, as the present to pass unseized.

He managed to equip himself with letters of recommendation to various people in Buenos Aires prior to his departure. Later, while in Montevideo, he talks of 'a temporary stay for the purpose of obtaining new ideas'. On arrival in Buenos Aires at the end of September he was presented to the viceroy and gives a longer explanation for his visit.

---

7. University College London, Brougham Papers 44,938. Fanny Kinder to Lord Brougham, St Johns Mews Fulham, 6 February 1833. The births of three of these daughters are recorded in the newspapers in 1825, 1827, 1828. The addresses recorded for the family are all in London. In 1828 they were living at Portland Place, in 1833 his wife was writing from St John's Mews Fulham, in 1844 Thomas was writing from 1 Regent Place East, Regent's Square and in 1846 from 1 Clifton Place West, Hyde Park Gardens.

The Viceroy very readily comprehended, what I have found it very difficult to instill into people both here & in Monte Video viz. that without having actually any business on hand, I am come to look about me & to acquire information. I had been told by several that it would be necessary that I should assume some distinct character which embarrassed one somewhat as it would have compelled me to enter into an explanation at length to his Excellency; as had I represented myself as a Merchant I should at once have subjected myself to be told that the regulations of the Government did not permit my being here in such a Capacity & should have been supposed to be a smuggler & had I avoided intirely the Mercantile character & represented myself as coming solely to look about me, then in case that the regulations hereafter encourage me to form an establishment I should have been liable to the imputation of practising deceit on the Viceroy.

As a result of his explanations he was able

to obtain the highest possible sanction of public authority for my safe residence here, having before explained the uneasy situation of foreigners not so circumstanced. I am therefore at present the only stranger whose residence here is so acknowledged.

From Kinder's account we learn that he was singled out for attention by Sir Sidney Smith in Rio and was able, exceptionally, to accompany Captain McKenzie on his official mission to Buenos Aires. It appears he also acted as interpreter at a meeting between Captain Lee of the *Monarch* and General Elío. All this suggests that Kinder's visit may have had some official sanction. It is known that British merchants plying their contraband trade with the Río de la Plata were sometimes entrusted with unofficial political missions. An example was James Paroissien who carried secret correspondence from Carlotta Joaquina on board the merchant ship *Mary* in November 1808. Kinder had sailed from Madeira in the same fleet that carried Lord Strangford and Sir James Gambier as Britain's ambassador and consul general to Rio and, although he was not on board the same ship, the weather permitted 'an interchange of visits and dinner parties which was very little interrupted during the whole passage.' It is quite possible that Kinder became familiar with Strangford during the voyage and was subsequently used by him to carry messages to the Río de la Plata, ironically on the same ship that was carrying Sir Sidney Smith's undoubtedly subversive dispatches.[8]

However, it is surely also no coincidence that in Montevideo Kinder stayed with Francisco Juanico and in Buenos Aires with Tomás Antonio Romero both of them among the leading local businessmen. One must conclude that Kinder was better connected, and his mission of more importance, than he was prepared openly to admit. As he himself wrote,

> I had become acquainted with most men of any estimation in Buenos Ayres & with the viceroy General Liniers, who frequently honoured me with invitations to dine at the Fort & several times made me one in his Sunday parties at a small country house about eighteen miles south of Buenos Ayres ...

He describes negotiations carried on by

> my friend Lieutenant Stow Commanding H. M. Brig *Steady* ... as the then representative of the British Government, about the English vessels in the river & the interests of British subjects embarked & ashore, [which] came ultimately to be carried on almost wholly by me.

Later, when the viceroy Cisneros published his new commercial regulations in November 1809 Kinder claims that he assumed, unofficially, the role of a consul and called a meeting of British traders to coordinate their response.

---

8. For the rivalry of Strangford and Smith, see J.Street, 'Lord Strangford and the Rio de la Plata, 1808–1815', *The Hispanic American Historical Review*, 33, 4 (1953) pp.477–510.

Kinder went to great lengths to inform himself of the contraband trade and how it operated. As he himself explains,

> I had as good information as the nature of the case would admit, being personally acquainted with the Supercargoes of most of them as well as with their Spanish consignees, and could detail was it necessary the means resorted to in most of the instances when I have marked them as trading by contraband and several of the Supercargoes permitted me to take from their invoices the gross amount of their investments. With respect to the amount of the others I obtained it by enquiries through those acquainted with the parties concerned and I believe that I am not wrong above five per Cent of the gross amount.

He also used his contacts in Buenos Aires to get hold of official information. This included lists of illegal trading ships entering the ports, the composition of the military units, the complete budget for the viceroyalty and the new commercial regulations published by the viceroy Cisneros.

The most mysterious circumstance in this story is the absence of Thomas Kinder's name from the list of passengers on the *Northumberland*. There can be little doubt that he was on this ship as the information he gives about his fellow passengers and about the Chinese is borne out exactly by the ship's passenger list. So why was his name not included? Most of the passengers appeared to have come on board at Gravesend whereas he boarded at Portsmouth, so perhaps his name was never added to the list. There are, however, three other possibilities. In the passenger list there is a mysterious entry which reads 'William Wooden [or Woolen] native'. Kinder makes no mention of this passenger and it is a possibility that this odd entry in some way relates to him. The other possibilities are that he was on some special mission which required anonymity or that he was unofficially taken on board as a passenger, with his fare being pocketed by the captain, and therefore not entered in the official ledger.

Whatever the motives for the journey, the contacts Kinder made in the Río de la Plata helped determine his future activities as a businessman.

Much of the information he acquired was shared with Robert Staples, with whom he lodged during part of his stay in Buenos Aires, and who acted as Britain's first consul in the Río de la Plata. Staples incorporated much of the same information in his consular report of 1812, translating into English the financial balance sheet that appears in Spanish in Kinder's narrative.[9] Staples later became consul in Mexico but was forced to resign in 1824 because of the involvement of his firm, Messrs Staples, in contracting a loan for the Mexican government. George Canning, the Foreign Secretary, wrote on this occasion that 'it is one of the express conditions of the Consular Office in Spanish America…that the holders of it should abstain from all commercial dealings.'[10]

The nature of Kinder's business after his return from South America seems to have been various. In 1819 he is listed as a member of a committee of London 'merchants, manufacturers and shipowners' opposed to the Foreign Enlistment Bill because 'its operation may prove extremely injurious to the manufacturing and commercial interests of this country in its intercourse with Spanish America.'[11] He also acted as agent for ships bound for South America; in 1821 he is acting as agent 'for freight or passage' on board the brig *Bull Dog* sailing from Liverpool.[12] He became an associate of Robert Staples in 1823, acquiring an interest in the Real del Monte mines in Mexico, acting as agent in London to raise money to buy out the mine's owner the Conde de Regla. Kinder fell out with the partners in this enterprise and his attempt to stop the formation of the Real del Monte Company resulted in his unsuccessfully suing John Taylor in Chancery in 1825.[13] The next year he is cited as one of the Directors of the

9. National Archives (Kew) FO 72 157 Robert Staples to Castlereagh, 22 June 1812.
10. George Canning to Lionel Hervey 20 July 1824 in Charles K. Webster, *Britain and the Independence of Latin America 1812–1830: select documents from the Foreign Office Archives*, 2 vols, Oxford University Press (Oxford, 1938) pp.455–6; R.A. Humphreys, *British Consular Reports on the Trade and Politics of Latin America 1824–1826*, Camden Third Series vol 63, Royal Historical Society (London, 1940) p.331; Dorothy Burne Goebel, 'British Trade to the Spanish Colonies, 1796–1823', *The American Historical Review*, 43, 2, (1938) p.315.
11. *Morning Chronicle*, 24 May 1819.
12. *The Times*, 19 December 1821.
13. Robert Randall, *Real del Monte: A British Mining Venture in Mexico*, Institute of Latin American Studies and University of Texas Press (Austin and London, 1972) pp.31–44; Anon, *An Inquiry into Plans, Progress and Policy of the American Mining Companies*, Murray (London, 1825).

Peruvian Mining Company whose company address was at Kinder's offices in Basinghall Street. Referring to this venture, the *Quarterly Review* wrote "'news from the mines" [is] regularly manufactured from St James' Street down to Charing Cross, to catch the city gulls, who in return lay their daily baits for the gentlemen of the West.'[14] In 1825 he purchased two large estates in Mexico and in 1826–7 he and Staples are financing the speculations of General Wavell in Mexico.[15]

Between 1822 and 1825 he was principal contractor for the Peruvian loan and successfully sued his bankers before the Lord Chief Justice in the King's Bench in December 1823 because they refused to honour his cheques.[16] On this occasion he was represented Lord Brougham. Payments on the loan had to be suspended in October 1825 and in 1826 he had to tell shareholders that he did not have the funds to pay the half yearly dividend. In 1824 he was contractor for the Manchester and Salford Equitable Loan[17] and in 1838 was a member of the London Committee of the Midland Grand Junction Railway.[18]

In 1832 Kinder went to Mexico and spent three years unsuccessfully trying to recover property which he and Robert Staples had purchased and which he alleged was valued over £200,000.[19] He wrote a long and detailed account of Mexico in the 1830s which is located in the Brougham papers.[20] In 1842 he took action against Lord Ashburton[21], who had been appointed ambassador to the US, and others over the property, alleging that those he accused had bribed deputies in the Mexican legislature to pass an act forbidding foreigners to own property. The case was heard in

14. Quoted in Anon, *An Inquiry into Plans, Progress and Policy of the American Mining Companies*, Murray (London, 1825) p.115. See also Henry English, *A General Guide to the Companies formed for working Foreign Mines*, Boosey and Sons (London, 1825) pp.93–4.
15. National Archives (Kew), E 192 5 Staples to General Wavell 10 March 1827; Holdsworth to Kinder 23 June 1826; Kinder to Holdsworth 6 September 1826
16. *Caledonian Mercury*, 28 December 1826.
17. *The Examiner*, 26 August 1838.
18. University College London, Brougham Papers, 45,923 Kinder to Brougham, Mexico 10 June 1833; 30,655 Kinder to Brougham, Mexico 1 October 1834; 4,257 Kinder to Brougham, Royal Institution 5 July 1841.
19. University College London, Brougham Papers 30,656, Observations on Mexico, 22 November 1834.
20. University College London, Brougham Papers 30,656, Observations on Mexico, 22 November 1834.
21. *Bristol Mercury*, 12 February 1842.

1844 and Ashburton and his fellow accused were found not guilty.[22] Kinder did not let the matter drop and asked the Foreign Office to intervene. When Lord Aberdeen refused, he petitioned parliament. In pursuit of his claims in Mexico Kinder approached, at different times, Lord Palmerston, Lord Brougham, Lord Aberdeen and finally the prime minister, Sir Robert Peel. His vain attempts to get the British government to act to protect his rights in Mexico raises interesting questions about the nature of what historians have called 'the imperialism of free trade'.[23] A long letter he wrote to Peel in 1844 is included as Appendix B and sets out many of the issues as he saw them. It is the authentic voice of a man who had earlier complained to Lord Brougham that he was treated rather 'like an alien enemy of the realm and a personal adversary than a British subject, for no other reason than that I have complained of wrongs sustained abroad and given a little trouble.'[24] This matter remained unresolved at his death in June 1846.

The International Context

When Thomas Kinder sailed from Portsmouth in April 1808 Britain's relations with the Iberian states were undergoing important changes. In the eighteenth century Britain had maintained a close alliance with Portugal based on four treaties which had been concluded between the two countries between 1641 and 1703 and which gave the British a privileged position in Portugal's overseas trade. The British merchant community in Portugal and Madeira enjoyed religious freedom, organised itself as a factory and appointed its own judge conservator. In exchange for granting Portuguese wine preferential tariffs, the British were able to have relatively unrestricted access to Portuguese markets and through Portugal to the markets of Brazil. Britain provided a guarantee of Portugal's independence and in return was able to use the magnificent harbour of Lisbon as an advance base for the Royal Navy.

22. *The Times*, 2 July and 3 July 1844.
23. The relations of British bankers and bondholders in Mexico with the British Government is discussed in Barbara Tenenbaum, 'Merchants, Money and Mischief', *The Americas*, 35, 5, (1979) pp.317–339.
24. University College London, Brougham Papers 4,257 Kinder to Brougham, Royal Institution 5 July 1841.

As a result of these agreements trade between Britain, Portugal and their empires rapidly expanded. Portugal's empire in the Atlantic was, in terms of territory, the largest European empire, its vast land mass in Brazil, Maranhão and Angola exceeding that of France, Britain and even Spain. In addition Portugal controlled the strategically important islands of Cape Verde, Azores and Madeira which commanded the sea routes from Europe to the South Atlantic. Ever since Portugal established its independence from Spain in 1640, it had faced a dilemma in European power politics. Threatened on its land borders by Spain, which after the accession of the Bourbons in 1699 was in ever closer alliance with France, it became increasingly dependent on Britain for its defence, but the alliance with Britain, while it offered protection to Brazil and the other colonies, left the land frontiers exposed to invasion from Spain. Although Portugal became involved in the War of the Spanish Succession and eventually in the Seven Years war in alliance with Britain, its colonial possessions remained largely free from outside threats. The wars brought on by the French Revolution, however, presented this dilemma in an especially acute form.

Since the outbreak of the war against France in 1793 British policy makers had disagreed on the best means of confronting the old enemy. While some sought to build continental coalitions, others believed Britain should concentrate on acquiring the overseas possessions of the enemy as had been done successfully during the wars of the eighteenth century. The rationale for the latter policy was that, although it would not by itself defeat the French, it would weaken France and its allies economically and help Britain to retain vital markets for its exports—a factor that came to be of increasing importance as France occupied more and more European territory and closed its ports to British goods. So, during the 1790s the British war effort was focussed largely on expeditions to capture West Indian islands, on war in the Mediterranean and on securing the territories of the East India Company against French subversion. This last policy had led to British forces being sent to occupy Portuguese Goa in 1799. When the French had invaded the Netherlands in 1795 the then stadholder, Willem V, had surrendered the Dutch colonial possessions to

Britain. The British had duly taken control of the Cape, Ceylon and Indonesia, a success which compensated for the failure to secure French Saint Domingue. The Cape was returned to the new Batavian Republic in 1802 but, after the renewal of the war the following year, Britain moved to re-annex what was seen as the strategic key to navigation between the Atlantic and Indian Oceans.

After the collapse of the Peace of Amiens Britain had to face an effective coalition of France and Spain, who increased their pressure on Portugal to close its ports to British commerce and Lisbon to the British fleet. The Portuguese prince regent, Dom João, was forced to pay a huge indemnity to secure his country's continued neutrality. Britain, for its part, made it clear that, should Portugal be invaded, its defence could not be guaranteed and its empire would be in danger.[25] Meanwhile Britain was faced with the prospect of a united French and Spanish fleet competing for the control of the seas and of Spain's South American territories falling into French hands and becoming completely closed to British commerce. So, as Napoleon assembled his army of invasion and the rival fleets manoeuvred in the Atlantic during 1805, Britain prepared once again to occupy the Cape. General Sir David Baird sailed at the end of August 1805 escorted by a fleet commanded by Sir Home Popham and with Brigadier General William Carr Beresford as his second in command. Baird and Beresford landed at the Cape early in 1806 and on 18 January received the surrender of the colony.

The ease with which the Cape had been captured encouraged the mercurial Popham to concoct a scheme for a raid on the Spanish settlements in the Río de la Plata. This idea had been in Popham's mind ever since 1804 when he had met Francisco de Miranda, a Spanish adventurer who was trying to persuade the British government to support an insurrection in South America.[26] In fact the idea of an attack on the Río de la Plata had been increasingly canvassed in commercial circles ever since

25. Martin Robson, 'British Intervention in Portugal, 1793–1808', *Historical Research*, 76 (2003) pp.93–107.
26. For a recent discussion of these plans and the origin of San Martín's campaigns of liberation see Rodolfo H. Terragno, *Maitland & San Martín*, Universidad Nacional de Quilmes, (Buenos Aires, 1998).

the Seven Years War and had taken on the complexion almost of a crusade. An anonymous book, published in London in 1806, had suggested that the Río de la Plata region would assume great importance for Britain with the inevitable decline of the West Indies that would follow the abolition of the slave trade.

> The temperature of the climate is such as to supersede the necessity of cultivating the land by African labourers. Free and voluntary labourers could be employed, because the mildness and serenity of the climate would ensure health even to European cultivators, and afford abundant returns. With capitals, activity, and a spirit of adventure, none of which, on so inviting and tempting an occasion would be wanting, the plains of the Río de la Plata might be made to yield an ample profit to the capitalist, comfort and prosperity to the inhabitants and a large revenue to the government. Here the poor emigrants from the highlands and islands of Scotland, and from Ireland, would find a real asylum from poverty, want, oppression, and slavery. The hardships and horrors which they often, nay, commonly encounter, when they go under the indentures to America, are such as to inspire regret, and a longing after their bleak and howling mountains, though now converted into sheep-walks.

It went on to predict a future painted in ideological colours every bit as vivid as those propagated by the French Revolutionaries.

> A people inhabiting Río de la Plata, and enjoying at the same time the blessings of a free government, would be a new and grand experiment in human nature: an experiment from which we might reasonably augur the happiest and the most glorious effects. [27]

---

27. Anon, *A Summary Account of the viceroyalty of Buenos-Ayres or, La Plata including its geographical position, climate, aspect of the country natural productions, commerce, government, and State of society and Manners. Extracted from the best authorities.* R. Dutton (London, 1806) pp.41, 42–3.

The Viceroyalty of La Plata

The Spanish settlements along the Río de la Plata were indeed a tempting target for, ever since the creation of the viceroyalty of La Plata in 1776, silver from the Peruvian mines had been shipped to Spain through Buenos Aires. The viceroyalty had been created as a response to the growing concern in Madrid for the security of its empire. Since the sixteenth century the Río de la Plata settlements had been part of the viceroyalty of Peru. Not only were they governed from Lima but their commerce was, in theory, all directed towards Peru from where they received the imports which came via Panama and across the Andes. This arrangement made no geographical sense but what mainly concerned the Spanish authorities was that the Río de la Plata ports had become the focus for an extensive contraband trade. Contraband not only undermined the Spanish trade monopoly but ensured that there was a constant outward flow of bullion. As the export of locally produced commodities was forbidden, the only way the contraband traders could be paid was in silver. Silver smuggled from Peru to avoid the tight controls and taxes of the Crown, found a ready outlet among the privateers and illicit traders whose ships frequented the Río de la Plata. Even more serious from Spain's point of view were the encroachments of the Portuguese who had established a port at Colônia do Sacramento opposite Buenos Aires in 1680. Sacramento became the chief resort of the smugglers and the gateway through which the Brazilian Portuguese penetrated Spanish markets with their sugar, tobacco and slaves. Securing control of Sacramento became a major objective of Spanish policy and the port changed hands constantly throughout the eighteenth century. Apart from the Brazilian Portuguese, it was ships' captains from Europe and, after 1783, the United States who braved the hidden shoals of Spanish bureaucracy.

The authorities in Madrid were under continual pressure to reform the commercial regime. In 1748 the old *flota* system for organising colonial trade had been abolished but it was not until the reign of Carlos III (1759–88) that a radical overhaul of the whole structure of Spain's empire was undertaken. Between the end of the Seven Years War and 1779 a series of measures were introduced which collectively became known as *comercio libre*. By these decrees the trade of the Río de la Plata was gradually opened to all the major sea ports in Spain and then to other colonial ports, although free trade with non-Spaniards remained forbidden. Even this was breached in 1791 when the import of slaves from Brazil was legalised and in 1798 when permission was given to *porteño* merchants to buy ships from Brazilians and North Americans.[28] Limited as it was, *comercio libre* led to a rapid expansion of the economy of the Río de la Plata and in particular to the mass export of hides, horns and other animal products.

Even so, it was the threat posed by the Portuguese that precipitated the major change in direction of the Spanish government. In the 1750 Treaty of Madrid a new boundary agreement had been signed by which Portugal agreed to give up Sacramento in return for Spanish recognition of Portuguese expansion in the interior beyond the old Tordesillas line. However, this had been followed in 1763 by a restoration of Sacramento to Portugal at the end of the Seven Years War and by increased British interest in the Río de la Plata and the Malvinas (Falkland Islands). It was concern for the defence of this region that eventually persuaded Carlos III in 1776 to establish the new viceroyalty and to send a major military expedition to wrest Sacramento from Portugal once and for all. The time was well chosen, for Britain was preoccupied with the incipient revolt of some thirteen of its American colonies and Sacramento fell once again, this time finally, into Spanish hands. The area of the new viceroyalty, which was established in 1776, was expanded to include upper Peru and the silver mines so that its revenue would be commensurate with the costs of its defence. The establishment of the viceroyalty was followed in 1782 by the Ordinance of Intendants which placed the provinces of the viceroyalty under French-style intendants who assumed the role of the former provincial governors.[29] One of the first of these to be appointed was the Marqués de Sobremonte who

---

28. Jerry W. Cooney, 'Oceanic commerce and Platine Merchants, 1796–1806: the Challenge of War', *The Americas*, 45, 4 (1989) pp.509–524

29. The establishment of the new viceroyalty is discussed in detail in John Lynch, *Spanish Colonial Administration, 1782–1810*, Greenwood (New York, 1958) chapter 1.

became intendant of Córdoba. After 1783 a Real Audiencia was also established to keep a close watch over the comings and goings in the river.

The new viceroyalty had an immense hinterland and controlled both banks of the Río de la Plata. Its capital, Buenos Aires, at once became one of the most important ports of Spanish America and its economic activity rapidly expanded. By 1795 330,000 hides a year were being exported and the revenues from trade passing through Buenos Aires had risen from 114,000 *pesos* in 1779 to 732,000 *pesos* in 1795. The population of the city meanwhile doubled and stood at 42,000 at the time of the British invasion in 1806. In recognition of the importance of the region's commerce a *consulado* or chamber of commerce was established in 1794 with Manuel Belgrano as its first secretary.[30]

The outbreak of war between Britain and Spain in 1797 severely restricted direct trade and exports to Spain fell from 5.4 million *pesos* in 1796 to just 100,000 *pesos* in 1798. This made the merchants of the city more than ever dependent on the contraband traders and on the neutral Portuguese to the north. In order to mitigate the depression caused by the war the Spanish authorities allowed trade to be carried on through neutrals. Among the most influential agents who brokered this 'neutral' trade were Thomas O'Gorman (whose Mauritian wife became Viceroy Liniers's mistress), the American William Pius White (who was one of Kinder's informants) and Tomás Antonio Romero with whom Kinder lodged in Buenos Aires.

The British Invasion[31]

The viceroyalty of Río de la Plata was believed by the British to be poorly defended and Commodore Popham clearly envisaged plundering Spanish silver just as Drake had aimed to do with his expeditions to Panama and

---

30. For a good summary of the economic changes see David Rock, *Argentina 1516–1982*, University of California Press (Berkeley, 1985).

31. Many accounts of the British attack on the Río de la Plata have been written. See especially Ernestina Costa, *English Invasion of the River Plate*, Kraft (Buenos Aires, 1937); John D. Grainger, *The Royal Navy in the River Plate 1806–1807*, Scolar Press for the Navy Records Society (Aldershot, 1996); José María Bueno Carrera, *La Defensa del Río de la Plata*, Almena (Madrid, 2000); Ian Fletcher, *The Waters of Oblivion*, Spellmount (Stroud, 2006).

Nombre de Dios in the sixteenth century. Popham claimed that his scheme had been informally approved in discussions with Pitt and Grenville and this was enough to convince Baird to detach troops from the Cape garrison for the raid and to appoint his second-in-command, Beresford, to lead them.

Without any authorisation from London, Popham and Beresford sailed on 14 April 1806 and touched at St Helena where they took on board more troops and sent dispatches to London asking for orders. The little force, numbering only 1,400 men, reached the mouth of the Río de la Plata on 8 June. The original target had been Montevideo but Popham urged an attack on the capital and in the end, as Beresford wrote later, 'it was our proper lack of food that decided us to take Buenos Aires.'[32] After surveying the river Beresford landed his forces a few miles downstream from Buenos Aires on 25 June. The following day, a large force of irregular cavalry confronted the British outside the village of Reduction but were driven off allowing Beresford to reach the River Chuelo which barred his advance on the city. On 27 June Beresford seized enough boats to bridge the river and drove the Spanish forces from a fortified position on the opposite bank.

It was at this point that the Spanish viceroy, the Marqués de Sobremonte, having sent the contents of the various treasuries and his own personal money into the interior, left with his cavalry bodyguard for Córdoba, appointing Hilarión de Quintana as governor of Buenos Aires to negotiate with Beresford. Beresford refused to discuss terms and demanded the unconditional surrender of the city to which Quintana had to accede. On 6 July Beresford sent a small force after Sobremonte which took possession of the contents of the treasury at the town of Luján 50 miles from Buenos Aires, returning with it to the city on 10 July. Over a million dollars in silver were then dispatched to London.

Thomas Kinder was not, of course, present at these events but they were still very fresh in the minds of the people he met in the city. His main source of information was 'an American Gentleman who furnished

---

32. Beresford to Baird 2 July 1806 quoted in Ernestina Costa, *English Invasion of the River Plate*, pp.26–7.

me with part of these particulars.' This American was presumably William Pius White, a contraband trader, who had provided Whitelocke's army with information and whose house had for a time been the general's headquarters. Kinder's account of Beresford's capture of the city gives a vivid picture of how the events were remembered two years later. It was believed in Britain that Beresford's success had been due to the 'inclinations of the People, desirous to better their condition from a Change of Government' but he concludes that the failure to defend the city was mainly due to apathy and incompetence.

> Never having seen an enemy, [they] had no conception of what it was. When the Gen[eral] landed, no attempts were made to oppose him, or even to reconnoitre his Army, nothing further being known than the reports of the Country people, or what is much the same thing, the exagerations of a body of men on horseback, whom they are pleased to call Cavalry... These men fled at the first discharge, & though not a man was hurt, swore that the bullets rained upon them, that there were six thousand of the Enemy, all Grenadiers as big as Patagonians... The Spanish horsemen might be 2000 in number, but not one of them could be brought to face the English, flying into the country in all directions.

Kinder's American informant then added some picturesque detail that had no doubt been improved in the telling over the previous two years. 'One of the horsemen gallop[ed] by his window, after the action, at full speed, of whom he learnt afterwards that he kept his way with all possible expedition till he got to Cordova, 400 miles into the Interior.' The next day he witnessed 3,000 Spanish infantry turning out to defend the city; the colonel

> halted his Column merely to have a Gossip with these two men in a Gig. He told them that the Viceroy had ordered him out to occupy the entrances into the City but that it was only sacrificing the lives of the men, as resistance was of no use. Just then a horseman arrived to report the advance of the English, adding some nonsense about the Caps of

the Grenadiers & their regular encampment in tents the night before, & their ferocious appearance, at which our 2 Spaniards shook their heads, & agreed it was all over with them.

Sobremonte, Kinder learned, was 'struck with the general panic, & fled without even seeing the enemy,' while 'those who then participated in his fears, & acted the same dastardly part, have circulated the cry, that he is a Traitor.' Ineffective as Sobremonte was as a viceroy and captain general he had, in fact, supervised operations until Beresford had reached the outskirts of the city. At one level the viceroy's actions were sensible and responsible. To remove the treasury and retreat to a safe place in the interior where the regular troops of the viceroyalty could be assembled to mount a counterattack was a rational if unheroic response[33] and the viceroy, as captain general, did subsequently attempt to lead his forces against Auchmuty's army when it was marching to attack Montevideo.

Beresford was well aware of his precarious position, attempting with only 1,400 men to hold a city of 40,000 inhabitants, while the colonial army and thousands of irregulars were still at large. Moreover, the shallowness of the Río de la Plata meant that Popham's warships could not get near enough to the city to lend practical support. So Beresford decided that the only sensible course to take was to establish a government acceptable to the population. He decided that although the contents of the public treasuries could be considered the spoils of war, private property, including privately owned bullion and ships, would not be touched. He also guaranteed freedom of religion and the continuation in office of government functionaries. So far so good, and in his proclamation he expressed the hope that

all good citizens will unite with him in their exertions to keep the town quiet and peaceable, as they may now enjoy a free trade, and all the

---

33. Almazan gives a rather more favourable account of Sobremonte's actions than is usually presented by English historians. See Bernardo Lozier Almazan, *Beresford Gobernador de Buenos Aires*, Galerna (Buenos Aires, 1994) pp. 54–59.

advantages of a commercial intercourse with Great Britain, where no oppression exists, and which he understands has been the only thing wanting by the rich provinces of Buenos Ayres, and the inhabitants of South America in general, to make it the most prosperous country in the world.[34]

Historians have been critical of the way Beresford exercised his authority, and Kinder offers the observation that, 'I have heard many Spaniards say, that had Gen[eral] B[eresford] possessed the talents of a Politician as well as those of a General, he might have kept it until the arrival of succours.' In declaring Buenos Aires annexed by Britain Beresford had turned his back on any idea of encouraging an independence movement. This was very much in accordance with British policy and later instructions issued by the British government confirmed this course of action. However, it meant that he lost the opportunity of dividing the population and separating the creoles from the peninsular Spanish. An anonymous author, writing in 1808 after Beresford's return from South America, clearly identified the importance of the independence issue: 'were we to declare the country independent of Spain, under the protection of the British Government, there is not a man among them but would fly to us with joy, and regard us as protectors.'[35] However, the fact that he opened the port to British commerce, but not more generally to the commerce of all nations, created the impression that the closed commercial regime of Spain was being replaced by an equally closed commercial regime which favoured the British.

As soon as news of the expedition reached London and the Cape an expeditionary force of 3,000 men began to assemble in London under Sir Samuel Auchmuty, while Baird dispatched 2,000 men from Cape Town as reinforcements under Colonel Backhouse at the end of August. Meanwhile resistance to the British was being organised in Buenos Aires

---

34. Missing footnote
35. Anon, *Notes on the viceroyalty of La Plata, in South America; with a sketch of the manners and character of the inhabitants, collected during a residence in the city of Monte Video, by a Gentleman recently returned from it* Stockdale (London, 1808) p.109.

and Montevideo. Although Kinder noted that 'he [Beresford] & his Officers are generally liked here,' Beresford's rule had the effect of uniting the inhabitants of the two cities in seeking to expel the British. In the countryside cavalry forces were assembling under Juan Martín de Pueyrredón, the *porteños* with the encouragement of the church were systematically harassing the British troops, while a French naval officer in Spanish service, Santiago de Liniers, was given the task of organising an army of reconquest by the governor of Montevideo. Beresford knew some of what was happening around him and on 1 August dispersed Pueyrredón's forces at Perdriel outside the city, but neither he nor Popham was able to prevent Liniers crossing the river on 3 August. The fight for Buenos Aires began on 10 August and ended with Beresford's surrender two days later. According to Kinder, 'when the number of the English became known, & it was seen that they were no bigger than other men, every one became ashamed of his former pusillanimous conduct.' Then, fearing the punishment that might follow if Spain ever regained control, 'when the present Viceroy attempted to retake the place, he was joined by numbers sufficient to ensure success.'

Kinder has little to say about the controversial events that followed the British surrender—the apparent disregard of the terms of surrender by the Spanish and the escape of Beresford and Colonel Pack from captivity—and concludes his account by saying, 'it is a common observation that to his invasion is owing the present freedom of the Country from a state of foreign subjection' and, with rather less judgment, 'if ever the Colony is again governed by the Mother-country according to laws which check her prosperity as heretofore, the experiment [of British rule] would certainly succeed.'

The Fall of Maldonado and Montevideo

On 9 October 1806, two months after Beresford's surrender, Colonel Backhouse reached the Río de la Plata and on 29 October, in co-operation with Popham, captured Maldonado to use as a base for future operations. On 5 January 1807 Auchmuty's force arrived and joined forces with Backhouse. The army, which now numbered around 5,000 men, evacuated Maldonado and headed for Montevideo, landing just down river from the city on 16 January. On 19 January the British met a large Spanish force commanded by Sobremonte himself who had arrived with reinforcements. In the ensuing battle the Spanish were defeated, the viceroy leading the flight with his cavalry. A second battle was fought on 20 January and again the British were victorious and Sobremonte's cavalry, this time in the absence of the viceroy, again fled from the field.

Auchmuty now began formal siege operations while Liniers in Buenos Aires tried to organise a relief force. The siege lasted from 20 January to 3 February when the city was taken by storm. As was reported to the House of Commons on 16 April 1807, 'although Monte Video was taken by assault in the morning, yet the shops were open, and the inhabitants seen going about their business, without any embarrassment, before 12 o'clock the same day.'[36] Auchmuty sent the governor of Montevideo, Ruiz Huidobro, and some of his officers to Britain as prisoners of war. A month later, on 5 March, Auchmuty sent Denis Pack to take possession of Sacramento, immediately opposite Buenos Aires. Sobremonte was arrested and deposed on 10 February by a Junta that had taken power in Buenos Aires consisting of the Cabildo and Liniers as commandant of the armed forces.

After the fall of Montevideo Auchmuty summoned Liniers to surrender Buenos Aires, a demand which was contemptuously rejected.[37] Auchmuty and Liniers never enjoyed the good relations that had existed

---

36. *A Narrative of the Operations of a small British Force under the command of Brigadier-General Sir Samuel Auchmuty, employed in the Reduction of Monte Video on the River Plate AD 1807*, Written by a 'Field Officer on the Staff in South America.' Stockdale (London, 1807), p.55.

37. See copy of Auchmuty's letter dated 26 February 1807 and Liniers' reply in National Archives WO 1 162, Sir Samuel Auchmuty to Viceroy or persons professing the supreme authority, Monte Video, 26 February 1807.

between Beresford and the French general and in his account of the campaign Auchmuty wrote that:

> the Spaniards in South America are superstitious to a wonderful degree, which places them entirely under the dominion of the priests and this crafty Frenchman, whose influence and popularity is sufficiently proved by his usurpation of the government of Buenos Ayres, to the exclusion of the Viceroy; who since its recapture, has not been permitted to return to that metropolis.[38]

Kinder reached Montevideo about eighteen months after the siege and, again, was able to glean a lot of information from those who had taken part in the fighting or who had witnessed Auchmuty's capture of the city. Introduced to Bernardo Lecoq, who had commanded the Montevideo garrison in the battle on 20 January, he comments

> he is about 72 years of age, and by no means differing materially from any other man of his years. The Spaniards all ridicule the Idea of such a man being sent out to fight Sir S. Achmuty & efforts were made to prevent him, but he was senior & obstinate. During the battle he held his snuff box in his hand when a Cannon ball shot off the left side of his hat. He nevertheless took his snuff very composedly, because (as I ventured to suppose) he was probably not immediately aware of what had occurred. Be that as it may, he certainly showed firmness enough to entitle him to great praise on that account.

By the time Kinder reached Montevideo Britain had become Spain's ally against Napoleon and that circumstance, together with the decisive victory over Whitelocke's army, had dissipated any sense of bitterness the earlier fighting might have caused. Kinder found huge admiration for the British and especially for Auchmuty.

---

38. *A Narrative of the Operations of a small British Force under the command of Brigadier-General Sir Samuel Auchmuty...* p.15.

Repeated enquiries were made of me respecting very many of the individuals of our nation who were at Monte V[ideo] while it was in our possession, as well Mercantile Men as Naval & Military. Sir S. Achmuty is respected by all in the highest possible degree.[39] The good order he preserved in his army & the precautions he took effectually to prevent any of those evils so greatly to be feared in a city taken by storm have endeared his name to every Spaniard & to use the words of one of them 'They all loved him as though he had actually been a Spanish General'. They greatly blame Whitelocke for the disorders said to have been committed by his troops during the attack upon B[uenos] A[ires] & many say that Sir S. Achmuty would have taken the city with half the number of men... and would not have suffered the same excesses to be committed.

Later he repeats this opinion as his own, 'Sir S. Achmuty would probably have induced surrender [of Buenos Aires] without the expence of a single cannon ball.'

Whitelocke's Surrender

Soon after Auchmuty had left Britain, the government, now deprived of the guiding hand of Pitt who had died in January 1806, decided on a second ambitious scheme to conquer the Spanish colonies. William Windham, the Secretary for War and the Colonies, devised a plan to send an army which was to conquer Chile and to cooperate with the forces in the Río de la Plata. Robert Craufurd was appointed to command this expedition which consisted of 4,300 men. He sailed on 12 November 1806. At the end of March 1807 Lieutenant General John Whitelocke, who had been appointed to overall command of what was rapidly

---

39. Eighteen years later the British Consul in Monte Video could write, 'There are also a few who had been admirers of British discipline whilst this place was in possession of General Sir Samuel Auchmuty, who are now anxious for British occupation.' Thomas Samuel Hood to George Canning, Monte Video, 31 January 1825 in Humphreys, *British Consular Reports on the Trade and Politics of Latin America 1824–1826*, p.80.

becoming a large army, left Britain with 1,800 additional reinforcements and reached Río de la Plata on 10 May 1807. A month later, on 14 June, Craufurd's force, diverted from its original destination, also arrived.

Whitelocke's assault on Buenos Aires began with a crossing of the river and a landing at Ensenada thirty miles downstream from Buenos Aires on 28 June. After a difficult march the advance guard outflanked the Spanish defence and inflicted a severe defeat on Liniers at Coralle on the outskirts of the city. This victory was not followed up and the assault on the city only began on 5 July. Suffering heavy losses, the British forces captured the Plaza de Toros and the Residencia, taking a thousand prisoners and thirty guns. However, the columns that entered the centre of the city were trapped in isolated buildings and forced to surrender. In all the army lost 3,000 men killed, wounded or taken prisoner. On 6 July Whitelocke accepted a ceasefire and negotiated terms for the exchange of prisoners and the withdrawal of his army from both Buenos Aires and Montevideo.

On his return to Britain, Whitelocke was court martialled, the hearings beginning on 28 January 1808 and the sentence being handed down on 24 March, only three weeks before Thomas Kinder left for South America.

Once settled in Buenos Aires at the end of September 1808, Kinder established contact with as many of the leading figures in the city as he could, including William Pius White, Santiago de Liniers, who by then had become viceroy, and many of the officers who had fought the British. The events surrounding Whitelocke's assault on the city were still fresh in people's minds and the outcome of the court martial was known, so Kinder felt it was unnecessary to give another account of the events. However, as with Montevideo, he records some of the opinions he heard from the Spanish.

All agree in the brutality & incapacity of this man [Whitelocke]. After the capitulation, he was invited to dine in the fort with Liniers, who likewise invited the Staff of both Armies. On entering the fort, he observed the Spanish Officers collected together, who as at present owing to the great scarcity of European manufactures, were probably very ill clothed. He expressed his surprise to a Mr O'Reilly who was in conversation with him at his being invited to dine with all these blackguards. He probably knew that he was not understood.

Another officer told Kinder that the 'ill success of the attack [was due] entirely to the badness of the plan & the incapacity of the General.'

However, Kinder also found some sympathy for Whitelocke. The governor of Montevideo, Francisco Xavier Elío,

who was at Buenos Ayres the whole time & to whom the people of Monte Vedio attribute the greatest part of the success, has delivered …his testimony in favour of General Whitelocke, in order that it may be made any use of in England in any way that can be made of any advantage or consolation to him. … The Spaniards shake their heads & say it is extremely severe that he should be deprived of all his honours & declared incapable & *unworthy* to serve his Majesty in future, & set up partial defences for him by declaring that others deserved worse of their country than he did; some being inveterate against Gower, some against Crawford, & nearly all against Pack.

The Spanish were particularly severe in their comments on Craufurd, which are significant in view of the high reputation Craufurd has always enjoyed among historians of the Peninsular War.

They all agree that he might have withdrawn his Column along the beach, or even have joined other detachments by the street with little loss. If I may judge from the manner in which the Officer who received his sword related the transaction to me, that officer thinks his conduct on that occasion very pusillanimous. The Commandant of the Grenadiers of Liniers[40] told me that Colonel Crawford addressed himself to him, enquiring in terms of great anxiety if he was safe from

---

40. Juan Florencio Terrada.

personal danger. This took place in the confusion that ensued immediately on the surrender of his Brigade, when the Mob entered the Church & were pillaging the Soldiers of their Caps, of muskets & bayonets in the utmost confusion. That officer answered that [he] would be responsible for the B[r]igadier's safety, & offered him his Arm protected by which he escaped from the Mob... The Commandant expressed to me his opinion that Crawford was a man of the most attainments of any in this expedition, but I observed that though he probably did not intend that I should draw any inferences discreditable to the bravery of that officer from what he related to me, he abstained from any opinion on that head, or as to his military talents.

The British forces in the Río de la Plata had from the first suffered from desertions, a severe problem which generally tended to deplete the manpower of British forces overseas. The Spanish had made particular efforts to persuade soldiers from Beresford's army who had been taken prisoner, many of whom were Catholic, to desert and similar offers were made to the soldiers captured during Whitelocke's assault. Beresford, indeed, had issued a proclamation threatening the death penalty for anyone caught trying to persuade British soldiers or sailors to desert.[41] It was not only men who deserted but some of the women who had accompanied the army also decided to remain behind in the Spanish colony. On his arrival in Montevideo Kinder became aware of the large numbers of deserters from the British army at large in the city.

I have been greatly sorry to see numbers of Englishmen wearing the Spanish uniform. I have not had opportunity to ascertain satisfactorily the actual number, & therefore hope that 2000, the number I have been told are in Garrison here, & in quarters at Buenos Ayres, greatly exceeds the truth. They have been tempted by the large wages given, which amount to 16 Dollars a month, to a private a very large

41. *Por Guillermo Carr Beresford, Mayor General, Comandante de las fuerzas de S. M. Britanica, empleadas en la Costa Oriental de la America del Sur, Gobernador de Buenos-Ayres, y todas sus Dependencias.* Buenos Aires, 19 July 1806.

allowance in a country where the necessaries of life are cheaper than in almost any other. They are mostly very fine men, & have the grace to show some embarrassment at facing the English Officers.

Later he was to comment on the former British soldiers who had set up as boot makers in Buenos Aires.

Whitelocke's Defeat and British Policy towards South America

Historians, particularly military historians, have had little good to say about Whitelocke, but it is worth looking again at his reasons for agreeing to a ceasefire and the withdrawal of his army. By taking this action Whitelocke saved his army and obtained the release of all prisoners, including those captured with Beresford. He then explained that there was no value in holding Montevideo if Buenos Aires was not under British control. He asserted that if he had renewed the attack he might have taken the city but would not have sufficient men to control it and considered that it was better to evacuate a province 'which the force I was authorised to calculate upon could never maintain, and which from the very hostile disposition of its inhabitants, was in truth not worth maintaining.'[42] In his official dispatch he repeated 'how little advantage would be the possession of a country, the inhabitants of which were so absolutely hostile.'

These phrases are indicative of rather more than a general seeking to justify military failure. Whitelocke understood the futility of wasting soldiers' lives to conquer a country that could not be held against the obvious determination of its inhabitants. After the first day's fighting the British held a part of the city and it was suggested to the general that he might bring up heavy guns from the fleet and begin a bombardment. This

---

42. Quoted in Ian Fletcher, *The Waters of Oblivion*, Spellmount (Stroud, 2006) p.117; see also John Whitelocke, *Buenos Ayres. Truth and Reason versus Calumny and Folly: in which the leading circumstances of General Whitelocke's conduct in South America are explained*, D.N. Shury (London, 1807).

he refused to do. It would be a policy of brute force which had no moral justification and which would, in his opinion, inevitably cost the lives of his soldiers and of countless civilians.

Kinder believed that Whitelocke was quite wrong and that the British were liked and respected above all other foreigners but a book published in Buenos Aires in 1807 warned the *porteños* that

> England has raised itself to the colossal (though precarious) height that we see today, not by virtue of the number of its inhabitants, nor by the riches of its soil (which are the solid bases of real power) but by the use of criminal force against the rights of nations and by a system, followed without interruption, of destroying other nations to raise itself on their ruins.[43]

Already, in May 1807, the new Secretary for War and the Colonies, Lord Castlereagh, had penned a memorandum to the Cabinet drawing lessons from Beresford's failed attack on the Río de la Plata. In this he sketched a future line of policy which would 'relieve us of the hopeless task of conquering this extensive country, against the temper of its population.' The British, he argued, 'in looking to any scheme for liberating South America…should not present ourselves in any other light than as auxiliaries and protectors.'[44] A sea change in British policy was about to take place and Whitelocke understood how pointless his military enterprise was in the new world that was emerging. As the historian H.S.Ferns wrote in 1960, 'in agreeing to evacuate the River Plate, Whitelocke's incompetence was the foundation of his wisdom… Whitelocke as well as Castlereagh made British policy in South America … but Castlereagh was right and Whitelocke's action ensured that he could never go wrong.'[45]

---

43. Pedro de Estala, *Quatro cartas de un Español a un Anglomano en que se manifesta la perfidia del gobierno de la Inglaterra, como pernicioso al genero humano, potencias Europeas, y particularmente á la España*, Real Imprensa de Niños Expósitos (Buenos Ayres,1807).
44. Quoted in H.S. Ferns, *Britain and Argentina in the nineteenth century*, Clarendon Press (Oxford, 1960) pp.47–8.
45. Ibid. pp.39 & 49.

Portugal, Madeira and Brazil

News of Whitelocke's decision to evacuate the Río de la Plata only reached London in September 1807. By then another crisis affecting South America had arisen. Following the Treaty of Tilsit, which was signed on 7 July, Napoleon had begun to put pressure on Portugal to join the Continental System and to close its ports to British goods. He also planned to seize control of the navies of Denmark and Portugal in his attempt once again to challenge Britain's supremacy at sea. Britain had responded with a pre-emptive strike against Denmark (16 August-5 September). Determined now to secure control of Portugal and its fleet, Napoleon assembled an army on the French frontier under General Junot and secured the agreement in principle of the Portuguese Prince Regent to close his ports. Britain responded by warning Portugal that the continued possession of its colonies was at stake and by assembling a force to occupy Madeira.

Britain may have contemplated the permanent annexation of Madeira but had no intention, after the debacle at Buenos Aires, of trying to occupy Brazil. Instead it encouraged Dom João to remove the Portuguese court and government from Lisbon to Rio de Janeiro—a move which would abandon Portugal itself to the French but would secure the Portuguese colonial empire, the Braganza monarchy and the all important Portuguese fleet. Although this move was also the preferred option of one faction at the Portuguese court, Dom João delayed his decision until Junot's army had crossed the Portuguese frontier and was approaching Lisbon. The fleet with the royal family on board eventually sailed on 29 November 1807 escorted by four British warships. On the way to Brazil Dom João put his signature to a new Anglo-Portuguese treaty opening the trade of Brazil to British commerce.

The change in emphasis of British policy is obvious. The swashbuckling, piratical interventions of Popham and Windham had given way to a policy of co-operation with local allies to achieve what, after all, was the main objective—the defeat of Napoleon and the opening of South

America to British commerce. Nevertheless Britain did not immediately reverse its decision to annex Madeira. Originally the intention had been to send Sir John Moore from Sicily but in November the force assembled in Britain was placed under the command of none other than General Beresford, newly returned from his adventures in the Río de la Plata. Not only had Beresford's reputation not been damaged by his exploits in Buenos Aires but his experience as governor of that city was seen as a positive recommendation for the Madeira enterprise. Beresford, in his own person, was to provide the bridge between the old policy and the new.[46]

Beresford reached Madeira on 24 December 1807 and, as he had done in Buenos Aires, refused negotiation and demanded the immediate surrender of the local authorities. He occupied the governor's residence and on 31 December declared the sovereignty of King George and began to administer the oath of loyalty to the island officials. Religion and private property were guaranteed and Beresford and Admiral Hood decided that no prize money would be distributed. So far it was a repeat of his performance in Buenos Aires but this time he had nearly 3,600 men with him, not a mere 1,400. Beresford governed the island until the end of April 1808 when it was formally restored to Portugal and its governor reinstated. Beresford, however, remained until August in command of the British garrison until he was relieved by General Mead. During his short period as governor Beresford was extremely active, carrying through investigations into the finances of the islands, reforming the local armed forces and making a number of changes to the way the island was administered. He also abolished the soap and salt monopolies and opened the island to trade by British merchants in British ships.

Thomas Kinder reached Madeira on 1 May 1808 and stayed until 9 June. His account of the island forms a substantial one sixth of his narrative and much of it is descriptive of the island, its public buildings

---

46. For the British occupation of Madeira by Beresford see D. Gregory, 'British Occupations of Madeira during the Wars against Napoleon', *Journal of the Society of Army Research*, 66, (1988) pp.80–96; Malyn Newitt and Martin Robson eds., *Lord Beresford and British Intervention in Portugal 1807–1820*, ICS (Lisbon, 2004); Paulo Miguel Rodrigues, *A política e as questões militares na Madeira no período das guerras Napoleónicas*, Centro de Estudos de História do Atlântico (Funchal, 1999).

and the comforts and discomforts of life. He had read, and was ready to correct, the account of the island that John Barrow had given in his book *A Voyage to Cochinchina*, which had been published in 1806[47], and he made observations of importance on the activities of the British community which was chiefly involved in the wine trade.

As he was to do in Buenos Aires and Montevideo, Kinder sounded out what the local population felt about the English.

> The inhabitants were at first very much irritated at seeing their own governor turned out of his station and house, & the civil authority taken possession of by Gen. Beresford, the Portuguese flag being lowered to give place to the English, and complained bitterly that the troops of that nation from which they expected nothing but protection, and on account of an Alliance with which their Sovereign had been forced to fly to his dominions in S[outh]America, should enter the Island as a conquered country, and not as protectors to defend it for its lawful prince against those who had dispossessed him of the crown of Portugal.

He thought that the islanders would have resisted if they had been given any leadership.

> They were enraged against their own governor that he had surrendered the place on the terms to which he had submitted, and no doubt had he first communicated them & taken the sense of the people upon them, a spirited resistance would have been opposed to the landing of the British troops.

However, once in control, Beresford had succeeded in making himself well respected.

---

47. John Barrow, *A Voyage to Cochinchina in the Years 1792 and 1793*, Cadell and Davies (London, 1806).

[He] took every means to render himself and his country popular here, & made and enforced many regulations of police, the benefit of which was very generally felt and liberally acknowledged. Therefore when orders arrived for the civil government to be reestablished on its former footing, and for General Beresford merely to retain the command of the troops in the Island, they scarcely knew whether to grieve or rejoice… regretting to lose the advantage of Gen. B[eresford]'s government from a continuation of which they had expected further improvements, and though their national pride was gratified at seeing their former governor again take possession of the Castle, they could not but be sorry for that event having a utter contempt for the Person who happens to be invested with that authority, who is a very nonsense-minded, mean-spirited, stupid man, and is led by a sett of the lowest people of the place.

Kinder comments favourably on Beresford's governorship. 'General Beresford has caused the streets to be cleaned of the numerous swine which were formerly suffered to wallow in them,' he notes with approval. Later he observes that the island batteries fire salutes to even the smallest merchant vessels which during 'Gen[eral] Beresford's government were prevented from giving that useless trouble.' However, he did not approve of all the measures Beresford had taken to win local support. 'The Men conduct themselves with great regularity and decency affording to the Portuguese an excellent example of neatness, & conciliating them by treating their religious prejudices [with] respect.' However,

in one instance which came within my notice, I thought too much deference was paid by the authority of the Gen. to the religious prejudices of the natives. Though it is both politic & liberal to provide that no annoyance should interfere with their … ceremonies, any participation in them may well be decreed a step beyond propriety. At the Chapel of Nossa Senora del Monte, there was a procession a few days after our arrival here to celebrate (as I believe, for I was not very solicitous for accurate information) the finding of the Cross. The band of the Buffs was ordered to attend on this occasion, and marched at the head of the procession the whole fore noon.

Beresford had been sent with an army large enough to secure the island and hold it for Britain. Clearly the lessons of Buenos Aires were in the mind of the government, although in the event the island surrendered without any resistance and there was no rising against British rule as had happened in the Río de la Plata. Kinder, not entirely aware of these considerations, was extremely critical of the waste involved in maintaining such a large British garrison.

> The English nation has but little reason to be satisfied with the arrangements made for taking and keeping the Island. In this instance, as in every other, they are made to pay a sum greatly exceeding what is necessary in order that the ministry may have it in their power to bestow more good places on their adherents.

The garrison, for example, had

> a medical staff, a Commissariat &c fully sufficient for an army of 5000 men ... but there was no provision made, or orders issued, in case the force to remain here should be so small as to have no need of them... As the country derives in the eyes of the Portuguese, much lustre from the conduct of Brig[adier] Gen. Beresford in the government he has held, I shall not go so far as to say, that himself & his Aids de camp might be transferred with advantage but it is thought that the deputy Adjutant General, as well as the Dep[uty] Quar[ter] Master General might well be spared.

Madeira's economy was based on its wine trade and on servicing the shipping which used Funchal as a port of call. The English had dominated the wine trade since the seventeenth century and had developed the varieties of fortified wine that passed under the generic name of Madeira. There was a structural connection between the wine trade and the international shipping. Madeira wine had large markets in India and America and the fleets that anchored there called at least in part to take on supplies of wine. The log book of the *Northumberland*, for example, records days spent clearing cargo space in the ship for taking on wine in Madeira.[48] According to Kinder:

> the whole produce of the Island does not, in middling years, exceed 15 or 16 thousand Pipes, ... & when we consider the number of houses Established there, many of which contain several partners, and the expensive manner in which the resident partners live, we are obliged to conclude that the per centage they gain on their sales must be very exorbitant... Houses have been named to me, as having sold 5000 pipes in one year. This, averaged at £40 a pipe would be £200,000, & an enormous profit would be made, but in these years, all the other houses who had only the remaining 10[000] or 12000 pipes to divide among 15 or 16 firms at least, appeared to be doing as well as usual, and I know of no instance of failure where they have confined themselves to the regular trade.

As far as the visiting fleets were concerned Kinder counted 'three India or China fleets including that I came with, two West India fleets, one of which was of 40 sail, the Brasil fleets of 4–5 sail in which I went away & several single ships.' These ships brought with them so many goods for sale that

> the glut of English Manufactures which the closing of the continental markets against us occasioned in every port left open to our speculators was beginning to be felt there, & I have been since informed that several of those I saw there who brought with them & received since [such?] large investments of dry goods as Cottons, Woollens, &c have failed.

---

48. Journal of the *Northumberland*. British Library L/MAR/B 141 P.

The opening of the ports of Brazil led to a similar glut in the market. It clearly took British exporters time to understand the limitations of the non-European markets they were so anxious to penetrate.[49]

Thomas Kinder left Madeira on 9 June and reached Brazil on 23 July. He stayed there a month before leaving on board the *President* for the Río de la Plata. The narrative of his stay at Rio de Janeiro, however, is not included in this MS and is lost—although it is possible that Robert Southey had access to it when writing his *History of Brazil.*

Background to Revolution in the Río de la Plata

When, in the absence of the viceroy, the people of Buenos Aires and Montevideo rose up and forced the surrender of Beresford's army, it was a revolutionary moment. The ease with which Beresford had brushed aside the viceregal forces and taken the city had, in the words of one historian, 'cracked the monumental edifice of the Spanish empire and began the process by which it collapsed into rubble.'[50]

Although the unexpected arrival of a British army had found the authorities totally unprepared and had elicited a spontaneous response from the citizens, the political changes which followed had origins which were more fundamental. The establishment of the viceroyalty of La Plata in 1776 had brought prosperity but also social tensions. With the new viceroy came a crowd of Spanish bureaucrats and a new Spanish military establishment, inevitably reducing the importance of the *cabildos*, the old governments of the cities which dated back to the early seventeenth century.

Until the last quarter of the eighteenth century the Spanish settlements of the Río de la Plata had been relatively neglected and were perceived in

---

49. This point is discussed at length in D.C.M. Platt, *Latin America and British Trade, 1806–1914*, A&C Black (London, 1972) Chapter 1 'The Market'.
50. John D. Grainger, *The Royal Navy in the River Plate 1806–1807*, Scolar Press for the Navy Records Society (Aldershot, 1996) pp. xi–xii.

Madrid as peripheral to the main concerns of the empire. Buenos Aires and Montevideo were at best minor ports which served the scattered cattle country of the pampas and which exported hides and some other natural products. Inland en route for the Andes lay the small towns of Córdoba and Mendoza while to the south of Buenos Aires the frontier with the native American 'Indians' was barely seventy miles away. The left bank of the river, the so-called Banda Oriental, was protected by the fortress town of Montevideo which had only been founded in 1726. Inland lay the great Jesuit missions and to the north the ill-defined frontier with Brazil.

With the new viceroyalty, Buenos Aires, and to a lesser extent Montevideo, began a period of rapid growth in some ways comparable to the growth of Rio de Janeiro after the arrival of the Portuguese court in 1808. Theatres, newspapers and schools appeared, books were imported and medical services improved. Historians have spoken of 'the Crown's need for a fiscal reconquest' of the whole Río de la Plata region and of a 'closer and more dependent relationship with Spain' being created.[51] Although prosperity spread, the creation of the viceroyalty had led to a significant influx of Spaniards of all classes and peninsular Spaniards continued to form the political, military and commercial elite. In his memoirs Manuel Belgrano, secretary of the *consulado* from its formation in 1794 to 1806, spoke for the Creole community when he wrote, 'I realized that the colonies could expect nothing from men [the Spanish merchants in the *consulado*] who placed their private interests above those of the community.'[52]

Because of the successful defence of the city against the British and the major role that the military were to play in the establishment of the Argentinian republic, historians have paid particular attention to the Bourbon military reforms and how they affected the society of the Río de la Plata. The new viceroyalty was defended by a number of regular

---

51. Mark Szuchman, 'From Imperial Hinterland to Growth Pole: Revolution, Change, and Restoration in the Rio de la Plata', in Mark Szuchman and Jonathan Brown eds., *Revolution and Restoration. The Rearrangement of Power in Argentina, 1776–1860*, University of Nebraska Press (Lincoln and London, 1994) p.3.
52. Manuel Belgrano, 'The Making of an Insurgent', in R.A. Humphreys and John Lynch eds., *The Origins of the Latin American Revolutions 1808–1826*, Knopf (New York, 1965) p.277.

regiments with an officer corps of Spaniards, while the frontiers were protected by an irregular mounted force known as Blandengues. Before the events of the British invasion few local Creoles were attracted into the regular army, which remained rather detached from local society, giving no indication of the key role the military were to play in the coming revolution. On the other hand the local militias in which the Creoles served lacked training, discipline and even proper arms. This was comically illustrated when the militia assembled to oppose Beresford in 1806 but found that the bullets with which it was issued did not fit the firearms.[53]

Although there was no strong Creole political movement prior to 1806, and nothing resembling the plots and conspiracies that seethed beneath the surface in Brazil, there were many educated Creoles who were ready to take a leadership role once this was required of them. In spite of all the authorities could do to prevent the circulation of newspapers and propaganda, echoes of the French Revolution and the subsequent European wars reached the Río de la Plata via the contraband traders. In 1791 a pamphlet concerning events in France was confiscated and in 1794 a group of French residents was arrested and eventually deported. In both cases the Count of Liniers, brother of the future viceroy, was involved, which makes it less surprising that suspicion of French sympathies eventually fell on Santiago de Liniers as well. There was also acute anxiety at the possibility of trouble among the black population of the city.[54]

It is clear that the British believed that Creole resentment of Spain had brought the *porteños* to the verge of revolution. This was not only due to the propaganda spread in Britain by Francisco de Miranda, who after all was from Venezuela, but came from the distorted images presented by contraband traders, many of whom had suffered losses and detention at the hands of Spanish authorities. In particular the British believed that the commercial restrictions of the Spanish government had so alienated the population that the promise of free trade would be enough for them

53. Tulio Halperin-Donghi, 'Revolutionary Militarization in Buenos Aires 1806–1815', *Past and Present*, 40, (1968) pp.84–117.
54. Ricardo Caillet-Bois, 'The Río de la Plata and the French Revolution', in R.A. Humphreys and John Lynch eds., *The Origins of the Latin American Revolutions 1808–1826*, pp.94–105.

to throw off Spanish rule. 'If the trade is thrown open all the inhabitants would willingly acquire and keep the place for the British nation without troops,' wrote an American trader to Commodore Popham in 1806.[55]

Spanish imperial authority was an imposing structure but Beresford's attack on the city showed how ill prepared the viceregal government was to defend the colony. The viceroy responded slowly to the reports of the arrival of the British force, the troops he sent to oppose Beresford ran away and he himself retreated to Córdoba in the interior taking the treasury with him. Kinder was in no doubt that the departure of the viceroy was looked upon as desertion by the *porteños*. Moreover the Spanish bureaucracy showed a disposition to collaborate with Beresford who guaranteed to them the possession of their offices. The initiative to reconquer the city passed to the citizens and to the Cabildo. Almost at a blow the authority of the viceroy had collapsed and a 'popular' government, or at least a government supported by the population, had taken control. The revolutionary implications of this transfer of power, however, were not immediately apparent as the Cabildo was largely made up of coopted peninsular Spaniards whose loyalty to Spain was not in doubt.

The Arming of the Río de la Plata

The citizens of Buenos Aires had taken enormous patriotic pride in the reconquest of their city and large numbers of Creole volunteers came forward to fight Beresford.[56] It was, however, the arrival of a regular officer, Santiago de Liniers, with troops from Montevideo, which made a successful attack on the British possible. Liniers had been appointed commander of the army of *reconquista* by the governor of Montevideo,

---

55. Grainger, *The Royal Navy in the River Plate 1806–1807*, p.16.
56. An example of the exalted language in which the *reconquista* was celebrated: 'En el siglo de los sucesos grandes: en el siglo de la heroicidad y del valor: en el siglo en fin en que resucitada la hedad de los Leonidas, de los Themistocles, de los Aristides todo es memorable, todo grande, todo portentoso, eran demasiados quarenta e cinco dias para que pueblo lleno de entusiasmo, de patriotism y de valor sufriese vergonzosamente las cadenzas con que el orgulloso *Breton* meditaba perpetuar su esclavitud.' *La Reconquista de Buenos Ayres. Rasgo Encomiastico*. Real Imprensa de los Niños Expósitos (Buenos Ayres, 1806).

Ruiz Huidobro, and after the defeat of Beresford he was formally appointed as commandant of Spanish forces in the viceroyalty. However, it was soon made clear to him that his authority rested on a popular mandate, when he found that the pressure of popular opinion prevented him from carrying out his side of the surrender terms agreed with Beresford. After his victory over Beresford Liniers realised that there might well be a further British attack and began to take measures to raise a proper defence force. During the closing months of 1806 a new military structure was created consisting of the regular Spanish regiments and new units of infantry, cavalry and artillery raised among both the Creoles and the Spanish population. The irregular Blandengues were included and an artillery corps was also raised among the 'Indios, Morenos y Pardos'— Indians and mulattoes. Kinder includes in his narrative details of the military establishment as it was in 1808–9 and in Appendix A are details of the structure Liniers created in 1806.

The new regiments were based on territorial and social categories, the Spanish for example being divided according to their provinces of origin into Basques, Andalusians, Catalans and Galicians while the Creoles were enrolled as Patricios and Arribeños.[57] These new units chose their own officers with the result that a new officer corps began to emerge with a power base in certain sectors of the community. An important role was also played by wealthy sponsors who were prepared to enlist their own corps. In general the creation of the new army saw a decisive shift in power towards the Creoles and away from peninsular Spaniards and this trend was intensified when the Creole militia regiments were reorganised as a permanent professional army in 1807.[58] Altogether the military units enrolled 8,584 men, roughly a third of the male population of the city.

The new army soon faced a stern test with Auchmuty's attack on Montevideo. Not all the units behaved well and Liniers himself was not able to relieve the city, which fell on 3 February 1807. Following this

57. Members of the Legión Patricia were always known as Patricios and were recruited from Buenos Aires. Arribeños were those from inland.
58. Tulio Halperin-Donghi, 'Revolutionary Militarization in Buenos Aires 1806–1815', *Past and Present*, 40, (1968) pp.89–92.

disaster a Junta was formed in Buenos Aires headed by Manuel Belgrano (described by Kinder as 'an Italian in character, cautious, artful & intriguing'), which declared the viceroy deposed. The city was now ruled by the Cabildo and Audiencia with Liniers as commandant temporarily in control of events. After the defeat of Whitelocke, a victory in which the Creole citizens had played as great a part as the newly organised military units, General Elío was sent as governor to Montevideo while Liniers received an interim appointment as viceroy in May 1808.

Politics in the Río de la Plata after the Departure of Whitelocke

The British invasions had united all sections of the population in the Río de la Plata. Peninsular Spanish, Creoles and the lower orders of the city and countryside had come together to defeat the invader. With the final departure of the British at the end of September 1807, the unity began to crumble and rival factions emerged, often focussed on one or other of the new military formations. If the fundamental split was between those Spanish who wanted to restore the old order and the new Creole elite who sought more power for themselves, there were also fault lines that ran between the traditional merchant class and those who had profited from free trade under the British. A rift of an even more fundamental nature also appeared between the cities of Montevideo and Buenos Aires, whose jealousy of each other had been intensified by the development (after 1799) of Ensenada de Barragán as a deep water port for Buenos Aires, which reduced the capital's dependence on Montevideo.

For a while the prestige of Liniers maintained some sort of stability but in March 1808 events in Spain threw all attempts to restore a kind of normality into total confusion. On 23 March Carlos IV of Spain was forced by Napoleon to abdicate in favour of his son Ferdinand VII. Ferdinand in his turn was imprisoned in France and abdicated in favour of Joseph Bonaparte. Joseph was not accepted in Spain and in May an insurrection broke out with regional Juntas declaring in favour of Ferdinand. On 25 September a Central Junta was created to act on Ferdinand's behalf, but this was to cause problems in America. Whereas the legitimacy of Ferdinand was almost universally accepted (even though he had abdicated) the legitimacy of the Central Junta was not. While some people were prepared to accept the Junta's authority, others wanted local Juntas to be appointed, while others yet again supported the claims of Carlotta Joaquina, the wife of Dom João VI of Portugal, who claimed the right to act as regent in America on behalf of her brother Ferdinand VII.

One consequence of this insurrection was a reversal of alliances as Britain now became a close ally in the fight against Napoleon and began to provide active support for the Juntas in Spain and their counterparts in Portugal. When this news reached Río de la Plata the British, instead of being viewed with hostility, suddenly found themselves treated as friends and allies.

The events in Spain confused still further the political alignments in the Río de la Plata and the new viceroy Liniers found that he was deeply compromised by the fact that he was French by birth and was believed to be Bonapartist in sympathy. In spite of this, he was able to consolidate his position in the latter half of 1808 with the support of the Creole regiments, the Church and the Audiencia. The provincial intendants and the old viceregal bureaucracy also declared in favour of Ferdinand VII and offered their support. Opposition was confined to the Cabildo and to Montevideo where General Elío openly defied Liniers' authority.

However, Liniers now began to face criticism on a number of counts. There were those who resented the influence of his mistress, Mrs O'Gorman, known as 'La Perichona'; others objected strongly to his liberal commercial policy which in effect opened the port to foreign traders and nullified the privileges hitherto enjoyed by Spanish merchants; and there were those who believed that he should be suspended from his office because, contrary to royal regulations, he had allowed the marriage of his daughter to the brother of his mistress. The Cabildo also objected to Liniers's attempt to recruit for the new army outside Buenos Aires. If opposition was concentrated in the Cabildo, it was because Liniers appeared to be ignoring the economic interests of the Spanish merchant elite. As the historian Halperin-Donghi put it, 'there is no doubt that, by ignoring the commercial interests of those who controlled the Cabildo and favouring, in a necessarily arbitrary manner, other people with a perhaps less solidly prosperous backing, Liniers was aggravating a conflict which it would have been in his interest to attenuate.'[59] Rumours of an armed showdown between the Cabildo and the viceroy were already circulating in October but it was on 1 January 1809 that the Cabildo, with the support of some of the Spanish militia regiments, tried to stage a coup. On this occasion Liniers was saved by Cornelio de Saavedra, the commander of the Patricios regiment, who disarmed the militias supporting the Cabildo and who subsequently emerged as the real power in the city.

Kinder's Commentary on Events in the Río de la Plata

Thomas Kinder reached Montevideo early in September 1808 and from that date until March 1810 he was an eyewitness of events in the region. When he arrived he found that 'the news of Peace was already arrived from Spain, & that we should be received on the most friendly footing.' Everybody he saw 'wears a cockade with the initials of Ferdinand the Seventh, the ground blue and red, intending by those colours to express the union betwixt England & Spain.' Although the British were now considered as allies against Napoleon, he found that the governor had 'no powers to grant any favours beyond assistance to such vessels as may put in for refreshments; nor can he permit trade until authorized.' He had to

---

59. Tulio Halperin-Donghi, *Politics, Economics and Society in Argentina in the Revolutionary Period*, Cambridge University Press (Cambridge, 1975) p.135.

convince the authorities that he was not seeking to trade but would be 'glad to avail myself of the present favourable opportunity to satisfy my curiosity.' Governor Elío, whom he described as 'a man of much quickness & intelligence & very Gentlemanly', then 'yielded his objections.'

The most dramatic event that Kinder witnessed in Montevideo, and which he described in some detail, was the attempt by Liniers to assert his authority and to replace Elío as governor, an incident which showed how quickly a rift had appeared between Montevideo and Buenos Aires.

One evening there, I was surprized by repeated cries of 'Vive Elio'. Vive el Rey. I found on enquiry that they were caused by the arrival of a new governor named Michelina, a Cap[tain] in the Navy sent by Liniers to replace Elio. The people did not chuse to part with Elio, & Michelina who entered the town at eight o'clock in the evening, was glad at 3 in the morning to embark in a boat in the bay ... in order to cross a corner of it and return by land ... to B[uenos] A[ires] fearing he should lose his life if he retreated by the gate and was perceived by the populace.

Kinder inquired into the reason for this and discovered that just as the city was preparing to proclaim Ferdinand VII,

an emissary of Bonoparte arrived & took occasion to recommend to the Governor to postpone it for a short time untill he received further advices from Spain. Elio demanded why, on which the emissary told him that, prior to his departure from Europe, Ferdinand VII had again abdicated the throne & that Joseph Bonaparte was king to the great joy of all Spain, throughout the whole of which tranquillity prevailed.

Elío rejoined that far from postponing the proclamation he would carry it out that very evening, 'being determined not to acknowledge any other king. Ferdinand was accordingly proclaimed, and the emissary proceeded by the first opportunity to Buenos Ayres.'

Liniers had written to all the intendants on 17 August.[60] According to Kinder:

> a proclamation appeared addressed to the People & forwarded circularly to all the Governors within the Viceroyalty recommending patience and unanimity of opinion, apologizing in some measure for aparent want of confidence in not sooner communicating respecting the state of affairs & the intelligence brought by the Emissary (who is expressly alluded to) & observing that in the absence of fuller advices it was resolved to proclaim Ferdinand VII which was accordingly ordered everywhere to be done...: it recommends them to wait with patience the fate of the northern [mother?] country & to be determined by it.

This whole episode aroused further suspicions as to Liniers' loyalty as 'it is very loosely & insiduously worded.' Elío reacted strongly against this proclamation and

> returned to Liniers's a very harsh reply (which I have not seen) inferring a falling off from his allegiance due to the family of Spain & declaring that he would be at war with any nation, province, city or individual whomsoever whom should swerve from their duty to Ferdinand VII·

Liniers replied 'that the proclamation was not his act, but that of the Cabildo assembly' and

> in consequence of his offence Elio was recalled to B[uenos] A[ires] under the pretence however of his presence being necessary in order to be a member of a junta to be formed according to the general orders of the supreme junta of Seville of the principal men in each province or Colony.

---

60. *Circular que el Excmo Senor Virey dirigio el 17 de Agosto de este ano a todos los Gobernadores y Xefes de las Provincias, baxo el titulo de reservada.* Copies of this circular and other official public documents were sent to London by Alex McKinnon and can be found, in most cases with translations, in National Archives (Kew) FO 72 90.

Kinder then explains that, although the Cabildo of Montevideo was prepared to obey the viceroy, Elío summoned a *Cabildo Abierto*, an open assembly of the citizens, which gave him its support. Kinder observes that 'the jealousies between Monte Video & Buenos A[ires] are so great, that it is quite sufficient that Elio is popular in M[onte] V[ideo] to cause the people in B[uenos] A[ires] to side with their Viceroy' and he suggests that one reason for this stand off was the belief in Montevideo that Buenos Aires had refused to come to their rescue when the city was attacked by Sir Samuel Auchmuty.

Later Kinder was to modify his opinion of Elío.

I now think that the part he has taken has probably been with a view of making his loyalty evident in Spain & so obtaining promotion (perhaps the Viceroyalty) in case of success against France in Europe or, in the Contrary event, to obtain a rich reward for delivering over the left bank of the River Plate to the Princess Charlotte, wife of the Prince of Brasil.

Elío was subsequently appointed viceroy and, when his authority was not accepted by Buenos Aires, did invite Portuguese troops from Brazil to help him assert his authority. Kinder's views are so prescient that one suspects he may have written this passage some time after he heard of Elío's appointment.

Kinder then speculates on the role of the emissary of the Central Junta in Spain, General José María de Goyeneche.

After the answer he [Elío] wrote to the Viceroy, he was summoned here not to be a member of a junta as I before supposed, but distinctly to give an account of his conduct & such summons was not only sent by Liniers, but by the Sen[or] Gorgonache who had just then arrived from Spain as an emissary from the Junta Suprema, with unprecedented powers such as gave him a control over all the Viceroys & Governors in the Country. G[orgonache] was well convinced of the motives which actuated the 2 individuals, & issued the summons for Elio's attendance & departed for Peru, but [Elío] instead of obeying has involved G[orgonache] in the charges of treachery circulated against the Viceroy.

Although Goyeneche later led royalist forces in Upper Peru he was suspected at the time, like Liniers, of being Bonapartist in sympathy and was certainly acting on behalf of Carlotta Joaquina.
Having expelled the man sent to replace him as governor, and having refused the summons to come to Buenos Aires, Elío was effectively in rebellion.

Not content with disowning the supreme power, it has been attempted to make all swear allegiance to the Cabildo or Junta of Monte Video, & in consequence numbers have quitted the place & yesterday arrived here all the marine officers near 50 in number.

Liniers, according to Kinder, decided to deal with the situation gently. '[He] has probably thought that the arrival of intelligence would set all right, & has consequently contented himself with summoning particular individuals.'

Kinder crossed to Buenos Aires at the end of September and obtained lodging at the house of Tomás Antonio Romero, a leading merchant and friend of Liniers, one of whose aides de camp was also resident in the house. On 29 September he was introduced to the viceroy as he was returning from Mass. 'He contented himself with observing that if he could afford me any facilities he should be very happy to do so, [and] that under the present circumstances he was peculiarly happy to see me there as an Englishman.' Kinder then took his leave,

having returned my thanks to the General for the kind expressions he was pleased to use towards me, & expressed as well as I was able the pleasure which in common with every other Englishman I felt at the close alliance subsisting between Spain & England.

Such apparently innocent social formalities were witness to a veritable revolution in international relations. Later Kinder observed:

I have always supposed that my having received no invitations from General Liniers for a considerable time after my first introduction, arose from his unwillingness to give umbrage to the old Spanish party by noticing any stranger; but the heads of that party had since been banished by him, & were thought of only with contempt.

Although Kinder came to like the viceroy personally, he had no illusions about his abilities or his character, describing him as

a man most culpably careless in the administration of his duties, so inactive that all his inferiors neglect their duty, & so easy & good natured that all his enemies escape punishment & every one else can obtain from him what ever they chuse to ask… it may be also doubted whether he possesses any other good qualities more than great good nature & humanity, together with some courage, & openness of disposition.

Later, after getting to know Liniers better, he writes:

The character I have already given of him appeared pretty correct on a nearer acquaintance. He was of too easy a temper, careless rather than radically unprincipled or extravagant, affectionate to his family & very easily swayed by those around him. His conversation was fluent and lively. He was certainly not a little vain, but strange as it may seem after the part he has acted I cannot forbear saying that I did not think him very ambitious. He always placed his comfort in sitting down on his Estate with his family around him, & occasionally to divert himself with his dog & gun & he solicited of the king a grant of a large Island in the Parana as the place of his ultimate retirement.

When Kinder arrived in Buenos Aires the French armies were undertaking the conquest of Spain in the name of King Joseph (Bonaparte) and by March 1810, when he left, the French were in control of the whole country apart from Cádiz. In these circumstances the appointment of a French naval officer as viceroy of Río de la Plata naturally raised questions about how he would respond to orders from Joseph's government in Madrid. Kinder considered this issue at some length.

The fiscal who wrote the proclamation I have before mentioned, probably thought he was adapting it to the sentiments of the Viceroy in the sentences to which I have alluded & Liniers signed it when presented, thinking no doubt it was as well to leave his determinations in an ambiguous state until the fate of Spain became decided when, if such are the sentiments of the people, he would, for the sake of avoiding additional commotions, submit to the orders of Bonaparte & probably his national vanity would be gratified by so doing. But certainly he does not possess, the Spirit of Ambition & intrigue so prominent in Frenchmen of the present day & so far I think from being likely actively to promote the subjection of this colony to France, in case Spain is subjugated, that if the people remain in the same sentiments they now so loudly profess, I doubt not that, as he is a Soldier of great courage, he would again lead them against the invader. The honours which, in consequence of a contrary conduct he might hope to reap in France, & the advantages or pleasure of returning there, could be but little use to him. He has been here 24 years or more, has once married here, & his children are now under the care of his wife's sisters, with whom, as well as with many other families & individuals here he is on terms of the strictest intimacy.

Alex McKinnon, whose letters to Canning are the other major British source for this period, thought that the hostility of Elío towards Liniers was partly due to 'an apprehension pretty clearly expressed that doubts the loyalty and sincerity of Liniers to the cause of F[ernando] 7th and of Spain.'[61]

Although suspicions of Liniers's Bonapartism never entirely disappeared, most people came to the same opinion as Kinder, and the viceroy's enemies began to focus their attacks on his character, his family

---

61. National Archives (Kew) FO 72 90, Alex McKinnon to Canning, Montevideo 11 June 1809.

and those with whom he associated and especially on his suspension of the commercial regulations to allow virtual freedom of trade.

> The objections to Liniers, among all the rational people, is his attachment to a French Lady, married here to one O'Gorman, who is now in Chili enjoying himself upon some appointment given him there by Liniers, while she & her brothers, in the name of the Viceroy govern the Viceroyalty. Liniers himself is perfectly careless of money, so much so that were he to die now his children would be left utterly destitute; but on the other hand he grants every favour & extricates out of every difficulty in the face of law & of justice, those who are interceded for by Mrs O'Gorman, whose favour it needs much money though very little delicacy in the application, to purchase… Her brothers would any where be looked upon with contempt, as rising from their sister's disgrace, but are besides men of known meanness; notwithstanding which Liniers last week had the imprudence to marry his eldest daughter to one of them in spite of the remonstrances of his brother the Count, the whole of his late wife's family, his confessor & every person of worth who has sufficient intimacy with him to venture to express their minds.

The tensions that had been growing between Liniers and the Cabildo ever since the departure of the British came to a head at the end of 1808 when the membership of the Cabildo had to be renewed. The events which followed, the attempted coup by the Cabildo on 1 January 1809, are the most important developments that took place while Kinder was actually in Buenos Aires and he gave a lengthy account of them. The constitutional issue appeared to be whether to recognise the legitimacy of the Central Junta (which the Creoles and Liniers were prepared to do) or to establish a local Junta in the name of Ferdinand VII (as the Cabildo and Elío in Montevideo were advocating). However, Kinder was in no doubt that this was in reality a coup by those wishing to restore the old commercial system.

The members of the late Cabildo are all Spaniards except one... The natives of old Spain are all of the same party, entertaining, to a man, the same illiberality towards every one who can possibly interfere with their gains, nay more, thinking it impossible that any one can gain, without their experiencing a consequent loss. Had these men succeeded, I doubt not, from what I have heard many of them utter as their sentiments, that every stranger would immediately have been imprisoned, & probably many of the principal Creoles & from experience, the temper of the troops is so well known that all now congratulate one another on seeing their houses safe from pillage & their families from insult.

After the coup failed Kinder heard that

Papers are said to have been seized indicating the plans of the revolutionists, who contemplated a complete change in most of the departments of Governments & revenue, especially a removal of all the present officers of customs, together with an Instant embarkation of all the foreigners which must have been attended with confiscation of property to such as have outstanding debts, or indeed every species of property which they cannot instantly remove. These plans are rendered probable by the known sentiments of the party which indeed I heard several express in the course of the morning of the 1st... while they flattered themselves with complete success & by the spirit of monopoly, known as the first spring of all their movements, which alone, & not the service of the king, was the motive for wishing a change in the Customs-house department, intending to introduce such as would countenance them, but suppress the contraband proceedings of all those who are not of their party. It is true, that a more venal set of men than the present cannot be found, ... but still no patriotism can be a moment supposed in favour of the revolutionists, because they are all known as great smugglers.

His commentary continues with an assessment of the Cabildo's opponents.

> The 2nd party consists of Liniers & those personal adherents who, deriving profit from the commercial advantages by winking at & even favouring contraband, or protection from their enemies by his power, find their prosperity attached to his, but these men are not sufficient to sustain him, but for the aggregation of the third party which is the entire body of Creoles, who finding him equally with themselves hated by the Spaniards &, not as yet knowing the extent of their own force here, supported his case solely with the hope of crushing the common enemy & gaining one step towards independence, & likewise because they do not know where else to look for a head.

This analysis did not fully recognise the latent struggle for power between the Cabildo and the viceroys, which had its roots in colonial times. The Cabildo, dominated as it was by peninsular Spaniards, had tried to seize the opportunity provided by the British invasion and the events in Spain to wrest power from the viceroy. Initially they had seen in Liniers an instrument to achieve their goals but, as Kinder points out, Liniers had adopted a liberal commercial policy which had fatally alienated the Spanish merchants who supported the Cabildo.

> The attempt of the Cabildo to depose him, was invited by 2 or 3 favorable circumstances – the marriage of his daughter with Cap[tain] Perechon disgusted every body & was besides contrary to law, which expressly prohibits any servant of the king in these Colonies to marry himself or his children without the king's consent, declaring that any Viceroy so acting shall by the act itself be dismissed & enjoining the officers of Royal Revenues not to pay his salary.

The Cabildo leaders used this as an excuse not to recognise Liniers's authority and provocatively asked the judges of the Audiencia to instruct them to whom to submit the names of their successors for approval, as the viceroy had relinquished his authority.

The arrival here of the late Governor of M[onte] V[ideo] Don Ruez Huidobro who is said formerly to have received a commission from Charles IV to succeed the Marquis del Sobremonte in the viceroyalty, though it probably was never the intention of the Cabildo to employ him, furnished them a stalking Horse to allure some of the people, as he is said to have lent himself to their plans.

The Creole leaders, however, fearing what might happen if a Spanish-controlled Cabildo was able to depose the viceroy,

determined to have a Cabildo composed of at least a majority of Creoles, a measure never to be expected, unless by intimidating the Cabildantes to elect such a one by the appearance of force, or by inducing the Viceroy to cancel their election & name others.

Kinder's description of the events of 1 January is one of the best passages of his narrative.

About 11 o'clock the great square was filled with people & occupied all sides & at the entrances by the 3 Corps in the interests of the Cabildo, viz. the Catalans, Biscayans & Gallegos. The great bell was also rung to excite alarm & draw together the populace… At the same time some of the members of the Cabildo harangued the populace, who immediately hallowed out 'Long live Ferdinand 7th & the Cabildo and down with the Frenchmen'. These cries continued till towards two o'clock, several emissaries being sent from the Catalans, to the quarters of the Provincial Artillery to request Guns, & lastly threatening to come & take them, when two Cannon were brought, & pointed down the streets in which they were expected to appear & the whole vicinity terrified with the momentary expectation of a battle… About two o'clock a violent shower of rain came on & dispersed the populace, the three forementioned regiments remaining formed in the square, & now beginning to fire on such of the opposite party as happened to enter the Square & shew themselves at the entrances.

Liniers was faced by what appeared to be a successful coup. Not only were the names of the new Cabildo presented to him but he offered his resignation and was forced to agree to name a Junta (similar to those which had been set up in Spain) to represent the authority of the imprisoned Ferdinand VII. Although he was to be president of the Junta, such a move would have entrenched the power of the Cabildo.

He had consented to this arrangement, when the Colonel of the Patricios [Cornelio de Saavedra] accompanied by the Commandantes of the other Creole corps entered the Room with a file of Soldiers with fixed Bayonets, & striking the table with his drawn sword swore he would kill any body who dared to talk of a Junta. The Bishop rose in extreme panic & embracing him, begged he would mention the form of government, testifying their instant submission to his pleasure in the most abject manner. Saavedra declared his determination to uphold the present government, & addressing himself to Liniers told him, that the Cabildo had been grossly imposing upon him, that the wish of the people was quite contrary to their report, requesting him to go into the Square & satisfy himself of the truth of his statement & content the people with assurances of his again governing them. They entered the Square, by that time in complete possession of the Patricios, the Biscayans, Catalans & Gallegoes having dispersed & fled immediately they perceived the cannon of their opponents. The cannon were then planted in front of the Recova, pointed towards the Town house & the Square was again full of people (the shower having ended) who now greeted Liniers with uninterrupted 'Vivas'. After this, no shots were fired, the Patricios having, not only uninterrupted possession of the Square, but of the quarters of all their adversaries, from whence they took the arms they held, thus virtually disbanding them.

In all some fifty people had been wounded by the firing.

Thus concluded the events of the day, an order being issued to illuminate the City, the troops remaining under Arms in the Square, & in the fort Centinels being posted at all the Avenues leading thereto at every turning for the distance of several Quadras, where indeed they yet remain (Jan16) challenging every body that passes after night-fall… The members of the Cabildo together with several of their adherents remained under arrest in the fort till the third instant when…[they] were embarked on board one of the small vessels of war in the Port & in 2 or 3 days more commenced their voyage for an unknown destination.

Liniers dealt with the conspirators by fines, confiscations and forced loans, which Kinder heard amounted to two million dollars. Although Liniers was reinstated as viceroy, power in the city had now passed to the Creole leaders, and in particular to Cornelio de Saavedra the commander of the Patricios regiment. Kinder concluded, 'this man appears to me likely to hold a good while the influence he possesses as it is founded on military command & he has prudence to attend to his popularity with his soldiers.'

Kinder's Views on Commerce and Politics

Kinder was assiduous in seeking to understand the commercial situation in the Río de la Plata and it is significant that, when he first arrived, he stayed at the house of Tomás Antonio Romero, one of the leading merchants of the city who had had extensive dealings with 'neutrals' and contraband traders and who must have been his principal source of information. In his description of the smuggling operations Kinder demonstrates how close had become the identification of British interests with the notion of free trade and good governance.

During the period between the outbreak of war with Britain in 1797 and the British invasions contraband trade had flourished. Although Kinder seems principally to have been interested in British trade, much of the contraband was handled by Germans, Danes and Brazilian

Portuguese. As for Americans, Kinder comments that the 'confidence which the Americans have been obliged to repose in them [Spanish agents], has been in almost every instance abused.' As the purchase of foreign built ships was legal, a common device of the smugglers was to arrive with what was said to be a newly purchased ship which was alleged to be in ballast but in fact was loaded with contraband goods. Romero was closely involved in this form of smuggling.[62]

Kinder formed an over-optimistic opinion of the commercial opportunities on his arrival in 1808: 'such a scarcity of most articles is felt as will insure in all probability good profits to the first shippers of goods, should the trade be opened. It proves the consumption of the interior to be very great.' In the event so many traders hastened to take advantage of the peace that there was soon a glut, as had been the case in Madeira.

During the short period of British control of the Río de la Plata ports (effectively from July 1806 to August 1807) there had been virtually free access to the market. The departure of the British, however, saw the old commercial regime restored—at least nominally. Contraband traders now had to run the gauntlet of Spanish officials, the customs authorities and the general hostility of the legal Spanish merchants towards rivals seeking to undercut them.

Any illegal trader who arrived in the Río de la Plata had to find a Spaniard willing to act on his behalf and take his goods off his hands.

The trade being from beginning to end contraband, it has been in almost every instance necessary to make complete transfers of property into Spanish hands in order to protect it, & the law being silent in behalf of the stranger, the merchant has been able to remain with the proceeds of sales... foreigners establish it as a rule, that no consignment quits the hands of a Spanish Merchant here without his contriving at least to clear 25 p[er] cent upon it if he does not detain the whole, & as numbers have built splendid houses, & started up

62. Jerry W. Cooney, 'Oceanic commerce and Platine Merchants, 1796–1806: the Challenge of War', *The Americas*, 45, 4 (1989) pp.509–524.

rich men suddenly, having been known to have had only 5 or 6 consignments... In consequence, every Merchant here is a decided enemy to the establishment of free trade, & to Englishmen being permitted to settle as Merchants.

Even under Liniers's liberal rule, 'ships have been seized & detained upon suspicion alone, & even now [it] depends more upon the standing of the nation whose flag they bear, or upon the interest of the individuals who speak in their behalf, than upon the law.' Although there was no protection in law,

> the system of smuggling is so organized here that it is nearly a certainty that any vessel permitted to remain in harbour a week, clears her cargo, even though the Viceroy should dispatch his principal officers aboard to watch it. The profit to the Officers is so great that Spanish integrity cannot withstand it.

Liniers's involvement in the contraband trade appears to have been well known. One of the consignees was 'Sarratoa, Brother in Law of Liniers, but who never appears in the affair & transacts all by means of an agent versed in these affairs.'

> The Viceroy waits for authority from Spain before he conceives himself authorized in the least to relax from the laws, but he is known as the friend of an open Commerce, & the people who suffer in their purses & in their personal convenience by the Monopoly, which is the consequence of consignments being limmitted to Spanish merchants, will all be glad if the English are permitted to establish themselves.

Liniers's relaxed attitude in granting licences to foreign traders had provided him with the revenue to pay the troops—a policy which proved invaluable when the Cabildo tried to overthrow his government in January 1809.[63]

---

63. Rock, *Argentina 1516–1982*, p.73.

The Spanish merchants, according to Kinder, believed 'it impossible that any one can gain, without their experiencing a consequent loss'—a neat expression of the dominant thought on economic matters. However, the British assumption that free trade would be to the benefit of everyone was not necessarily true of the specific situation in the Río de la Plata where market conditions were very inelastic and the capacity of the world market to absorb hides, which was the main export of the viceroyalty, was limited—although tallow apparently found a ready market as a result of the war with Russia. The Spanish merchants were not entirely wrong.

Kinder gives a detailed account of how the smuggler had to operate.

It is well known that the laws of Spain prohibit absolutely, the entry of foreign manufactures in foreign Ships… Each requests leave to sell his cargo, & combats the denial he receives & the various orders issued for him to quit the anchorage by pleas of want of repairs & by the interest he has made to support those pleas… The reasons alledged … against his granting leave to sell are the existing laws, the danger to the commerce of Spain & hurt to the revenue all evidently falsehoods because none of those who alledge them are ignorant that everything gets ashore, but all the individuals from the Viceroy (or at least from Mrs O'Gorman) downwards are aware that though revenue could not but profit greatly from permitting a regular entry, they must necessarily lose the hush-money each either gets or hopes to get…

The smugglers

have to arrange with the Commandante of the Vessels in the harbour, with the Cap[tain] of the Port, with the Cap[tain] of the Resguardo whose especial business it is to prevent contraband, besides paying the Guards on board the Ships, & ashore, with immence wages to all the boatmen, cartmen, Porters, & every other description of person who must necessarily be privy to the business, added to all [of] which prior arrangements, a prudent smuggler always carries twenty or thirty onza's

... in his pocket to provide against unforeseen incidents. When the expence of bribing all the nest of hornets is considered together with the risk of bad faith in your consignee, at whose mercy you are immediately after having committed yourself by one illegal step, it cannot be wondered that so few have escaped total loss.

The corruption inherent in this system provided officials, from the viceroy downwards, with an extremely profitable source of income.

A former Cap[tain] of the Resguardo at M[onte] V[ideo]... so completely made his office his own, that after having for the first few months pursued the smugglers with such vigour, as to make it evident that nothing could escape him, or go ashore without his consent, was accustomed to undertake the landing (ensuring himself the property) of any cargo on receiving for his own use, the said circular duties & he being able to compound with the other departments at a lower rate than any merchant could, cleared for himself an immense regular profit.

The smugglers for their part were sometimes able to blackmail the officials and their Spanish collaborators.

It cannot be supposed that any of these rascals are such bad calculators as to trust their offices, & perhaps their lives, in the hands of one, whose circumstances they do not know to be such that he cannot denounce them without ruining or deeply prejudicing himself.

To compensate for the risks, the consignees expected to make a profit of between 50 and 100 per cent on the cargoes they bought.

Kinder points out that legalising the trade would have been of immense value to the state revenues. The total value of goods brought in by British and American vessels in 1808–1809 was 'two Millions Sterling, nine tenths at least of which was smuggled in & an equal bulk of return produce smuggled out.' Had this trade been legal, the ... whole amount of duties paid to the Government could not have been less than 500,000 [dollars?]. I suppose the average return cargo of the vessels given in the list would be worth £10,000 each at the very least, the duty on which would amount to a considerable sum. It will be seen that the value of the return still greatly falls short of those imported, to compensate which about 1,500,000 Spanish milled Dollars, such as have been restruck in England, were smuggld on which a duty of two per Cent might very easily have been levied had their exportation been permitted.

The Viceroyalty of Cisneros

Although Liniers had triumphed on 1 January his enemies had taken their case to the Central Junta in Spain, while a growing crisis in mercantile circles and in the finances of the state, caused in part by the growth in defence expenditure, was rapidly undermining the viceroy's position. The early part of 1809 saw the French triumphant in Spain as another British army, that of Sir John Moore, was driven in headlong flight from the country. With the prospect of Spain succumbing to Napoleon, the Creole leaders began to talk about independence. Kinder succinctly summed up the deteriorating position.

Towards the middle of 1809 the remittances from Peru were stopt, in consequences of expences incurred to suppress a fermentation which the state of affairs in Spain had given rise to in the Upper Provinces; especially La Paz where they have always manifested a spirit of independence & revolt.[64] The Custom house produced nothing & consequently the troops were unpaid & the officers in the different departments were some quarters [sic] without having received their

---

64. The rising in La Paz had begun in July 1809 and was headed by the Cabildo which, in imitation of the failed coup in Buenos Aires, tried to establish itself as a local Junta in the name of Ferdinand VII. The rising was suppressed in October by Goyeneche with an army sent from Peru.

salaries. At the same time the market beginning to fall deprived the speculators of their hopes of great profits & the land holders were dissatisfied with the little incouragement given to the export of their hides which they fancied would have gone off quicker through the regular channel, being too bulky & of too little value to be smuggled when any other produce could be obtained to ship.

Kinder also thought there was a rapid growth in the desire for complete independence from Spain.

During my more enlarged intercourse with the better informed resident[s] at Buenos Ayres I found that the spirit of independence had pervaded every order except the merchants natives of Spain & the officers in high Civil Employ. Even the Clergy, with the Exception of the Bishop & two or three of the higher dignitaries, were much decided revolutionists. Not a Country Curate in the whole Viceroyalty, but is a warm partisan of independence the ideas of which had even broken into the Sanctuary of the bishop's residence whose chaplain [a] Dominican friar greatly esteemed by all who knew him & holding the important office of chief deligate from the tribunal of inquisition at Lima used very frequently to chat with me & advance Doctrines which any Spaniard would have deemed highly inflamatory & treasonable.

General Liniers himself was under great alarm at this growing discontent, & even once went so far as to express to me his fears of the effect which the news contained in a London paper which I had in my hand might occasion if it transpired & became generally known in the City. He saw his popularity decline, & his family seemed to be in hourly apprehension that a popular commotion might deprive him of his power.... As a palliation the General began to think of opening the port to English trade & by that means obtain a revenue which would enable him to pay the troops & the civil departments & thereby secure their adherence.

However,

> When the General had resolved to open the Port & another week
> would have seen the enactment probably on liberal terms, every body
> was surprised by the arrival of the aid de Camp of Don Balthzer
> Hidalgo de Cisneros to announce the landing of that officer at Monte
> Video with commission from the Supreme Junta to supersede General
> Liniers as Viceroy.

The new viceroy had come to re-establish Spanish authority over both the
Creoles and the rebellious Cabildos of Buenos Aires and Montevideo. It
was to be the last stand of the old colonial system for Cisneros was also
determined to clamp down on contraband and on the illegal activities of
foreigners in the city. Kinder watched the unfolding of events.

> At the same time as the Aid de Camp announced this General's arrival,
> we learned by post that the inhabitants of Monte Video & especially
> the Governor had received him with acclamations, notwithstanding
> that when he landed he had shewn very evident marks of
> disconfidence in them & want of boldness by the trepidation with
> which he made his first steps on the pier. As both General Liniers &
> Governor Elio had dispatched vessels to Spain, each to justify himself
> & to criminate the other, the people of Monte Video hailed the
> coming of the new viceroy as a certain sight of the triumph of the
> Governor. Those of Buenos Ayres on the other hand were greatly
> incensed when they heard that General Elio was to be removed from
> his Government of Monte Video, in order to be promoted to the
> employ of Inspector General of the Troops of the Viceroyalty & the
> procedure of the New Viceroy did not tend to conciliate them.

Cisneros proceeded to Sacramento and sent General Nieto to Buenos
Aires as its governor.

In addition to all this he gave pretty strong proofs that, although the colonies had been declared integral parts of the Spanish Empire, it was not the intention of those who had named him to depart any more on that account from the old Spanish mode of Governing them for, being waited upon by a deputation of English in Monte Vidio to enquire on what footing their commercial affairs would be placed, he answered that no innovations having been made in the Laws of the Indies he must confine himself to them.

The consternation caused by these actions in Buenos Aires led to talk of resistance. 'Saavedra & others strongly urged General Liniers to continue at their head & not to obey a requisition he had received from his successor to pass over to Colonia.' However, Liniers readily gave up his office and obeyed the new viceroy. Kinder speculates once again that Liniers may have been calculating that if Joseph Bonaparte consolidated his control over Spain he would be duly returned to power as a nominee of Napoleon. When Liniers was allowed to return to the capital after a few days he was met 'by a crowd who conducted him triumphantly to a house he had hired near a Fort & several of the military Commanders hastily drew out their corps to do him honor.'

Cisneros was, from the start, dangerously isolated but

after observing narrowly the temper of the military, he ventured to disband three of the Corps of Hussars & the Light Infantry of Rivadavia, & restored their arms to three Corps which had been deprived of them by Liniers in consequence of the affairs of the 1st of January, viz the Catalonians, Galicians, & Biscayans.

In this way he succeeded in restoring the military ascendancy of the *peninsulares*.

The new viceroy's greatest problem was a lack of funds, and this forced him to address the issue of contraband trade.

During the whole of this time Cisneros demonstrated the greatest jealousy & dislike of the English, & actually caused an account to be taken of all the strangers resident at Buenos Ayres & commensed by ordering away some Portuguese. His own necessities however compelled him to furnish the greater part of us with just grounds for remaining in Buenos Ayres for he had early begun to be distrest by the very low state of the public treasury & was at last instigated by the numerous representations he received from the Creole Landholders & others to take into consideration the opening of the port.

He was strongly opposed by the Spanish merchants but when these failed to raise a loan for him he determined to move towards opening the port, and

assembled a council composed of the members of the Royal audience, of the Finance department, & of some of the Military commanders & two representatives of the Landed Interest, to whose deliberation he submitted the measure.

On 6 November Cisneros went further than Liniers had dared to go and · published new regulations for trade which partially opened the port to foreigners on payment of duties. The foreign traders were not told of the new regulations and Kinder reports that he called a meeting 'to consider of the conduct the English merchants ought to pursue, & represented the danger to which their interests would be exposed should they warehouse their cargoes on the faith of an enactment to the performance of which the government had in no manner pledged itself to us.' This claim is surprising because Alex McKinnon, who had arrived in the Río de la Plata in June, claimed in a letter to Canning that 'the British merchants [are] here represented by a committee elected from their own number (of which they have been pleased to name me as president).'[65]

At this point Kinder's commentary on events comes to an abrupt end.

---

65. National Archives (Kew) FO 72 107, Alex McKinnon to Canning, Buenos Aires, 4 February 1810.

In this manner the Port was at length opened, and the market which had begun to be unprofitable soon became ruinous. Affairs continued in a pretty even tenor till the month of March 1810 when I left the River Plate, the old Spaniards discontented at the opening of the Port which destroyed their profitable monopoly, & the Creoles anxiously hoping for news of the Political death of Spain, which might render the liberation certain.

Affairs had not proceeded 'in an even tenor' at all. In December Cisneros had ordered the expulsion of all foreigners from the city but, after protests from the committee of British merchants and the officer commanding the naval vessels in the Río de la Plata the order had been partly rescinded.[66]

The Revolution of 25 May 1810

Thomas Kinder had left Buenos Aires before the revolutionary events of May 1810, but he does include a letter he received from a friend, probably Alexander Greaves who was a merchant resident in the city since 1807. This gives a detailed account of the events of 21 to 25 May which resulted first in the establishment of a Junta with Cisneros as president and then in the deposition of the viceroy and the establishment of the revolutionary Junta headed by Saavedra. The historian Halperin-Donghi confessed he 'would not attempt to reconstruct—on the basis of an account of the proceedings that is hopelessly condensed and a mass of subsequent testimony that is excessively verbose—the arguments expounded at this meeting.'[67] So this long letter is of particular importance because it is dated 25 May and is apparently one of the very few first hand accounts of the events to be written at the time. On the evidence of two of his letters written in 1812 and 1813 the historian Arnoldo Canclini called

---

66. National Archives (Kew) FO 72 107, Alex McKinnon to Canning, Buenos Aires, 4 February 1810.
67. Halperin-Donghi, *Politics, Economics and Society in Argentina in the Revolutionary period*, p.153.

Greaves 'un notable cronista de la época'. This letter to Kinder, which is of outstanding importance, bears out this judgment.[68]

For Greaves the events of May 1810 could only be understood in terms of the rivalry between 'Europeans' and 'Americans' and he praised the fact that the Revolution had not resulted in violent confrontation between the two groups.

> On the part of Americans, nothing is heard but expressions of the most earnest desires that the Europeans would look upon them as brothers, and would unite sincerely with them in the general good. This conduct on the part of the natives is the more commendable, as they have the whole of the force in their hands, and as they have not wanted provocations in the conduct of the Europeans, to make them feel in their turn the vexations which they have so long made the Americans to suffer.

Although the May revolution did not lead immediately to political stability, it did resolve the position of the foreign merchants which had so preoccupied Kinder. According to H.S.Ferns, three days after the events of 25 May, 'in response to a petition from the "*labradores y hacendados*" the prohibitions on trade were relaxed. Within a fortnight export duties on hides and tallow were reduced from 50% to 7.5% and within six weeks the prohibition on the export of bullion was removed.'[69] Free trade had at last replaced *comercio libre*.

---

68. See entry for Alexander Greaves in Maxine Hanon, *Diccionario de Británicos en Buenos Aires*, M. Hanon (Buenos Aires, 2005).
.69. H.S. Ferns, 'Britain's Informal Empire in Argentina, 1806–1914', *Past and Present*, 4 (1953) p.65.

Kinder the Englishman Abroad

Kinder's narrative belongs to the much-studied genre of travel literature. Apart from important political and economic analyses, it contains a wealth of observation and detail on the places he visited and the people he met. Some of the information he provides is surprising and unexpected. His account of the mutiny of the Chinese on board the *Northumberland* shows something of the complexity of issues faced by the East India Company in operating what was in effect a maritime passenger service between Europe and the East. In the Río de la Plata he comments on domestic arrangements and on the relations between different classes of inhabitant. There were few schools in Buenos Aires, he notes, 'unless the day schools where the Children of the Slaves mix indiscriminately with those of their Masters can be called such.' As for the native Americans:

> In the Barracas I have observed that the natives of the country (I mean the Indians) are employed as labourers. I have frequently endeavoured [to] ascertain why they are not employed in the City as domestic Servants. I am told that they do not understand the language & that they are stupid & that they only come out of the Country in gangs of 8 or 10 together & will never engage themselves without the whole gang or at least half of it is hired.

He describes public festivals at La Recoleta in Buenos Aires which usually ended with someone being knifed, and the appalling conditions under which cattle were slaughtered in the cities. No doubt educated by the traditions of the Grand Tour he tries to describe the cathedrals and churches he visited but is more enthusiastic in his descriptions of the horses, their harness and the mode of riding. 'It is probable that for a silk handkerchief you may have any you fix your eye upon & may very likely get an excellent horse in very good condition but of course only Grass fed.' Life on the pampas fascinated him—bull riding, taming wild horses, slaughtering cattle by ham-stringing them at the gallop and sleeping rough under a hide or a poncho. As for the gaucho,

> with a Saddle a Lassoo, a Knife & a Poncho they are able to meet their little wants as they arise, living always on horseback or in the fields, supplying themselves by the Lassoo with a fresh horse as often as they are displeased with that they have, sleeping in the air or under a hide, eating without even the addition of salt, beef all the year round.

The people of the country, he believed, were crying out for commercial freedom and the good government that would come with it.

> Such is the life of a large portion of the lower class, who with due encouragement might be made serviceable in Agriculture, as well as in all those numerous modes of day labour so necessary in a thriving City, but at present are barely to be distinguished from the Indians, the difference between these being in their features, not in their dress or customs.

There are also the descriptions of the people he meets.

> Donna Francisca Sorrelea smokes cigars & has a lap dog, but these two vices apart, is as neat & nice a woman as any English Lady. She takes out her cigars with equal indifference, whether in her friend's Chamber, or in the Viceroy's drawing room, having acquired this habit at Ascension, where she resided many years…

And here is Ruiz Huidobro, who according to Kinder was 'a very polite man, not ill informed & a very great favourer of all that is English':

> his Wig I suppose had come from Rosses & was always dressed & powdered with the utmost regularity & a Lady of my acquaintance once told him she was sure he slept in his pantaloons that he might not derange their fitting by pulling them on & off. With all his formality,

His Excellency had quite good temper enough to bear a jibe of this sort. What would have been the case if the Ladies lap-dog had licked the blacking off his boots I cannot tell.

Like so many travel writers Kinder becomes the hero of his own narrative. Self-doubt is not the stuff from which travel narratives are made and, his sea sickness apart, Kinder provides yet another cameo portrait of the Englishman at large, seeking to master the world through free trade, good Protestant values and being a sound judge of horseflesh.

He likes to pass judgment on military matters and in Montevideo claims to have taught the local Spaniards to play chess: '[and] cannot but take great merit to myself on the score of public spirit in thus varying the amusements of this very dull place.' He never hesitates to mention the important people with whom he became friends and, like his contemporaries during this time of war, is intensely conscious of his English identity. This asserts itself from time to time through caustic comments on Catholic religious practice in Madeira and in the readiness with which he is prepared to sum up the national characteristics of Portuguese, Spaniards and French. Unlike so many British abroad, however, he is determined to overcome his inability to speak Portuguese and Spanish and mixes as much as possible with the local population. His objective of gathering information was admirably served by his affable and open personality and his confidence that English ways and English principles were universally admired and imitated.

Alex McKinnon, whose account of events in the Río de la Plata in 1809 to 1810 complements that of Kinder, was much less flattering with regard to the English—but then he was angling for an appointment as Britain's consul in the region. He described to Canning in November 1809:

disgraceful circumstances… amongst the Englishmen, *who are at least dressed like fine gentlemen.* We have had very lately, horse whipping before breakfast, – pulling noses at dinner – boxing after by way of desert – and by daylight, duelling with pistols. Some of our ship masters have given sumptuous banquets and a ball to the convicted and transported female mutineers of the Ladyshore botany bay transport, and to other women of the same description. And two Sundays ago the same captains entertained them on board their ships, saluted them with a number of guns on going aboard – again when sitting down to dinner, and in the evening in leaving the ships.[70]

Kinder's Narrative

Thomas Kinder's account of his journey to Madeira and the Río de la Plata between April 1808 and March 1810 was acquired by the John Carter Brown Library in Providence Rhode Island in 2000. It is catalogued as Codex Eng 207. The manuscript is contained in a single bound volume inside the cover of which are notes that provide some indication of its history. They read as follows.

1. A printed catalogue entry: 'Southey (R) His Journal, made during a voyage to Madeira and the River Plate: This voyage was undertaken in 1808, the opening being dated "Funchal" May 4th, in that year'
2. In ink: 'Robert Southey Keswick 1813'
3. In pencil: 'From the Castle Howard Library'

The manuscript is clearly a copy of a lost original and is the work of Thomas Kinder not Robert Southey. Part of it takes the form of diary entries, part is in the form of a narrative based on diary entries and written up later, and part consists of what are best described as lists or appendices. Finally there is a letter, probably from Alexander Greaves, detailing the events of May 1810. There is also reference to another manuscript which is now lost. This is the diary or narrative of Thomas Kinder's residence in

---

70. National Archives (Kew) FO 72 90, Alex McKinnon to Canning, Buenos Aires, 2 November 1809.

Rio de Janeiro where he stayed on his outward journey in 1808 and on the homeward journey in 1810. He writes:

> As in the year 1808 I only spent one month at Janeiro which place I revisited in 1810 when I had somewhat more time, and more leisure to observe what surrounded me I propose to affix my description to that part of my journal which relates to my homeward bound voyage, and making no mention at present of any thing which occurred during my first residence there, refer my friends to my next sheet which commences with my departure thence for the Río de la Plata.

In the preface to the second part of his *History of Brazil*, published in 1817, Robert Southey wrote, 'I am beholden to ... Mr Thomas Kinder for a volume of Noticias del Paraguay, and the prose Argentina, both in manuscript, and for his own valuable Journal.'[71] This appears to refer to at least two if not three items, one of which is presumably this manuscript which was part of Southey's library. It may also refer to the account of Kinder's stay in Rio which he wrote separately and which would have been of greater importance to Southey. Kinder also wrote an account of Mexico based on his stay in that country in the 1830s which has never been published.[72]

Thomas Kinder apparently composed this narrative to be of interest to his 'friends'. That the manuscript was put together after the event and is not, strictly speaking, a diary contemporaneous with the events described, is made clear in the first paragraph where the author writes, 'I shall endeavour to retrace them [his observations] as accurately as my memory will permit.' Sometimes the present tense is used to indicate a diary entry but this is occasionally modified with a comment. For example, writing of Funchal harbour Kinder says, 'such is occasionally the violence of the storms that the spray dashes to the top of the Loo Castle which I think is not less than 200 f[eet] – having since frequently

---

71. Robert Southey, *History of Brazil*. Part the first. Longman, Hurst, Rees and Orme (London, 1810), Part the Second 1817.
72. University College London, Brougham Papers 30,656, Observations on Mexico, 22 November 1834.

seen it I think I have somewhat overrated the height.' On page 50 the text ends abruptly and an entry reads 'London March 1811' suggesting that this part of the text at least was added or revised after Kinder's return. Later he writes explicitly that his friends 'may well be glad to have been saved from the perplexity naturally arising in notes regularly taken, by the sentiments committed to paper to-day being contradicted by those of to morrow.' Nevertheless this sometimes happens, for example when he revises his opinion about why Elío had been summoned to Buenos Aires by Liniers. Originally he states that the reason was that Elío was required to join a new Junta that was being established. Later he admits this was unlikely and Elío had been summoned 'distinctly to give an account of his conduct'. In September 1808 he apparently sent back to Britain an initial draft of his narrative up to that point: 'I closed the former sheets of my remarks & leaving them in the *President* in order to their transmission to Rio de Janeiro & to England.'

The manuscript is, therefore, a mixture of diary entries with narrative composed from memory and with all the advantages of hindsight. It is clumsily written and not well put together. In one place, for example, the author discusses the growing rift between Elío and Liniers and then switches without explanation to a discussion of the horses of Buenos Aires. It is not difficult to see why the manuscript, in the form in which it has survived, was never published.

Editorial Matters

Small editorial changes have been made in transcribing the manuscript. The copyist was careless to the extent that some words are obviously misspelt and the letters in them transposed and some words and whole phrases are duplicated. These have been corrected and the duplications omitted. The copyist is very inconsistent in paragraphing the text. Sometimes single sentences stand for whole for paragraphs and sometimes the text goes on for pages without a break. I have taken the liberty of rationalising the paragraphs. Some small changes have been made to punctuation but only where this is necessary to understand what is being written. Ship names have been italicised and some of the upper case letters reduced to lower case where this makes for consistency. Some words and some parts of words are missing and the copyist makes frequent use of abbreviations. I have extended these abbreviations in order to make the text easier to read. Page breaks in the MS are marked thus //.

The Diary of Thomas Kinder

Funchal, May 4th, 1808

SEA SICKNESS AND THE MANY ANNOYANCIES which contrary to my expectations I have found attendant on the commencement of this my first voyage have hitherto prevented me from regularly committing to paper such observations as arose from the novelty of my situation at the time when the occurrencies which gave rise to them were passing under my eyes. I shall endeavour to retrace them as accurately as my memory will permit.

April 9th. On this evening I quitted London in company with Mr Brooke (secretary to the East India Company & secretary to the Governor of that Island) & Henry Kinder.[1]

As the Persons then about to sail were to receive their dispatches the same evening, it was generally expected that the fleet would sail immediately on their arrival at Portsmouth and having sent to six or seven stables before we were able to procure a chaise we concluded that the direct Portsmouth road would be so covered// as to make our chance of reaching Portsmouth on the following morning very small. We therefore took the Gosport road through Farnham and reached Gosport at half past eight on Saturday morning while many of the Pursers who did not leave London till Sunday morning & travelled the direct road did not arrive till late on Monday.[2]

---

1. Henry was presumably a relative of Thomas Kinder.
2. The two routes are the Portsmouth road which today is the A3 from London via Hindhead and Petersfield and the A31 and A32 via Farnham and Alton to Gosport.

Contrary winds caused the fleet to remain at the Mother Bank till Thursday 14th during which time I made enquiries for a passage to Rio de Janeiro in any of the Brasil traders waiting for convoy but without success as they were all extremely crowded with passengers but being introduced by Cap[tain] Lloyd of the *Sarapis* to Lieu[tenant] Grey under whose command are several victualling *[in pencil 'transports]* bound to Rio de Janeiro he was induced to direct Cap[tain] Brocklesby of the *Neptune* 238 tons burthen to take me on board at Madeira – I determined to proceed to this Island in the *Northumberland* Indiaman Captain Franklin[3] in order to avoid the inconveniences which I anticipate on board so small a vessel as the *Neptune* thus far, and induced by the proba[bi]lity// that I shall have some time for recreation in the Island before the Brasil fleet arrives.[4]

On the 14th therefore I passed my baggage at the custom-house and sent it on board the *Northumberland*,[5] and having purchased a few articles of necessary furniture for the cabin, H. K. and myself went on board in the afternoon but as the wind was still from the S.W. we expected after having made my arrangements again to go on shore and intended to have passed over to Ryde until the wind should change. But on arriving at the Mother Bank we found the ship under weigh.

The Commodore Captain Miller of the *Thetis* frigate[6] having taken ship to St Helens[7] the Indiamen were all moving to join him although the Captains were ignorant of his intentions he having hoisted no signal.[8] We therefore slept on board that night and early the following morning the fleet again weighed anchor and attempted by repeated tacks to round

3. John Robinson Franklin (born 1774 in Nova Scotia) had made two voyages to India between 1804 and 1807 as captain of the *Alexander*. Between 1807 and 1815 he made four voyages to the East as captain of the *Northumberland*.
4. The crew and passenger list is to be found in the log book of the *Northumberland* in the British Library L/MAR/B 141P. There is no record of Thomas Kinder among the passengers.
5. *Northumberland* (637 tons) was built in 1805 and made six round voyages to the East the last being 1816–17. Four of these were made under the command of John Franklin,
6. HMS *Thetis* was a 38–gun frigate built in 1782. In 1795 it captured the French storeships *Prévoyante* and *Raison* and in 1801 took part in Keith's expedition to Egypt. In 1809 captured the French *Nisus* (16 guns) and took part in the capture of Guadeloupe. Sold 9 June 1814. Captain George Miller was commissioned lieutenant 1794 and captain 1802. He commanded *Pallas* 1806 and *Thetis* 1808.
7. St Helens in the Isle of Wight.
8. The convoy was made up of nine Indiamen: *Northumberland, Europa, Lord Castlereagh, William Pitt, Sovereign, Alexander, Lord Keith, Euphrates, Sir William Bentley.*

the eastern extremity of the Isle of Wight. H.K. then quitted the Ship having first taken a few memorandums for stores to be bought// for me and put on board the *Neptune.*

At length towards evening the highland at the south of the Island was in sight but the wind was so very contrary that the Commodore perceiving that it be impossible for the fleet to make // any way hoisted the signal to return to anchor [at] St Helens.

The fleet put about and went with a fine side wind at the rate of seven knots for about an hour, when having nearly reached our anchorage the wind became favorable, we again put to sea and before bed-time were in sight of the light at the Needles.[9]

Being sea-sick I did not go upon deck till noon the next day (Saturday) when we were close in with Start Point on the coast of Devonshire.[10]

On Sunday 17th the Lands End[11] was perceivable till late in the day. We saw land no more till Friday 29th at day-break when the Island of Porto Santo rose over our larboard bow and over our starboard bow, Madeira was at intervals to be discovered, when the mass// of clouds with which it was enveloped occasionally divided & opened.

The Commodore stood in direct for the Channel which separates Porto Santo from Madeira contrary to what I was informed is the usual practice which is to go to the East of P[orto] S[anto] & round in between it & the "Desertas" (three rocky Islands bearing S.E.).[12] We fully expected to come to an anchor in the afternoon but the wind became unsetled & squally & after beating about the whole of that day we were unable to reach Funchal[13] bay till Saturday evening 30th.

We had what was generally thought a fine passage. Just before we entered the Bay of Biscay the wind became unfavorable and blew what the sailors call "half a gale of wind" It then became necessary that all the

---

9.   The rocks that mark the extreme western point of the Isle of Wight.
10. Start Point south west of Dartmouth is the southernmost point of the Devon coast.
11. Lands End south of Penzance is the extreme westernmost point of England.
12. The Madeira archipelago consists of the main island of Madeira and the smaller island of Porto Santo which lies 50 kilometres to the north east. The Desertas are three small islands that lie south east of Madeira. They are Deserta Grande, Bugio and Ilhéu Chão.
13. Funchal is the main town on the south coast of Madeira and is the capital of the archipelago.

trunks should be cleated (ie confined in their places by small pieces of wood nailed near the corners into the floor) and lashed to the sides of the ship by the handles. Except at that time and for a few hours on the 29th when within sight// of Madeira there was no danger of anything "fetching away" and rolling about during the whole passage.

At dinner we were accustomed to have bags of sand laid across the table at intervals to confine the dishes to their places (which however was scarcely ever necessary) and the strancheons[14] [sic] (which are poles passing from the floor to the ceiling between every two chairs to hold on by) were never put up. We dined about twenty two in company generally and had an excellent table. Soup, Fowls, Beef, Mutton, Pillau, Curry, Pies, or Puddings were almost all of them on table every day in different forms. We had plenty of excellent Milk at Tea and Breakfast & with the exception of the bread which was in general (for want of good leaven) very heavy, every eatable was very well cooked and handsomely served up.

The passengers consisted of six Ladies[15], two officers in the king's service[16], & two in the East India Com[pany's] army[17], a writer[18] in the Madras establishment[19], a free merchant[20], & four Cadets[21] who were thus disposed of. But it will be first necessary to give some idea of the interior// arrangement of an India ship. They have always a poop, the sternmost part of which is generally divided longitudinally into two compartments.

The larboard half was occupied by Cap[tain] Franklin, the starboard by three of the Ladies. Before those rooms is the Cuddy, or dining-room which is lighted from the roof, & from the sides & from the glass doors by which you enter it from the Quarter-deck. The only entrance to the

---

14. The word should be stanchions.
15. Mrs John Pattinson, Mrs O'Hara, Misses Corrie, Crisp, Cox and Keir, all bound for Bengal. British Library L/MAR/B 141P.
16. Lt R.Macdonald and Ensign Goodacres.
17. Captain R.Meares 17th Native Infantry and Lt G. Flint 7th Native Infantry.
18. G.H. Keene.
19. The East Indian Company territories were divided for purposes of administration between three presidencies: Madras, Bombay and Calcutta.
20. Alex Arnott.
21. The four cadets were John Buck, Sam Thornton, John Lewis, W.J. Gairdner. There was also a passenger described in the Log Book as a 'native' whom Kinder does not mention.

apartment first mentioned is from the Cuddy. They are called the round houses most impro[per]ly as they are perfectly rectangular.

There are commonly two small cabins opening on one side into the Cuddy into the corners of which they project, and on the other towards the Quarter-deck. They are called Quarter-deck cabins, and measure about 9 feet square. They are the most agreeable Cabins in the ship for Gentlemen as being surrounded with venetian-blinds and sashes the air may be admitted, or excluded at pleasure and opening immediately into the external air, the close smell of the ship hardly ever annoys those in them.// They are likewise less affected by the motion of the ship than the round houses, being nearer the center of the deck. To give a clearer idea, I lay down an outline of the rooms I have mentioned.

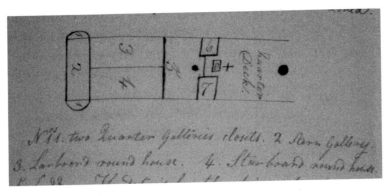

N⁰ˢ 1. two Quarter Galleries closets. 2 Stern Gallery. 3. Larboard round house. 4. Starboard round house. 5. Cuddy. The dot is for the Mizen Mast. 6 & 7 are Quarter deck cabins. 8. Staircase to descend to the Steerage. The X is the steering wheel, & and the larger dot the Mainmast head.

The starboard Quarter deck cabin was occupied by Cap[tain] Meares in the Com[pany's] service, the Larboard one by a piano forte belonging to the Ladies in the round house, but would have been occupied by me but my passage in the ship was so short that it was not worth the Captain's trouble to deprive the Ladies of their music, for which there was no other room upon this Deck.

I suffered much from not having//[22] [sic] to the extreme closeness of the ship below whenever the Port holes are shut down, which, of course, was always done at night, and even in the day-time. There is in every ship a most nauseating effluvia from the water which must get in from leakage and which nothing but a continual current of air can effectually correct. During the day time the above inconvenience was in a great measure obviated by the politeness of Cap[tain] Meares who constantly invited me to sit & read in his Cabin.

It is scarcely necessary to observe that as the Cuddy extends from one side of the ship to the other & is much longer in that direction than in the other, the dinner table is likewise so sett out, and occupies the whole room barely leaving enough for the servants to move round it. At night it is lighted by lamps swung from the ceiling, in which manner the passengers light their private cabins. To obviate the effect of the ship's motion, waiters are swung in the Cuddy over the table to hold the decanters & Glasses – and on the sideboard which is close by the Mizen mast there are frames for the glasses &c to be confined in their places. A movable stove is in cold weather brought// into the corner of the Cuddy & a chimney fitted over it. The deck under that just described is called the Gun deck. That part of it immediately under the round houses is called the great cabin & is often divided into two rooms the same size as the round houses.

In the *Northumberland* the Starboard room is occupied by three Ladies, the Larboard by Mr Keene, a gentleman in the service of the company at Madras in a judicial capacity. He is termed a writer because the servants of the company were formerly so designated, their occupations being purely commercial, but since extensive territories have been added to the Com[pany] the functions of a writer have become generally judicial and most of them endeavour to qualify themselves for the performance of those duties by the study of civil law. In the same cabin is Mr Flint, a young Lieutenant of Native cavalry at Madras.

To the friendly attention of these gentlemen I have been indebted for much comfort on board the *Northumberland*, for// not anticipating much

---

22. There is clearly text missing at this point.

illness I neglected to provide myself with preserves, or any of the little niceties which I looked upon as troublesome & frivolous until I became from sea sickness so much out of order as to have a distaste for the more solid fare of the Cuddy table. Their stores were then opened to me and I passed much time in pleasant conversation though frequently driven out of it to seek relief from the motion of the ship by moving nearer to its center.

Next in succession to these cabins are those called steerage cabins commonly appropriated to the Master, Surgeon & Purser, & when there are more of them than necessary for their accommodation, those unoccupied are given to Passengers.[23] A Lieutenant and an Ensign in the King's service jointly occupied the larger of these cabins. The free Merchant & one of the Cadets bought the use of another & I occupied a third. A plan of the deck will shew how they are disposed.//

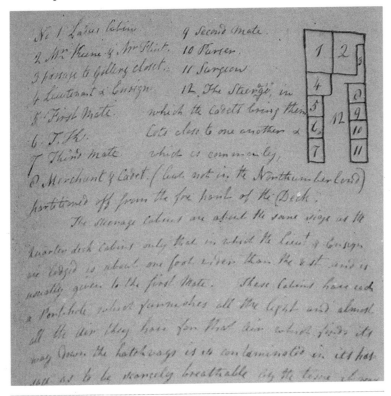

---

23. Chief Mate was Henry Kemp, the purser Walter Etty, the surgeon John Fallowfield.

No 1 Ladies Cabin

2 Mr Keene & Mr Flint

3 Passage to Gallery closet

4 Lieutenant & Ensign

5 First mate

6 T. K.

7 Third Mate

8 Merchant & Cadet

9 Second Mate

10 Purser

11 Surgeon

12 The Steerage in which the Cadets bring their Cots close to one another & which is commonly (but not in the Northumberland) partitioned off from the fore part of the Deck.

The steerage cabins are about the same size as the Quarter deck cabins only that in which the Lieu[tenant] & Ensign are lodged is about one foot wider than the rest and is usually given to the first Mate. These cabins have each a Port-hole which furnishes all the light and almost all the air they have for that air which finds its way down the hatchways is so contaminated in its passage as to be scarcely breathable by the time it reaches the cabins. When the Port is closed at night, the closeness is such as is unknown to one who has not been at Sea for then the only air that can come has first to circulate through the lungs of the whole crew sleeping in the forepart of the deck, & of the Cadets in the steerage. In blowing weather it often happens that the Port holes must be kept closed for days together// and even the hatchways almost continually shut.

I rejoice that I am not able to describe the effect of such a circumstance as the Port in my Cabin was not prevented from being open a short time during the worst part of the voyage. To dissipate in some degree the darkness of the steerage which must otherwise be cimmerian, four small pieces of very thick glass are let into the deck above it. They are so strong as to bear even the rolling of the water-casks over them without breaking notwithstanding which they admit light enough to read by when the eye has been accommodated to it by sitting at rest a little while after descending from above. One of them is likewise let into the center of each of the Cabin Ports.

To a Cadet the expence of his voyage to India is £110 & to those who occupy separate cabins proportionally more. The Cadet who occupies half a Steerage Cabin with the free merchant, told me he pays £50 more for that accommodation. Mr Keene & Mr Flint are charged £500 for the Cabin they occupy which sum includes their Mess expences.[24]

The Ship is very well provided with servants. There are three whose business it is to attend to the Cuddy besides the private servants of some of the passengers, and// several native Indian servants who being brought to England by passengers homeward bound are sent back as passengers and hire themselves out to wait on those who are unprovided.[25] Those who bring native servants from India deposit £50 to be reclaimed on the servant's return or death as an indemnification to the Company from the expence they would be at in keeping them from Slavery if turned off by their masters on their arrival here. Consequently as the passage of a servant costs £50 they are generally sent back that the money may be reclaimed besides which it generally happens that those who engage them in India pledge themselves to send them back.

The crew of the *Northumberland* was when she set sail the awkwardist it is possible to conceive of. The only Men at all conversant with the tackle were thirty Lascars.[26] When the India ships are in India they hire Lascars to supply the deficiency which [is caused by] death, desertion and pressing occasions, engaging to send them back, and as the owners are compelled by laws passed with a view of manning the British Navy to send their ships on the outward-bound voyage with a full crew of Europeans, the Lascars are taken home as passengers.[27]

Next come thirty Chinese, brought to Europe most probably to [*illegible*] some large leaky Chinese ship under a similar engagement to be returned.// These last were not at all acquainted with the Ropes. They would have returned direct to China, but no fleet will sail for some time,

---

24. For the rates in force in 1810 see Sir Evan Cotton, *East Indiamen*, Blatchworth Press (London, 1949) p.73.
25. The *Northumberland's* log lists eight servants.
26. The term Lascar usually refers to sailors recruited in South East Asia. According to the log of the *Northumberland* these were transferred to another ship early in the voyage.
27. Ships in the East could fill gaps in their crews with Lascars (Indian seamen) to the ratio of three English to one Lascar. The Lascars then were returned to India as passengers. Evan Cotton, *East Indiamen*, p.58.

and therefore they are sent to Ben-Bengal [sic] to be forwarded in country ships. They were unacquainted with the name of even a single Rope in English, and no soul in the ship speaks one word of Chinese.

Most of the Officers in the India ships are able to direct the Lascars in their own language the "Moors" & had the Chinese been kept in England till the next China fleet, it is probable the Officers could have made them understand what ropes they were ordered to hall[28] & they would have reached China as soon as they are now likely to do.

After these sixty passengers had been on board some time when the crew was mustered to be divided into watches, it was proposed that they should watch likewise, but they were to be divided into three companies of twenty each – each company to watch four hours during the day & four at night, whereas the regular crew of the ship is in two watches, six hours by day and as many by night. They were accordingly mustered and much amusement afforded by the efforts of the first mate to divide them & take their names.//

The Lascars who understood what was wanted murmured at being made to work without pay, and the Chinese looked very sulky though probably not aware of the precise drift of the business. The former however being made to understand that they must either watch and work or starve, submitted with much resignation & arranged themselves into three parties under boatswains chosen from among themselves and retired quietly from the Quarter deck.

The Chinese were likewise parcelled out by the mate, but no satisfactory mutual understanding could be obtained. Accordingly at night when the first watch after bed time was called they were all in their hammocks & not a man stirred, till one of the mates went below and cut the ropes at the foot of their hammocks & spilt them all about the deck. The confusion this occasioned was such that the man was glad to make his escape, & the Chinese stayed where they were. Next day they were all collected upon deck and made to understand that they must watch if they would eat, and one of them had just eloquence enough to make it evident that they all deemed it// very hard to be compelled to work without pay.

---

28. Haul.

A slight skuffle ensued, a guard was called up & and furnished with muskets and swords & men were placed at the hatchways the Chinese being told that they should not be suffered to go below either night or day until they consented to watch with the rest. Seeing that they were outnumbered they were prevented from breaking out in open mutiny but we observed them propose to one another to throw themselves overboard. No one was inclined to set the example and the mildness of the Cap[tain's] disposition added to a sense of its not being strictly proper to compel men to work who were passengers induced him to let them go below on a promise which their leader contrived to express that they would make "proper work" of it next day.[29]

Many of the passengers did not sleep easy that night, thinking the revengeful spirits of the Chinese might break out into some excess. They contented themselves with obstinately keeping their resolution not to watch at night - & the Cap[tain] having deprived them of a meal or two yielded the point. It is said however that he will be obliged for the health of the ship to turn them up when in warm latitudes. Besides the Lascars & Chinese there are twenty five recruits going to the Company's army in// India, who being put under the Captains command are made to keep watch & lend assistance when wanted.[30] The Ship's Crew consists of sixty five Germans, Dutch, Flemmings, French and natives of every country but England, and brought up to every trade but that of a sailor.[31]

During the voyage the fears of many on board were kept alive by an apprehension that we might fall in with the Rochfort Squadron[32], no satisfactory intelligence of it having reached England before we sailed. Our Commodore appointed each ship its station in line of battle, regulating the sailing of the whole by that of the leading ship the

29. There is no mention of this incident in the log of the *Northumberland* but twenty of the Chinese were paid as crewmen at the end of the voyage. Each Chinese received £14–18–8 and their leader £18–13–4.

30. According to the log there were 23 soldiers, 3 NCOs and two soldiers' wives, one of whom deserted in Madeira. British Library L/MAR/B 141P.

31. According to Cotton, *East Indiamen*, p.52, the *Castle Eden* in 1808 had a crew that was 'composed of natives of almost every nation in Europe, besides nine Americans and eighteen Chinamen'. The *Northumberland's* Ledger shows that 11 crew deserted in Calcutta, 2 died on the voyage and 11 were pressed by different warships. British Library L/MAR/B141GG(1).

32. The French Rochfort Squadron was later to feature in the events leading up to the Battle of the Basque Roads in April 1809.

Euphrates, which had that station assigned her as being by far the worst sailor in the fleet. She constantly carried all possible sail, while most had not half their canvas spread. By losing her main top gallant mast she detained the fleet half a day.

Early in the voyage the Commodore directed the fleet to Rendezvous her in case of separation but if that had not taken place in the gale off the Island he would probably have made the signal for the *Northumberland* & *Alexander* [33]to separate and have ordered the other ships round by the north west of the// Island while he provided for the safety of these two, by seeing them into Funchal Bay & then joining the main body of the fleet. The Cap[tain] of the *Pitt*[34] had urged the Commodore to put in without success but when the gale subsided that ship & the *Castlereagh* were out of sight & rejoined the fleet while laying to off this Island.

We passed the North east side of Porto Santo. The cultivation is nearly all on the other side as are the Inhabitants and Cap[tain] Franklin tells me there is a very pretty village[35] on the shore with good anchorage off it.* It is bounded where we passed by perpendicular cliffs [which] generally as far as I can judge [do] not reach above a hundred feet high the sea dashing violently against the base – the ground slopes gradually from the Cliffs towards two large conical hills (whose height I should estimate between 5 & 600 feet) which occupy the Eastern end of the Island. The western end is not so elevated but we remarked one hill beyond the rest standing alone and shaped like a sugar loaf. These hills did not give me any high ideas of the richness of this climate,// but brought to my mind the hills of Wales & as I have reason to believe their composition is mostly the same it is natural the verdure should resemble. The outline of the Island is however striking, & its effect augmented by several rough grotesque masses of isolated rock against which the sea dashes with great violence. I perceived a line of white running through a part of the cliff resembling a very long vein (*The length of the Island may be two leagues)// of

---

33. *Alexander* (614 tons) was built in 1803 and entered East India Company service making seven voyages between 1804 and 1817. On two previous voyages it had been captained by John Franklin but on this voyage the captain was Thomas Price.

34. *Pitt* was the name of a 775 ton ship in East India Company service 1785 to 1795. This may be the same ship.

35. Today known as Vila Baleira.

Quartz. Its diss[36] was towards the East at an angle of about 40. We next approached the eastern point of this Island (Madeira) called point S[t] Laurence[37]. It is lower land than any of the rest of the Island but is composed of masses of rock presenting their rugged points all of nearly equal height & perfectly barren for the space of a mile in length but very narrow.

I saw that one of them that projected into the sea had a natural arch of considerable size pierced through it. We next saw the Desertas on our left two of them of considerable size but barren rocks, and from their appearance inaccessible as they rise from the sea like two barns. As they lay to the South E[ast] of this place though distant they have some effect in sheltering the Bay when the wind is in that quarter & from a good object in the distance visible from all this side of the Island.[38]

We stood in for the shore and came within sight of the village of Santa Cruz[39] situate[d] in an open bay offering no better anchorage than this bay. This village was the first settlement in the Island, but the ground rises so abruptly immediately behind it that as the population increased it was

---

36. This may be a mistake for 'dip'.
37. Ponta de São Lourenço is a long cape at the extreme eastern end of Madeira.
38. The Desertas lie 37 kilometres from Madeira and would normally be visible from that island.
39. Santa Cruz is located on the western side of Madeira between Machico and Funchal. Machico was one of the first areas settled in the fifteenth century.

found inconvenient for want of ground sufficiently level to build upon. Indeed the effect of the whole Island excepting point St Laurence is that of the top of one// large hill. The shape of it when first we were able to make out its outline from the North was that of half an elipsis with a few points rising near its center. From point St Laurence to this place the shore rises in abrupt Cliffs except in the neighbourhood of S[anta] Cruz where the descent to the water is a little more gradual.

When within a mile of the Cliffs the lead was dropped and no soundings obtained. The known badness of the anchorage made the Cap[tain] extremely anxious to choose his birth[40] but the wind failed us and night coming on he was obliged to drop anchor before the ship had made the point he wished. The cable was out 35 fathom before the anchor grounded though within 200 y[ards] of the shore.

The best anchoring ground is nearer the west side of the bay in 25 & 28 fathom and even then it becomes so suddenly deep that anchors often lose their hold and ships are again driven to sea. As has now happened to the *Alexander*, which parted two cables and anchors and took a day's cruise at sea before she could bring up in the birth she now occupies. The *Northumberland* is more in the center of the Bay and every body is greatly surprized that she has not drifted. Five or six Ships have done so since we came here and the very night we anchored a small brig came foul of us across the bows and at the same time the *Alexander* was seen drifting towards our stern. Luckily she floated clear of us and went to sea or the damage must have been considerable.// She came within a few yards.

The night when we anchored was beautifully still and clear and the scattered lights rising from the beach had a very pleasant effect. Some of the convents at a distance up the country having their windows on a line with each other appeared to be illuminated: as I afterwards found was the case in honor of some Saint.[41] Captain Franklin and those who had been here before had during the voyage taken so much pains to prepare us to expect wretchedness and filth and nothing worth landing for to be seen in

---

40. Presumably 'berth'.
41. 29 April is the feast of St Catherine of Siena.

this Island that, notwithstanding we found the appearance of the Island after we passed point St Laurence pleasing and verdant and the height of the Cliffs & of the middle striking, and were much gratified with the neat light appearance of the white houses of S[anta] Cruz & of this place resembling an Italian Landscape and with the effects of the lights when evening sett in (which it does very quickly here, there being a very short twilight) we all went to bed not very eager for the approach of morning, having but moderate expectations of the gratification we should receive by going ashore. I for my part did feel more eagerness than the rest having been sea sick but the day before and being so thoroughly disgusted with the taste of ship water & buiscuit & heavy bread that the mere hope of getting a good breakfast & a draft of clear water & perhaps a little fruit (though not in the season for fruit) was quite sufficient to make me anxious to touch Terra Firma while those whose stomachs had accommodated themselves to that// diet were comparatively careless about it.

Having so much complained of the water on board ship some of my friends may suppose we were unprovi[ded] with filtering stones, I will therefore observe that we had one which provided us ample quantity of water but though all visible impurities are abstracted from water by filtra[tion] it compleatly retains any ill flavour it may originally (as is the case with all the water taken in at Portsmouth) have acquired in the spring or from being kept in vessels not perfectly clean for any length of time.

Cap[tain] F[ranklin] tells me that at the bottom of every cask there is always drawn off two or three Gallons quite muddy with the sediment precipitated from the water alone, even the purest water he has ever taken on board, with the exception of some he shipped at Banda or Amboyna[42] which was nearly pure having only a very small quantity of fine gravel in a whole cask. That water likewise drank perfectly tasteless to the last. Before I land myself in Funchal I will observe that the Thermometer was about 45 when I left England and at that point it remained for several days — every one complained of cold and every evening we had a fire in the Cuddy.

---

42. Banda and Amboyna (today Ambon) are two islands in the Banda Sea famous for their spices.

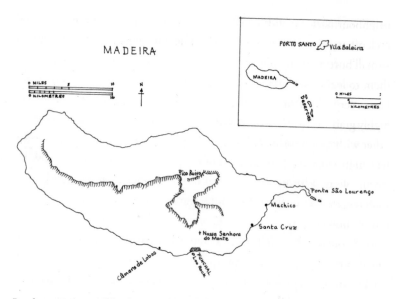

In about 5 days it began to rise gradually & was at 60 in the shade the day before we anchored here. This Island is between 32° & 33° parallel of the Latitude - & the 17th & 18th of the longitude.[43]

May 1st. Early this morning I accompanied the Purser on shore. To avoid the surf// which when there is any kind of wind from the S.S.W. or S.W. makes landing out of any boats but those of the Island dangerous & unpleasant, we ordered the boatmen to row to the West side of the bay instead of standing in direct for the town which is situate[d] due W[est] of the anchorage the *Northumberland* occupies. At this corner of the bay stands an isolated Rock of considerable height called the Loo.[44] Its natural shape approaches to a Square, so that filling up its irregularities with Masonry, a fort has been found inaccessible on every side except by the stair-case at top. This battery commands the whole anchorage.

Nearer the main land, and now connected with it by a stone causeway is another rock similar to the Loo, but not so high. Its top is occupied by a guard-house, and at the foot of it is a very good landing place as the

---

43. Its position is between 32°22.3N, 16°16.5W and 33°7.8_N, 17°16.65W.
44. The Loo Rock with its fort was a favourite subject for artists. Later in the century it was linked to the mainland with a causeway providing a seawall to protect the anchorage.

neighbouring water sheltered both by the Loo rock, and the guard-house rock offers safe anchorage, except in extreme stormy weather, to vessels of a small burthen and a good landing for boats at any time it is possible for them to leave the shipping. It is however very inconvenient because you have a very hilly walk before you enter the Town. Having landed we were highly gratified we were once again on terra firma, and congratulated each other with great sincerity on that head. We crossed a causeway full forty feet high which connects the landing place with// the main land. In stormy weather the sea washes completely over it from the W[est] and such is occasionally the violence of the storms that the spray dashes to the top of the Loo Castle which I think is not less than 200 f[eet] – having since frequently seen it I think I have somewhat overrated the height. Once in the year 1784 the sea washed quite over it.

The uncertainty I was in when I left London as to my taking passage by any ship which might touch at this Island had prevented [me] from furnishing myself with letters of introduction & therefore I accompanied the purser to the houses where he had business with the view to learning where I could hire apartments during my stay till the *Neptune* should arrive.

We approached the Town by a winding road over a steep hill planted mostly with vines, trained mostly over lattices about two feet above the ground leaving just room to crawl under and gather the fruit. We likewise saw the Banana, the prickly Pear, some Indian corn in the bottoms & abundance of vegetables especially cabbages & onions in great perfection. The onions of Madeira are famous for their mildness. There were some standard Peach trees, a few Oranges & Lemons & honeysuckle & geraniums. The whole appearance of the enclosures was that of the richest spring & the breath of the morning furnished// a balmy regale.

We walked the whole way over a very rough pavement resembling that of the badly paved towns in the north of England and not any better for being paved in the pattern of half squares, for the lines are made up of stones having acute or rugged edges while the center is filled up of smoother pieces thus:

All the roads in which I have hitherto been are so paved with the exception of one short level pavement terrace among vineyards in the country and I am informed nearly all in the Island are, only sometimes they do not take the trouble to preserve the pattern. The roads are mostly bounded by stone walls from 4 to 6 feet high the sides smoothed and whitewashed with a slanting coping on the top. The prospect is often bounded by them though the inequality of the ground enables us to see to a great extent below as though confined sideways. We entered the town at the distance of about half a mile from our landing place. The first houses we saw appeared extremely mean and certainly the exterior of every building in the town scarcely ever rises above meanness and never aspires to elegance.

The streets are all very narrow, and in the lower parts of the town and distant from the houses of the opulent, a delicate sett of olfactory nerves is not at all to be desired, although general Beresford[45] has// caused the streets to be cleaned of the numerous swine which were formerly suffered to wallow in them. The lower stories of all the houses of opulent people are used either for warehouses or stables; or are let out in meaner tenements by the occupiers of the upper part to the laboring part of the inhabitants – consequently, all on a level with the eye looks dark & rough there being no windows on the ground floor which is generally only entered from the street by folding wooden doors in stone door-cases. In large houses an opening through the lower story like an entrance into a

45. William Carr Beresford (later Lord Beresford) had commanded the British force which had occupied Madeira in December 1807. He had acted as Lieutenant Governor of the Island until it was formally restored to Portuguese rule at the end of April 1808. Beresford was still in the island commanding the British army of occupation when Kinder landed. For Beresford's subsequent career see Malyn Newitt and Martin Robson eds., *Lord Beresford and British Intervention in Portugal 1807–1820*, ICS (Lisbon, 2004). José de San Martín, the liberator of Chile and Peru served under Beresford at the battle of Albuera. See Introduction.

court in London discovers the staircase and gives a clear passage through into the back yard or garden.

I accompanied the Purser into the houses of several of the English merchants here and observed that the rooms were generally of good dimensions, from 10 to 20 feet square and often much larger having lofty ceilings commonly much higher in the center than at the sides. The rooms we entered were wainscotted chair high & coloured in distemper from the wainscot to the cornice, the ceilings of wood, sometimes painted & with light carved work in the pannels. The furniture is wholly English. In English houses we generally saw pannelled doors with locks let in and brass finger plates. The furniture consisted of Venetian-blinds to the windows, for we saw no curtains, & of convex mirrors with branches to hold candles, in some rooms a few coloured copper-plates in gilt frames & a cut// glass chandelier suspended from the ceiling. Tables, sofas & chairs of course. Sometimes a carpet but more generally a floor cloth covered the floor. The windows are sashed & open down to the floor into balconies either extending the length of the house or only serving for the windows immediately opening into them. The windows on the outside are commonly cased in stone cases resembling what we see in plans of Italian houses with an entablature above them.

House rent is high here especially in the country, but every opulent inhabitant whether English or Portuguese keeps a small cottage at the distance of a mile or two to which he may retire to avoid the heat during the summer as there is a difference of many degrees even a little way up the mountain.

After enquiring at two or three lodging houses for accommodation, I engaged the only vacant lodging I could find, but it appeared so little agreeable that I returned that evening on board the *Northumberland* determined that unless on the following day I could engage better I would regularly return to the ship as long as she remained at Anchor here.

May 2nd. I again came on shore in the morning and being informed that a ball was to be given in the evening at which General Beresford, and the Governor[46] were// to be present, I resolved I would this night try my lodgings hoping to see at the Ball all the fashionables of the Island both English & Portuguese. I therefore returned to the ship once more for the necessary articles of dress, notwithstanding it blew a very stiff breeze from the S.E. which drove so violent a sea into the beach as would certainly have stove in any of the ships boats.

The boats of the Island are peculiarly adapted for the service required of them. The[y] are built very light and hollow being high and pointed at each end alike, the keel being continued & rising above the body of the boat a foot, or more at each end. A walnut shell with a keel affixed would represent one of them pretty accurately.

In one of these boats we fastened ourselves on the bench and the boatmen being in with us several men launched us altogether through the spray into the sea wading up to their mid[dles] to push the boat off. We had a very rough row & notwithstanding our boatmen were dexterous enough to bring the head of the boat opposite the approaching wave we were – "dappled with the dashing spray"[47] till part of our clothing was completely wet through. But the most difficult matter was to get out of the boat into the ship, for as the ship's head was directly up to the wind she had no lee

---

46. The newly restored Portuguese governor was Pedro Fagundes Bacellar d'Antas e Menezes.
47. This appears to be a misquotation from Scott's Lay of the Last Minstrel which had been published in 1805. The line actually reads 'was daggled by the dashing spray'.

side, and our boatman having accidentally approached the ship a little
astern of the// gangway it was with the utmost difficulty we were able to
seize the ropes which were thrown towards us, & so very unsteady was the
boat that the moment I caught the rope it swung away & left me to get up
the side of the ship by a single rope, being considerably below the steps of
the gangway ladder. I esteemed myself fortunate to reach the deck with
only one wet foot, having dipped it as the boat swung off.

We returned to the shore in a larger boat constructed in a similar
manner for the purpose of conveying wine to the ships. The gale had
moderated, but the surf still ran high. The boatmen on approaching the
shore dropped the anchor just outside the surf & making signal to the
men who stood ready on the beach one of them came near and caught a
rope thrown from the boat by which they pulled towards the beach &
presented its pointed end in a direction to meet the surf.

This boat was too large to be drawn ashore as the smaller one was, for
though all are drawn up when not wanted for use, it is a work of much
labour and is done by a windlass turned by oxen. As soon as the boat was
drifted in sufficiently near, one of the men approached quite close to it,
watching his opportunity when the surf retired, and one of the boatmen
fixing himself on his shoulders was carried on shore on purpose to give
hint to us, how the business was to be performed (We were not slow in
comprehending it, and were carried on shore perfectly dry & safely). The
boatmen and attendants at the beach are all extremely strong, active &
dextrous men & very good swimmers, but the impositions to which
passengers are subject from not understanding the language & regulations
of the place are very great, as a boat can scarcely ever be had to any ship
though not distant half a mile from the shore for less than a dollar & if a
fleet is here or the weather a little rough and they believe the stranger must
have a boat 2 or 3 or 4 dollars are commonly demanded. There is a beach
master, to whom a reference may be made & the regulated price will be
awarded according to the service to which it is fully adequate.

The weather has gradually moderated since we arrived here and has
now for some days been so mild that the boats belong[ing] to the ships

may land without any other danger than the risk of wet feet & legs which very commonly happens but which is thought preferable to being landed near the Loo & walking over the hills into the Town. Many accidents happen here to boats coming from Ships with people who, not having been here before, do not know the landing place at the Loo & naturally attempt to come ashore on the beach close to the town where they observe all the boats either at anchor or drawn up. If the weather is at all rough they are sure to be swamped. When the India fleet first came off the harbour, these Captains who were not allowed by the Commodore to bring their ships to an anchor were anxious to send ashore in the same evening and the *Sovereign*// very narrowly escaped drowning, his boat being overturned by the surf.

I attended the ball in the evening & to my great disappointment found it an Assembly completely English. There were only three Portuguese Ladies in the company and about as many Gentlemen with the Governor. A limitted number of military Officers, the English merchants & their Clerks made up the company. The rooms which were too small were hung with festoons of artificial flowers & the floor was painted with flowers surrounding a large figure of a Centaur*.

On returning to my lodgings I found the place appointed for me to sleep in by my host so intolerable, that I refused to occupy it & ordered a bed to be made up for me on a sofa in [the] Parlour & the next morning I sett off in quest of other accommodation & engaged a bed room & my board at Mr Goodall's whose house from all I have since heard is by far the best lodging in the Island, and by a description of which my friends may judge of the inferior ones.

*The Centaur I suppose was painted when Sir S. Hood's ship so named was at anchor there.[48]

Two sisters, the belles of the place, have composed a lively dance so named very much in vogue.// The lodging I had just quitted was kept by

---

48. There were two admirals called Samuel Hood who were cousins. The Samuel Hood referred to here was born 1762 and commanded the fleet which brought Beresford's army to Madeira in December 1807. His flagship was the *Centaur* in which he later won considerable fame fighting the Russians in the Baltic. He died 1814. HMS *Centaur* was a 74–gun ship of the line built in 1797 and decommissioned in 1816.

an Irishman of the name of O'Brian, a very civil man and attentive to those in his house but unable from the constant change of company in his house during the stay of any ships in the Harbour, to allow me even a bed-room to myself miserable as it was.

Mr Goodall's is situated against the side of a steep hill immediately looking into the Sea, having only a row of low cottages & the Town wall between it and the beach. The entrance is from behind into the upper story the hill being so steep that we descend the height of two stories while passing the end of the house. After passing the hall are three & lofty rooms the windows of which command the whole bay with the Desertas in the distance. They are used as sitting rooms by the family & the boarders. Below them is a range of sleeping rooms one of which I occupy – there are no ceilings to them, the flooring of the rooms above and the rafters which support it being left bare. Whenever the rooms above are swept we receive through the crevices left in the ill joined floor a considerable proportion of Dust, and the same takes place whenever a battery of six cannon, which is close to the Town, is fired which happens very frequently, as besides saluting the ships of war entitled to that honor they even return the salutes of the smallest Merchants Ships which in Gen[eral] Beresford's government were prevented from giving that useless trouble.

The Portuguese expended also much powder in saluting the numerous saints in their Rubrick whenever the anniversary comes round. There is never a[n] interval of many days without an illumination more or less partial & a salute according to the rank & estimation of the Saint to be honored.

The walls of the Chambers are newly whitewashed. The windows are large old folding wooden doors, ill put together & fitting very ill, with a few panes of Glass in the Center of each. A bedstead without Curtains, a table, a chair & a looking-Glass compose the furniture. Numerous fleas & a few centipedes are to be seen but we have I believe no other inmates. The lower part of the house is let out to Fishermen, who enter their separate tenements from the street & we should know nothing of them if they were not accustomed to treat our ears occasionally with a song & our noses with a plentiful scent of fried fish.

Our party at the dinner table varies from 8 to 16, every exertion is made by Mrs Goodall to procure good dinners, but the variety which the Island affords is small & the meat of a very inferior quality.

As there is no pasture land in the Island, the cattle are fed on green Oats, and imported hay & what little they can pick up from lands lying fallow. I am told that most of what is produced at table as mutton is in fact// Kid. Some fine oxen are kept by the Merchants here, being the only animals used in the Island for draught, but the only good beef I have ever seen at table has been Irish corned beef.

A considerable quantity of good fish is caught near the Island. Fowls are dear, and ill fed. The oranges at this season are mostly brought from the western Isles[49] – the supply is therefore varying, and now there are none to be procured. The Butter is all Irish, the price varying according to the supply from 1/6 to 3/- per pound. There are at present a few Bananas brought to Market & the earliest strawberries appeared the morning we arrived. They were very tasteless, but have since continued to improve though still inferior to what are commonly seen in London. They are gathered on the North side of the Island where they grow wild. The Banana has a taste something like a very mellow pear but not so agreeable. I am told those produced here are much inferior to the growth of Tropical Latitudes. The Lemons of this Island are very large & fine. Besides the wine drunk in England by the name Madeira, there are three other sorts expressed from Grapes of different species grown here. They are called Sercial, Tinta, & Malmsey.[50]

The Sercial much resembles the common Madeira[51] but has more body & strength. The Tinta is like Port// in colour & takes its name from being used to coulour the Madeira which is naturally paler than it ever appears at table. It drinks like good claret. The Malmsey is reckoned superior to that of the Rhine. These three sell here for £72 per Pipe, whilst the best Madeira is shipped at 48 p[oun]d. The lodgers at Goodall's pay

49. The Azores
50. There are four 'classic' types of Madeira fortified wine: Sercial (the driest), Verdelho, Bual and Malmsey (the sweetest). In addition there is the Tinta, a red wine.
51. Either the Verdelho or the Bual.

2 ½ dollars[52] each per diem for board & lodging, which includes wine & porter at the discretion of the consumers. The dollar passes here for 5/6 St[erlin]g & is divided into 5 Pistoreens[53], which are again subdivided into the "bit" & "half bit" all of silver. The bit is ½ a Pistoreen – there are likewise pieces of 4 Pist[oreens] & half dollars, & half Pist[oreen]: they are mostly Spanish coins.

This Town of Funchal estimated some years since to contain from 10 to 15,000 inhabitants, has not within it any place of public amusement, neither is there anywhere any partial regular Assemblage of persons for the purpose of amusement except the Ball I have mentioned called the "Antimelancholic" and instituted immediately on the Island being ceded to the English.[54] The Portuguese inhabitants make up for the want of public places of resort by frequent large parties at their own houses, to which being once introduced, a respectable stranger is always welcome, and expected when convenient to him without the formality// of an invitation each evening. You there meet from 20 to 50 people assembled and are entertained with good Music both Italian & Portuguese and with Cards, and it frequently happens that a dance is proposed which as it begins late, keeps the party together till 2 or 3 o clock in the morning.

Very few of the men speak either English or French, it is not common to find above 5 or 6 in a large party who can converse in either. I have tried Latin upon several whom I have been told were good Scholars but they have all excused themselves by saying in Portuguese that the manner in which we pronounce the latin is very different from theirs. In these parties I have only seen three Ladies that could speak French, and one of these is an Italian.

If however their acquirements are to be judged of by their aparent ease & sprightliness of conversation & their taste & skill in music many of them may be deemed accomplished, but as books are never to be seen, & there is not in the Island a bookseller's shop, a Printing Press, or a reading-room

---

52. The dollar referred to was the Spanish silver real de a ocho or piece of eight.
53. The pistareen was a silver coin of two reales minted in Spain.
54. Following the arrival of Sir Samuel Hood and General Beresford Madeira was formally annexed to the British Crown on 31 December 1807. It was returned to Portugal 24 April 1808, just six days before the arrival of Kinder.

even for Newspapers, I fear that if I had been able to converse with them in their own language, I should have discovered that they have not been able to overcome the disadvantages incidental to the country they live in.

The English inhabitants associate merely among themselves// and preserve their nationality unaltered. The Clerks in the mercantile houses live [on] a footing of seeming perfect equality with their employers, and those who [reside] in English houses are mostly members of the "Antimelancholic Ball". Notwithstanding the little pains the English take to keep up their popularity, the Nation is much respected here. The inhabitants were at first very much irritated at seeing their own governor turned out of his station and house, & the civil authority taken possession of by Gen. Beresford, the Portuguese flag being lowered to give place to the English, and complained bitterly that the troops of that nation from which they expected nothing but protection, and on account of an Alliance with which their Sovereign had been forced to fly to his dominions in S[outh] America, should enter the Island as a conquered country, and not as protectors to defend it for its lawful prince against those who had dispossessed him of the crown of Portugal. They were enraged against their own governor that he had surrendered the place on the terms to which he had submitted, and no doubt had he first communicated them & taken the sense of the people upon them, a spirited resistance would have been opposed to the landing of the British troops. But being in possession of the power Gen. Beresford took every means to render himself and his country// popular here, & made and enforced many regulations of police, the benefit of which was very generally felt and liberally acknowledged. Therefore when orders arrived for the civil government to be reestablished on its former footing, and for General Beresford merely to retain the command of the troops in the Island, they scarcely knew whether to grieve or rejoice, feeling flattered that things should be placed on a footing of amity and protection such as they had been in the first instance wished and expected, but regretting to lose the advantage of Gen. B[eresford]'s government from a continuation of which they had expected further improvements, and though their national pride was gratified at seeing their former governor again take possession of the Castle, they could not but be sorry for that event having a[n] utter contempt for the Person who happens to be invested with that authority, who is a very nonsense-minded, mean-spirited, stupid man, and is led by a sett of the lowest people of the place.[55]

The English nation has but little reason to be satisfied with the arrangements made for taking and keeping the Island. In this instance, as in every other, they are made to pay a sum greatly exceeding what is necessary in order that the ministry may have it in their power to bestow more good places on their adherents. The expedition which came consisted of four regiments viz: the 3rd or Buffs, 1st battilion// and [the] 11th which now together with a detachment of artillery of about 80 men form the Garrison of the Island, & 25th & 63rd which were never landed, but proceeded, according to orders issued in the supposition that no resistance would be made, and their stay here be consequently unnecessary, to the W[est] Indies.[56] A medical staff, a Commissariat &c fully sufficient for an army of 5000 men, or more in actual service accompanied this expedition, but there was no provision made, or orders issued, in case the force to remain here should be so small as to have no need of them, and though orders as above mentioned have been received here for the government to be restored to the Portuguese, & there have been frequent communications from England since the distribution of the forces sent out was known there, none of the Gentlemen holding these needless offices have received instructions to return home.

The medical staff consists of a deputy inspector of Hospitals, a Physician to the Forces, 2 staff surgeons & an Apothecary to the forces, a deputy Purveyor, with 5 hospital mates, who are all unnecessary as the medical men attached to each other are quite equal to the duty. There is a deputy Commissariat with his deputy, and assistants and Clerks. There is likewise a deputy Paymaster general who receives £1000 a year for paying

55. For a discussion of these observations, see Introduction.
56. The regiments referred to are The Buffs (3rd East Kent Regiment of Foot); the 11th Regiment of Foot (the North Devon regiment); the 25th (The York) Regiment of Foot (King's Own Borderers); the 63rd (The West Suffolk) Regiment of Foot.

two regiments, for which duty, a district paymaster with a small salary would be fully sufficient. As the country derives in the eyes of the Portuguese, much lustre from the conduct of Brig[adier] Gen. Beresford in the government he has held, I shall not go so far as to say, that himself & his Aids de camp// might be transferred with advantage but it is thought that the deputy Adjutant General, as well as the Dep[uty] Quar[ter] Master General might well be spared. Many of the officers I have mentioned were promoted from inferior stations in order to occupy the more lucrative ones, they obtained when attached to this expedition and which seem therefore to have been created for them. The two regiments remaining here are composed of Men recently volunteered from the Militia, and are very fine regiments, in a high state of equipment & discipline.

The Men conduct themselves with great regularity and decency affording to the Portuguese an excellent example of neatness, & conciliating them by treating their religious prejudices [with] respect. Those whom I have seen accidentally led by curiosity into the Churches have conducted themselves with more reverence than the principal Actors in the mummery, the priests themselves, who are often seen to laugh in the midst of it: and when meeting any of the processions in the street I have never observed in them the smallest sign of derision. In one instance which came within my notice, I thought too much deference was paid by the authority of the Gen[eral]. to the religious prejudices of the natives. Though it is both politic & liberal to provide that no annoyance should interfere with their ~~prejudices~~ ceremonies, any participation in them may well be decreed a step beyond propriety. At the Chapel of Nossa Senora// del Monte[57], there was a procession a few days after our arrival here to celebrate (as I believe, for I was not very solicitous for accurate information) the finding of the Cross. The band of the Buffs was ordered to attend on this occasion, and marched at the head of the procession the whole fore noon.

---

57. The church of Nossa Senhora do Monte is situated in the village of Monte high above the old town of Funchal but has been swallowed up by the modern expansion of the city. Kinder is referring to the feast commemorating the finding of the True Cross which was celebrated on 3 May.

These ceremonies of the Romish Church which as protestants we are tempted to think most absurd were that day largely displayed, & a great concourse of people was drawn together to have their imaginations once more subjected to the influence which the production & adoration of reliques & images is known to have in superstitious minds, who but for the attraction which the music furnished would most of them have remained quietly at home, as I have been told that the former anniversaries of that day were never greatly regarded or attended by many people. On the other hand the English are not here subject to any of those inconveniences which I have frequently read of as annoying them in other Roman Catholic countries and I believe formerly in this.[58]

When the Churches are open for service we are permitted to gratify our curiosity by examining every part of them as long & minutely as we please, and if we chance to meet the Host in the Street it depends upon ourselves whether we pull off our hats or remain covered. This Island is a Bishop See & produces a revenue to the Bishop of about £3000 per Annum.[59] He has been now for some time at Lisbon. The Cathedral is in the Center of Funchal// having an avenue of trees about 150 paces in length leading from it to the Church & Convent of St Francis.[60] This is the only public walk in the town, as well as the only piece of level improved ground near it with the exception of a field made level for the military at the distance of about a mile. This walk is called the "Terreira de Sey" or walk of the See.

The Cathedral is of stone having a raised platform at the South side, and at the West end. The walls, as is the case with all the houses, are plastered white except at the Angles, and at the Doors where the stones being wrought into shape are left bare in their natural colour of Slate. The inside of the nave is similar, the Pillars which divide it from the side Aisles being clusters of four in one without capitals, & the Arches quite unornamented, the Architect having probably aimed at the Gothic. The entrance has likewise some pretentions to that style, as has a small circular

---

58. The freedom of worship accorded to the English was enshrined in the 1654 Anglo-Portuguese treaty.
59. The diocese of Funchal was created in 1514.

window over the doorway, but the rest of the exterior is quite plain and advances no pretentions to be classed in any style of Architecture.[61] Like the houses it has a tyled roof. The ceiling is high & resembles fillagree work being made of wood of a dark colour, in small hexagonal compartments either inlaid with wood of lighter colour, or painted and// gilt.[62] In the side aisles are several large Paintings, very well executed probably by Italian Artists, but I have not yet been able to learn where they came from. There are likewise three Altar-pieces one in the Choir

and one at the end of each transept.[63] These last mentioned divisions of the Church contrast greatly with the Nave, the pillars of compartments being profusely Gilt, the Altar tables hung with cloth of silver or of Gold & surmounted with candlesticks either gilt or of massive silver, of which last metal are many large chandeliers very richly wrought (suspended by common ropes from the ceilings) as well as a weighty and high balustrade extending across the entrance of the South Aisle of the Choir. The Aisles of the choir are hid by curtains of crimson cloth edged with gold lace, as are frequently the Altars in the transepts. The Altars at the Church of St Francis, & at that of our Lady of the Mount are much in the same style, as gaudy if not equally valuable.

60. The cathedral was completed in 1514. The Franciscan convent no longer exists having been closed in 1834. Today the Jardim de São Francisco occupies the site of the former convent.
61. The cathedral, which was the work of Gil Pedreiro Enes (Pero Anes), is considered to be an important example of the Manueline style.
62. The ceiling is made of Madeiran cedar and is inlaid with ivory.
63. The carved altar pieces are thought to have come from Flanders.

The Chapel of Sculls with a plate of which Mr Barrow[64] has complimented the taste of his English readers, belongs to the convent of St Francis, but is detached from the Church. It is a small room not above 15 feet by 12 & perhaps 15 feet high. The Altar & the furniture on it are in very bad condition. The entrance opens immediately into the piazzas, under which, at the other end, is the entrance into the convent. There is a window in one side of// it which admits light enough to dissipate all that fine sombre gloom which Mr Barrow has caused to be thrown over his plate, and one of the Pannels of the door being taken out is supplied by a grating, through which happening, accidentally to peep I obtained an unwished for sight of this Chapel, having from the outside appearance taken it for a stable or a wash-house. The idea of its dimensions, as well as every other idea except that of disgust which can be gathered from Mr Barrow's plate quite vanished on beholding the place and the false impressions given in that plate must be my apology for having written a single [word] about it.[65]

The convent contains about 80 friars, some of whom are reported very eloquent in the pulpit. There is one other monastery in the Island at Camara de Loubos and several nunneries in this place & elsewhere. The troops have been provided with quarters by causing the nuns in one convent to make room for the sisterhood of another, and the 11th Regiment inhabits the College formerly occupied by students of divinity who were dispossesed on a former occasion to make room for the troops under Gen[eral]: Clinton in the last war, since which time the College has remained unoccupied.[66] The church has by a recent order been appointed for the use of the English Garrison, a Chaplain having just arrived, who receives, (as I hear) a remuneration of 600£ per annum, which salary// as obviates the necessity of his resorting to other means for

64. John Barrow, *A Voyage to Cochinchina in the Years 1792 and 179*, Cadell and Davies (London, 1806) contains a description on pages 7–8 with the plate facing page 8.
65. This chapel no longer exists but a similar chapel, walled entirely with human bones, can be seen attached to the church of Nossa Senhora do Carmo in Faro.
66. A British force under General Henry Clinton had occupied Madeira during the War of the Oranges between July 1801 and January 1802. The College referred to was the former Jesuit College. The Jesuits had been suppressed in Portugal in 1759. The former Jesuit chapel had been allocated to the British as a regimental chapel with the consent of the Bishop.

any increase of income deprives a great many of the English resident here of the hope of having their children educated under his care.

May 26. Being Ascension Day was chosen for the entrance of two young Ladies on their noviciate in the nunnery of Santa Clara.[67] The Chapel in which this ceremony was celebrated is very well proportioned, & but for the prison-looking grates at the end contiguous to the private chapel would make an excellent ball room. The walls are painted like oiled floor cloth & the grating which is as strong and closer than that which confines the wild beasts in the Tower of London is hung round [with] a crimson drapery. Both the Chapels are spacious and the private chapel appeared to be richly decorated. A numerous company of Portuguese & English attended on the occasion, & I am happy to say that the opinions of most of the Portuguese with whom I conversed, & some of whom were of the Clergy, were given in disapprobation of the sacrifice we witnessed, the eldest of the young Ladies being under fourteen & the sister about 12 years of age. They subdued their distress during the ceremony but wept greatly at parting with their friends at the grating after their admission.

No wheel carriages are kept in this place. The Ladies pay formal// visits in Sedan Chairs attended by their Gentleman-usher. On other occasions they ride in Palanquins made very light & carried by two men who walk diagonally along the street, the hindmost nearly on a level with the other, easing the pressure which the pole of the Carriage bears upon the shoulder which supports it, by placing their walking sticks over the other shoulder &

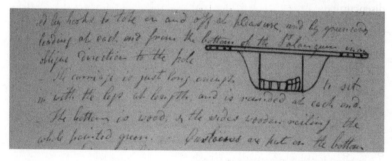

---

67. The convent of Santa Clara still exists. It was originally built by João Goncalves Zarco, one of the first discoverers of Madeira. His son founded and endowed the Franciscan convent.

under the pole of the carriage. In this manner a lady is carried up and down the steepest hills for several miles without stopping at a rate which it is inconvenient for an Englishman to keep pace with. The pole of the Palanquin is quite straight the body suspended from it, by two thin rods of iron, one at each end, perpendicular, attached by hooks to take on and off at pleasure, and by green cords [?] leading at each end from the bottom of the Palanquin in an oblique direction to the pole. The carriage is just long enough to sit in with the legs at length, and is rounded at each end. The bottom is wood, & the sides wooden railing, the whole painted green. Cushions are put on the bottom and a piece of linnen of some large glaring pattern printed on it, or else resembling a large shawl is thrown over the Pole as a shelter from the Sun & the Air. The Gentlemen walk if the distance is short but long walks into the country are only taken by// the English & not by many of them owing to the extreme steepness of the ground. The better sort of horses are ponies, some from the Western Isles; I have heard some from England & some from America. They are very high priced, a small one which I have been accustomed to ride being accounted worth 230 dollars, such a sum having been refused for him by his owner. Of course the hire of horses is expensive, for though a short ride on a rip[68] may be had for a dollar, you pay 2, 2 ½ and 3 for a good pony the whole forenoon. A man always accompanies each horse, & will keep pace with you by crossing & cutting off the ground in a most surprising manner as notwithstanding the extreme badness of the roads (I do not mean level ground, but ground disencumbered of loose earth and stones) every body canters or trots fast. As all the horses are rode with sharp [sic] with short curb bits they generally go exceedingly well up before & many are so well trained as not to require any tension on the bridle in order to keep them up, consequently their pace is very safe & though now & then the hind feet cannot be prevented from slipping, the riders neck is never endangered by a stumble. I have generally rode without whip or spur, & have prevented the man in attendance from goading my horse which has hardly ever been necessary. Mules of small size are likewise rode & some few asses.//

68. A worthless horse.

If the ride is long some additional men are sent to carry provisions, & if it is intended to sleep out of Funchal beds & cooking utensils are likewise provided. One man will carry provisions enough for a meal for at least six persons with wine, beer, plates &c and not give you much occasion to wait his arrival at your halting places. A sett of bedding, and a Portmanteau containing a full change of Ap[parel], as a provision against being drenched with rain when among the mountains, will be carried with ease by one man during a tour of any length. There are some few large horses kept by those who wish to shew off, but they do not answer so well, though being up they become equally sure-footed.

When long journeys are taken it is customary to procure introductions to the Vicars or wine-growers at the different villages who however can furnish you with no other convenience beyond a room to sleep, & the procuring fowls, eggs &c which you will probably have to dress & must sleep on the floor if you have not bedding with you.//

(this page stops short)

London March 1811[69]

The necessity of not going far from home, lest the Brasil fleet should come off the place in my absence prevented my making many excursions into the Country & restricted those I did make to a short distance from Funchal. I did indeed resolve to venture away for 3 days in order to ascend the Pico Ruivo[70] the highest point in the Island, estimated at 6000 feet, but the weather never became sufficiently settled to promise a pleasant journey. My rides therefore were confined within seven miles east & west of Funchal, and up the hill north to the elevation of about 2000 or 2500 feet.

The Chapel of Nossa Senora del Monte is situated about 1500 feet above the Town which it fully commands & beyond it one of the finest sea-views I ever saw. The road to the Chapel is one of the favorite walks of the towns people & on a Sunday or festival day we met always many small parties attired in their best, walking side by side to the sound of a Guittar plaintively

---

69. The insertion of this place and date seems to be further indication that much, if not all, the following text was written later.
70. Pico Ruivo de Santanna is 1861 metres and the highest point in Madeira.

struck by one of them who generally accompanied it with his voice. The best country residences are situated near this road which is bounded on both sides as high up as the Chapel by garden walls. Each house is situated within its own vineyard probably amidst a shade of Mulberies trees & accompanied by roses & honeysuckles. They all look towards the Sea, and are generally built in the highest part of the Garden belonging to them which is intersected with terrassed walks, over which the vine is frequently trained// to form Arbours & bowers, and in some places a double row of well grown orange trees offers a rich shade. The dwellings themselves are generally more cottages only designed as summer residences being so much more exposed to the Sea Air, than the town that the temperature of those situated near the Chapel is from 10 to 15 degrees less warm.

The rides to the East & West are more varied than that to the North (which is one continued, unbroken, steep ascent), the gullies & ravines which torrents have formed down the sides of the Island offer many singular & romantic points of view, and break the road into a series of ascents & descents, at times going along the edge of perpendicular precipices, & at times crossing the bed of a large mountain stream bestrewed with large masses of rock. Entering one of these ravines on foot from the beach, where its stream is discharged into the Sea, the sides gradually become higher as you ascend forming walls of rugged rock on each land [hand?] where however you may often see small terrassed Gardens & Cottages.

In this manner I traced for a considerable way up it the ravine which serves as the bed of the stream which 4 years ago made so much havoc owing to the bursting of a water spout in the mountains sweeping away several houses, and part of [a] Church which stood near the Beach into the Sea.[71] As the ascent along the bed of the stream is much more gradual than the ascent of the mountain, in the face of which the ravine is hollowed

---

71. This catastrophe occurred in 1803. In a flash flood a part of Funchal was swept away with up to 700 people losing their lives. The British Factory House was destroyed. After the flood the engineer Raynaldo Oudinot was asked to draw up plans to prevent a recurrence of the disaster. Oudinot was responsible for the rebuilding of the city, the construction of embankments and bridges and for extensive engineering works undertaken throughout the island. He died during 1807 shortly before the arrival of Beresford.

out, we found after walking up it for about two hours when night-fall obliged us to give// over the attempt to trace it further that the rocky banks on each side of us could hardly be less than between 4 & 500 feet high. We had the good fortune to find a narrow path leading up to one of the terrassed gardens I have mentioned and from it to the brink of the Ravine from whence we get across the country into the Chapel road before named.

The most distant excursion I made eastward of the town was to the County seat or "Quinta" of Mr Carvalho the greatest landholder in the Island.[72] He has chosen his situation so as to have the most extensive piece of level ground I anywhere saw in the Island for a garden situated at the height of at least 1500 feet above the Sea.

Here, although the spring was scarcely set in, I saw hedges of roses of various sorts & what I deemed the most beautiful profusion I had ever seen, a hedge 5 or 6 feet of the scarlet fuchsia, as full of flowers as ever I saw one of sweet peas in England. I was the more surprized because we had felt a sensible chill in ascending to this delightful spot, & had actually passed through several clouds which shewed it to be within reach of the influence of the gloomy atmosphere which, except in the midst of summer, almost uninterruptedly covers the more elevated parts of this beautiful Island.

The country to the west of Funchal is even more romantic than that to the east. I did not go further than to the Camera de Loubos[73], or the Chamber of Sea Wolves, a miserable dirty little place, so called because built close to a very romantic little cave formed by some high & grotesque rocks which project into the Sea, and form a very small basin, so perfectly land-locked, that it is as still as a pond however// rough the Sea may be outside. The water is deep in it, so that the craft may be moored against the banks. It makes a most excellent retreat for a few fishing boats, & should any enemy invade the Island a landing might be made here by the boats from the squadron, while the attention of the people is attracted by

---

72. This must be João José Xavier de Carvalhal, later Conde de Carvalhal. He was described in 1819 as 'the worthy proprietor of the largest estate in the island: his income is above £20,000 per annum; he was educated in England and has since travelled through the greater part of Europe. Any person respectably dressed is promptly admitted to traverse his noble domain and view his charming gardens.' Anon, *A Historical Sketch of the Island of Madeira* (London, 1819) p.29.

73. Câmara de Lobos. The word Lobos (wolves) was used for monk seals that used to live off the coast.

a demonstration in front of Funchal, in perfect safety, the place being left with two dismounted Guns only. By this means all the batteries which defend Funchal would be avoided & the Garrison forced to meet the Enemy in the field or capitulate.

The road to Camera de Loubos crossed two of the deepest ravines in the Island. One of them, the furthest from Funchal presents a most magnificent scene. It proceeds directly from the Central ridge which forms, as it were, the back bone of the Island to the Sea. Instead of a natural descent in the bed of the torrent, the mountain is cleft perpendicularly to its very foundation where the ravine commencing holds a strict course to the Sea with hardly more slope than of a peaceful river. The verdure & foliage on its lofty banks contrast grandly with the masses of rock which everywhere occupy its bed, which I should think must be 60 or 70 yards across at least.

I have to regret only having had a very imperfect view of this grand scene, as the part which I have tried to describe, is not seen in going to Camera de Loubos, the road only crossing the mouth of the ravine & the view I obtained of it was on another occasion when I was galloping back to Funchal in quest of medical aid// for one of my companions (Mr Etty of Lombard St.[74]) who had been kicked off his horse by the vicious mule of another of them (Mr Luccock of Leeds[75]) & whose thigh narrowly escaped fracture.

It will appear strange that my excursions should have been confined within such very short distances, but in Madeira, a ride of seven miles from home, is quite sufficient to occupy a very long morning. Whenever you quit the paved road, and attempt to deviate into any cross track, you find your way encumbered with loose stones, and by the unevennesses of the rocky road itself. I never saw in North Wales any tracks coming near

74. Bodley & Etty of 31, Lombard Street were lace merchants. Madeira was well known for lace making and embroidery.
75. This is John Luccock, author of *The Nature and Properties of Wool...* (1805) and *An Essay on Wool...* (1809) but chiefly remembered for his book *Notes on Rio de Janeiro and the southern parts of Brazil; taken during a residence of ten years in that country, from 1808 to 1818*, Samuel Leigh (London, 1820). See Herbert Heaton, 'A Merchant Adventurer in Brazil 1808–1818', *Journal of Economic History*, 6, 1 (1946) pp.1–23.

in difficulty to those in Madeira, and the agility & spirit of the horses in surmounting them surpasses what I could have had any idea of. Goats could scarcely be more provident & alert.

On the whole, comparing the picturesque beauties of Madeira with those of the only other mountainous countries I have seen, N. Wales, & the vicinity of Rio de Janeiro, I am tempted to give it the middle place in my estimation. It presents two or three views perhaps superior to either of the others. In general, it falls very greatly short of the variety & richness of Rio de Janeiro & its small extent bounded by a coast very little broken, makes it yield to Wales in variety of outline, while its more happy climate, gives it a variety & cheerfulness of tint which the happiest vallies in Wales can give no idea of, & vegetation extending to a height above the Sea little short of// the summits of the second rate hills in Wales. The dreariness of sterility is never perceived which so much strikes the attention there.//

Page 55 ends after only two lines

The Island of Porto Santo is governed by a sub-governor the supreme authority being vested in the Governor of Madeira resident in Funchal. His salary is only 3000 Dollars per Annum. The most useful production of P[orto] Santo is the lime-stone, of which there is none in the neighbourhood of Funchal where they build their houses with the Granite of the Island, and whiten them within & without with plaster made of the lime of P[orto] Santo.

The most esteemed product of Desertas is the Orchilla, which is though inferior to that of the Canaries & Cape de Verd Islands.[76] On the center of the largest of the three Islands is a level plain, which has been cultivated and is said to have produced good barley. The most southern of them is rented by a Portuguese Merchant Mr Vieira of the Crown. He pastures about 150 Sheep upon it, & has the only good Mutton [to] eat in Funchal, except what is procured from ships touching there.

The chief commerce of Madeira depends, as is well known, upon its wines. The whole produce of the Island does not, in middling years, exceed

---

76. Orchilla (Roccella Tinctoria) is a lichen from which a purple dye can be extracted. It was probably known to the Romans and was used in Europe from at least the 13th century to dye cloth.

15 or 16 thousand Pipes, & although a good deal of Tenerife & other wines are sold for Madeira in London & other Markets, I do not think that any considerable proportion of it passes through the hands of the Merchants of Funchal, but is imported directly from the places where it is produced. Consequently the profits of the greater part of the English Merchants depend almost wholly on the wine of// the Island, & when we consider the number of houses Established there, many of which contain several partners, and the expensive manner in which the resident partners live, we are obliged to conclude that the per centage they gain on their sales must be very exorbitant, as the returns are small in proportion to those in Mercantile Establishments of similar appearance in other countries.

Houses have been named to me, as having sold 5000 pipes in one year. This, averaged at £40 a pipe would be £200,000, & an enormous profit would be made, but in these years, all the other houses who had only the remaining 10 or 1200 pipes[77] to divide among 15 or 16 firms at least, appeared to be doing as well as usual, and I know of no instance of failure where they have confined themselves to the regular trade.

A considerable appearance of commercial activity & bustle is kept up at Madeira by the numerous fleets which touch there, and take in wine & fresh provision (when they can get any) consisting of Fowls, turkeys, goats vegetables & fruit. The passengers benefit the Shops a good deal, by purchasing what they forgot to provide themselves with before they left England, or what they may have felt the want of in the passage. During my stay of six weeks in Funchal, three India or China fleets including that I came with,// two West India fleets, one of which was of 40 sail, the Brasil fleets of 4–5 sail in which I went away & several single ships came to anchor in the Roads. While I was in Funchal the glut of English Manufactures which the closing of the continental markets against us occasioned in every port left open to our speculators was beginning to be felt there, & I have been since informed that several of those I saw there who brought with them & received since large investments of dry goods as Cottons, Woollens, &c have failed.

---

77. He presumably means 10,000 or 12,000 pipes.

Towards the close of my stay at Funchal, the weather became very warm *in the Town* at noonday. The Thermometer in the shade was generally about 77 but on the sunny side of the street, against a white wall it would rise to 113 or 114. No one would choose such a station to walk or stand in, but unavoidably in crossing the streets you would at times become subject for a few minutes to the influence of the Sun full upon you. Every sunny wall, as well as the tiled roofs of all the houses, are covered with small lizards timid & harmless enough, but very disgusting till habit makes the sight of them familiar. I used to be very much annoyed by the apprehension of their getting into my bed-room but it was not I suppose warm enough for them, nor were there many flies in it. These last are the greatest pests of the Island, as I believe they are of all middle latitudes.// In the tropics it is too hot for them nor do Lizards abound at Rio de Janeiro. Some few Centipedes which I found usually at night against the walls of my bed room were not entertained by me as agreeable visitors, although I believe the centipedes of Madeira have not the venom of those of hotter latitudes. Mosquitoes began to appear, but not of size or in number to produce considerable inconvenience.

I quitted Funchal June 9th at night to embark in the *Neptune* transport already under weigh with the Brasil fleet, under convoy of the *President* Frigate[78] & *Lightning* Sloop of War[79] the former having on board Lord Strangford Envoy to the Court of Brasil[80], the latter, among other passengers, L[ord] Claude Hamilton[81] who has been at Madeira some [time] for his health & now left it in the last stage of consumption, to try the chance of a still warmer climate and of a Voyage. He died in the passage.

78. HMS *President* was a 38–gun frigate. Originally a French ship *La Présidente*, it had been captured in 1806. It was commanded by Captain Adam McKenzie and Kinder later sailed on the *President* from Rio de Janeiro to Río de la Plata.
79. HMS *Lightning* was a 16–gun 'fire ship'. It was launched in 1806.
80. Lord Strangford (1780–1855) was appointed British diplomatic representative in Portugal, largely on the strength of having published a translation of Camões' minor poems entitled, *Poems, from the Portuguese of Luís de Camões, with remarks on his life and writings*, J. Carpenter (London, 1803). He was active in trying to persuade Dom João to leave Portugal and transfer his court to Rio in 1807. He was then sent to Rio to continue as British minister there from 1808–1815. Thomas Kinder accompanied him on this journey. He was later ambassador in Sweden, Turkey and Russia and was made Baron Penshurst. See J. Street, 'Lord Strangford and the Río de la Plata, 1808–1815', *The Hispanic American Historical Review*, 33, 4 (1953) pp.477–510
81. The Hon Claud Hamilton (1787–1808) was the son of Sir John Hamilton, First Marquis of Abercorn.

The fleet was likewise accompanied by the *Undaunted* Frigate[82] as far as the Tropic, and I had the pleasure of seeing a race of several miles between two of the swiftest frigates in the Navy, with a fair breeze and every stick of canvas set. The fleet was going at the rate of 5 ½ knots an hour or thereabout when they dropt astern & commenced the race. They over took us and passed us in a most majestic manner. The *President* had a little the advantage of her opponent.//

The *Serapis*[83] store-ship was likewise in company, having on board S[ir] James Gambier[84], Consul General at the Brasils & his family with whom & the commanders & passengers in the vessels of war the weather permitted an interchange of visits and dinner parties which was very little interrupted during the whole passage. As for myself, my time did not pass away in the most diverting manner possible. In the *Neptune* only 230 tons burthen I could not have the various accommodations I had enjoyed in the *Northumberland*. I had however, thought to quarantine myself against disagreeable company by agreeing at Portsmouth with the Captain that he should take none but myself. He did not keep his agreement, and admitted two empty headed young fellows whose chief occupation during the voyage were singing & sleeping. The weather being finer than in more northern latitudes, I was not so sea-sick as I had feared, and having obtained gradually the tone of my stomach and the use of my legs was sufficiently well to divert the time by reading Portuguese and reading in general. At length I even became so far a Sailor as to go out to the bowsprit end to try to harpoon the numerous bonetas, & Albacores[85] which were playing around us and two or three times in the finest weather did reach the top mast-head & go out to the ends of the main & for[e] yards to look at the fish which are seen as they glide through the water to much greater advantage from a position whence you nearly look down upon

---

82. HMS *Undaunted* was built in 1807. It was on this frigate that Napoleon was taken to the Island of Elba in April 1814.
83. Although Kinder describes *Serapis* as a storeship, this is probably HMS *Serapis* (30 guns) commissioned in 1782. Between 1807 and 1815 its Master was William Lloyd. It sailed for the Cape in April 1808. Ended service as a convict hospital ship in Jamaica where it was sold in 1826.
84. Sir James Gambier was appointed in 1808 to be Britain's first consul general in Brazil.
85. Albacores are yellow fin tuna. Boneta is the Atlantic bonito.

them.// These however were great efforts, and cost me no small degree of toil & fatigue, and as the motion is felt so much more when so far removed from the center of motion I used almost to apprehend that should the wind freshen I should become sick & gidy and almost unable to descend. We were constantly attended by large shoals of Bonetas & Albocores which were continually leaping some feet out of the water. We saw likewise flying fish innumerable & as our deck was very few feet above the waves many flew on board. One day we had nine or ten which made a good dish at our table, and though dryer, resembled small whiting in taste. Having arrived in the latitude of 9° North we were there becalmed & spent a fortnight in advancing the next 5 degrees where the S.E. trade winds at that season commences.

The trade winds south of the line blow always from S.E. or S.S.E. varying only a point or two, and north of the line they blow from the N.E. or N.N.E. The belt of calm which separates the two trades winds, changes its station according to the Sun's position. When the sun is near the Northern tropic, the calm Latitudes are found from 4^0 to 9^0 or even 12^0 north, when he is in the South Tropic, they will be found south of the Line. Each Trade wind seems to extend over about 20 or 22 degrees of Latitude but my little experience induces me to believe they are generally found to blow with fewest intermissions on the side of the //Equator where the Sun happens to be situate.[86]

The fortnight of calm weather we experienced in this Voyage was not only tedious, but subjected those of us who were in crowded or inconvenient vessels to much inconvenience. The Sky became perfectly surcharged with Clouds, without a breath of air stirring, & we were then deluged with water which seemed to fall rather in a connected sheet than in a shower. At such times, although the Thermometer did not indicate more than 80^0 to 82^0 I endured a heat much more oppressive than I ever remember elsewhere to have experienced. Our little cabin built upon the deck, and on that account, very agreeable in dry weather as more airy & less exposed to the nauseating effluvia of the bilge water, than such as are below deck, was not proof against the inundations and I had my bedding wet more than once.

86. This refers to the Equatorial Convergence Zone or Doldrums.

At length however we were relieved from these nuisances by a breeze which carried us with very little interruption to the end of our voyage. Two or three days after it sprung up we diverted ourselves with the usual frolics with splashing one another in honor of Neptune on crossing the Equator. We had but one man on board who had ever pretended to have crossed the line before, and by a little cross examination of him I satisfied myself, & had like to have satisfied those who stood by, that he had never been there, but I was afraid of spoiling the good humour of the crew, by throwing doubts about their being legally// sprinkled & opening a door to discussions among them as who should begin, & still more, by giving my fellow passengers a right to avoid the little fees for Grog levied upon the novices who pay for being smoothly shaved instead of being scraped a little with the edge of [a] barrel [?] hoop which fees, marvellously induce to cheerfulness & good temper.[87]

We had little other variety in our passage. The temperature of the trade winds is the most agreeable possible. The Thermometer hardly ever rises above 32^0 while the breeze is the most refreshing, and the air the most lightsome imaginable. Instead of being, as might be imagined, warmest under a vertical Sun, I believe it is generally found to be coolest, as the Atmosphere is generally obscured, & the wind fresher than is customary in the trades. But I have been told that when a vertical sun is passed near the Equator, calms are not infrequent, and all the inconveniences of them must doubtless in such cases be greatly augmented.

Two or three days before we made Cape Frio[88], five or six spermaceti Whales passed close to the Ship. Some of them appeared nearly as long as the Ship, and swimming gently along without any aparent effort among the Ships, they very soon out-stripped the fleet which was going about 6 knots. They did not appear to me ill shaped fishes, and as the sun shone brilliantly at the time, the colour of their backs were reflected with every lustre & variety. Salt water seems to be a very favorable medium for shewing changes of colour for I have always thought that the appearance of the

87. Crossing the line ceremonies were regularly observed by passengers and crew. Although their exact nature seems to have varied widely, today they still involve ritual shaving.
88. Cape Frio is a promontory on Brazil's southeast coast 113 kilometres from Rio de Janeiro.

Dolphins// darting about in the water, greatly exceeds the much talked of changes which they exhibit when dying.

On the 23rd of July we made Cape Frio distinct about a degree east of Rio de Janeiro, and doubled it at night-fall, & the following morning we perceived the picturesque coast which extends from Cape Frio to Rio de Janeiro on our Right.

The harbour mouth with the small Islands outside and the magnificent range of Granite Mountains which are on the left of the Entrance, to the south of it [was] before us. The fleet was at Anchor opposite the City by mid-day. The enchanting scenes which presented themselves as soon as we had neared the land were much too interesting ever to become even faint in the memory, and although I was [busy with] the many occupations in which I found myself engaged, on my arrival at Rio de Janeiro as well as by the multiplicity of new objects which continually presented themselves to my sight and which I wished first to arrange in my mind, [I was prevented] from putting any of my observations on paper during my short stay there. I do not despair of being able to describe them from recollection, as well as I could have done at the time. I have no hope of making any one as interested in the description, as I was in seeing the scene, but it will be more the fault of my talents for description than of my recollection, if I am not able to give a tolerably adequate description of them. As in the year 1808 I only spent one month at Janeiro which place I revisited in 1810 when I had somewhat// more time, and more leisure to observe what surrounded me I propose to affix my description to that part of my journal which relates to my homeward bound voyage, and making no mention at present of any thing which occurred during my first residence there, refer my friends to my next sheet which commences with my departure thence for the Rio de la Plata.[89]

(page ends after six lines)

---

89. See Introduction.

Towards the close of August a vessel arrived in the Rio de Janeiro from Gibraltar bringing dispatches to S[ir] Sidney Smith,[90] informing him of certain negociations commenced between the patriots of Spain, & the English Admiral, commanding the blockading Squadron off Cadiz, relative to a peace and alliance between England & Spain, which latter country had agreed that her colonies in S[outh] America should be opened to English commerce.[91] About the same time papers arrived in some vessels from Liverpool, from which the disposition of the English ministry to confirm & forward the negociations commenced at Cadiz was made known: in consequence of all which intelligence Sir S[idney] S[mith] resolved to dispach the *President* Frigate for the River Plate, in order to communicate to the governors of that province the news received, and to ascertain their willingness to comply with the stipulations entered into by the mother-country on their behalf. Judging that it offered me a most favorable opportunity of either collecting interesting information, or entering into commercial engagements, I obtained the permission both of the Admiral & of Cap[tain] Mackenzie[92], to take my passage in that vessel.

It was expected that she would be ordered to Sea on the 25th or 26th August but the necessary dispaches were not then ready, & on the 27th, having been informed she would certainly sail that morning, I took my luggage on board, with much reluctance at leaving Rio de Janeiro// so soon after my arrival there, without having had either time or opportunity to see much of the beauties of that country, or to satiate my curiosity as to its productions. But I entertain the hope of returning there in my way to Europe & cannot suffer so good an opportunity of visiting the Spanish Colonies, as the present to pass unseized. The dispatches were still

90. Vice-admiral Sir Sidney Smith (1764–1840) is chiefly remembered for his successful defence of Acre against Napoleon in 1799. He was appointed to command the fleet blockading Lisbon in October 1807 and escorted the Portuguese royal family to Brazil when they decided to depart at the end of November. While commanding the British ships in Brazilian waters he became involved with the intrigues being carried on by queen Carlotta Joaquina who hoped to have herself made regent of the Spanish colonies in the New World. Smith was recalled to Britain 1809.
91. The Spanish insurrection against the French army of occupation had occurred at the beginning of May. The squadron blockading Cadiz was part of the Mediterranean fleet commanded by Admiral Collingwood.
92. Adam MacKenzie (later Admiral Sir Adam MacKenzie), commissioned lieutenant 1790 and captain 1799. Served under Sir Home Popham as second captain aboard Admiral Gambier's flagship *Prince of Wales* at Copenhagen in 1807. Commanded *President* 1808 and *Bedford* 1809.

unready, and as the setting in of the sea-breeze before noon, prevents vessels quitting harbour that do not early get under weigh, I again returned on shore, and having some ground for believing that the papers could not be ready even on the following day, I engaged a party of Friends with whom to pass the 28th on the water among the Islands in the Bay, which I had not had any opportunity of visiting, being still ready to embark in the Frigate, if on reaching the water side we should discover her about to move. It so happened. The Admiral weary of any further delay, had sat up all the preceeding night preparing his dispatches for the various Governors & men of consequence in the Viceroyalty of La Plata, & Peru & Chili,[93] which dispatches chiefly consist of Copies of proclamations issued in the various Cities of Spain, reprinted together with such additional articles from the Spanish & English newspapers, as most tend to shew the actual state of affairs; and though he had not concluded, he resolved to avoid another days delay by ordering the Frigate out of harbour before the // Sea-breeze should prevent her going. Accordingly I quitted my party & on the 28th August before 10 in the forenoon the Frigate was out of the harbour of Rio de Janeiro.

She stood off & on till dark, and as the day was fine, I had a full opportunity of again seeing in many different points of view the beautiful entrance of the Harbour, as well as the lofty and romantic chain of mountains forming its southern boundary, their summits broken into shapes both grand & grotesque & clothed with trees nodding on their very Apex. The shore is indented most beautifully with numerous curves & small bays, and near the Harbour are several small Islands, which gave a very luxurious fore-ground to our view. The Admiral came on board soon after the vessel had cleared the entrance of the harbour, in his barge of 12 oars, having a Schooner in attendance in which to return as the distance would be much greater. On stepping on the quarter deck he returned the salute of the Officers of the guard of marines drawn up to receive him, & the bows of those walking the quarter deck and then

---

93. The Viceroyalty of La Plata was created in 1776 and included the silver mines of Potosí. Chile was a Captaincy-general within the Viceroyalty of Peru..

directing the guard to be dismissed & the Ship to take a good offing, he descended into the Cabin with his flag Lieutenant, Secretary & Linguist[94], in order to put the last hand to his yet unfinished dispatches. The stateliness of his entrance, & the dignity with which, as Admiral, he gave the above commands formed a striking contrast with his agreeable & conciliatory manner// in private society. As he occupied the principal Cabin thro which it is necessary to pass, in order to get into that which in such a case remains more immediately the Captains, I suffered the inconvenience (though somewhat ill as usual at Sea) of walking the Quarter deck from the time of his arrival on board, until dinner at 4 o'clock. During the preparations for dinner he came again on deck, conversing very freely with the Lieutenants of the Frigate and congratulated me on being thus far on my way to Buenos Ayres, where [he] told me he expected I should be well received, but cautioned me that I should wait the result of Cap[tain] Mc Kenzie's negociations with Mr Liniers[95] & ascertain the good dispositions of the Spaniards towards us, before I trusted myself among them.

At dinner I had to regret that the sea had in a great measure disabled me from taking a part in the conversation which the Admiral did me the honor to address so frequently to me, as to have enabled me to turn it so as to have furnished information most desirable to me, but I was compelled to leave the table shortly after the Cloth was drawn. The Admiral did not quit the Ship till night fell, when having made signals by burning blue lights for the Schooner to approach he descended into his barge, & Cap[tain] Mackenzie immediately ordered more Sail to be set & we have bore away for the Island of St Catherine's.[96] Cap[tain] MacKenzie very obligingly directed my Cot to be swung on the Larboard side of the great Cabin while himself occupies the Starboard, and as I now use with him// the same range of room which in

94. By 'linguist' is meant interpreter or translator.
95. Santiago de Liniers y Bremond. Born Jacques de Liniers in France in 1753, he entered Spanish service as a naval officer in 1788. He acted as governor of Misiones 1802–5 and commanded the forces that compelled Beresford to surrender Buenos Aires in August 1806. Appointed viceroy in May 1808, he was replaced in August 1809. Accused of plotting a counter-revolution, he was executed in 1810. See Introduction.
96. Santa Catarina is a small island off the coast of Brazil, situated at 27.30 south, half way between São Paulo and Porto Alegre.

the passage from England was occupied by 4, for sleeping, and in the day by 6, viz Cap[tain] MacKenzie, Lord Strangford, L[or]d Forbes[97] & Mr Bing, with Count Lipenhawsen [?] & Col Fonseca who had sleeping cabins fitted up outside, it may be supposed that I made the voyage as comfortable as a qualmish stomach would permit.

Lord Forbes came on board with intention of accompanying us as far as St Catherine's, but feeling doubtful of a passage back within the time he wished to return to Rio de Janeiro, he again went on Shore with the Admiral. On the 30th I was wakened in the morning by the Officer of the Watch entering the cabin to inform the Cap[tain] that two large sail were seen on her Starboard bow.

Cap[tain] M[acKenzie] got up & after going onto the quarter-deck ordered the Ship to be cleared for action when I expected to hear a great racket & to have been disturbed by the entrance of the men quartered to the 4 Guns in our sleeping cabin, in order to clear away our trunks, tables, wash-hand-stands &c but everyone went to his quarters in silence & I was suffered uninterruptedly to dress & shave myself, when in opening the Cabin door in order to go into the quarter deck I saw all the Guns on the main deck manned & the men belonging to those in the Cabin waiting at the door for my coming out. On reaching the Quarter deck it was just ascertained that the two vessels were the [illegible] ships Foudroyant[98] & Marlbro[99] beating to windward in order to reach Rio Janeiro, after a cruize of some weeks off the Rio de la Plata where they had experienced very bad weather// had exhausted all their fresh provisions and had had no communication whatever with the shore. Cap[tain] McKenzie went on board Commodore Moore's[100] ship, and supplied him, and Cap[tain] Schauenberg[101] with some fresh beef & mutton, after which each pursued his course.

97. James Ochoncar Forbes, 17th Lord Forbes (1765–1843). A Scottish representative peer.
98. HMS Foudroyant, 80 guns, was launched in March 1798. From June 1799 to June 1801 she was Nelson's flagship.
99. HMS Marlborough, 74 guns, was launched at Deptford in June 1807.
100. Commodore Graham Moore (1764–1843), later Vice-admiral Sir Graham Moore, was the younger brother of General Sir John Moore.
101. Charles Marsh Schomberg (1788–1835) was captain of Hibernia, Smith's flagship off Lisbon in 1807. He took command of Foudroyant in June 1808 for the voyage to Río de la Plata and ended his career as lieutenant-governor of Dominica.

These ships had quitted the station on being relieved by the *Monarch*[102] & *Bedford*[103]. Having altered the course which the frigate was keeping in order to join those vessels, we found on making the Island of St Catharine the following day, that we were a few miles to Leeward of the Entrance of the Channel which separates it from the Continent, with so unfavorable a wind that Cap[tain] McKenzie deemed the object for which he wished to go into harbour there of insufficient consequence to compensate the probable delay.

We then coasted at about 6 miles distance the whole length of the Island abreast of its eastern shore. It is one continued ridge of hills of a hundred f[ee]t elevation nearly totally covered with wood, of an agreeable aspect, but presenting no very prominent features. We could discover no inlet or bay along its Shores. The appearance of the adjacent continent was similar, its hills being occasionally seen through some of the breaks in the Island, in altitude & towards the South seeming gradually to decline.

On the 5th Sep[tember] we saw Point Castello a few miles to the North of Cape St Mary's, at the Entrance of the Rio de la Plata & fell in with his Majesty's ships *Monarch* & *Bedford*// when our Cap[tain] communicated his dispatches to Cap[tain] Lee[104] of the *Monarch*, & by his orders the three vessels doubled Cape St Mary's, & anchored abreast of Monte Vedeo on Wednesday the 7th Sep[tember] after having been baffled by Southerly Winds, and calmed since the 5th. The whole coast from point Castello is very low (with some small elevations in the distance) and covered with a short lively verdure bringing to my mind the Downs of Dorsetshire in Spring. We passed close to the Islands of Lobos & Flores, small barren spots full of Seals & aquatic Birds; and during our passage in their neighbourhood, we saw many Whales blowing in the water & numbers of Seals shewing their heads above the waves.

---

102. HMS *Monarch*, 74 guns, was by now a very aged ship. Launched in 1765, she was Vice-admiral Onslow's flagship at the battle of Camperdown in 1797. She was broken up in 1813.

103. HMS *Bedford* was launched in 1775 and was in action at the battle of Cape St Vincent. In 1808 she was commanded by Captain Walker.

104. Captain (later Admiral Sir) Richard Lee was commissioned lieutenant 1782 and captain 1794. Took command of *Monarch* 1806 and was involved in Sir Sidney Smith's blockade of Lisbon in 1807.

When we quitted Rio de Janeiro, the Thermometer at 12 at noon in the shade usually stood at or about 76^0 and we experienced but little variation till after we had passed the Island of St Catharine & approached the River Plate, when the southerly winds beginning to blew, it speedily indicated 57^0 at which temperature it remains settled.

The Senior Officer having determined that Cap[tain] McKenzie should proceed to Buenos Ayres, he resolved first to land at Monte Vedeo, in order to procure a small vessel in which to proceed up the river as well as to ascertain the state of affairs, as much as possible beforehand; and as the Vessel had hoisted the Spanish Ensign, & a flag of truce we had the satisfaction, in the morning to see a boat sent from the City// to inform us that the news of Peace was already arrived from Spain, & that we should be received on the most friendly footing, the Governor[105] having already ordered a vessel down the River to seek such English Ships, as might be cruizing at its mouth & inform them that orders were given for their being provided with refreshments, and treated as allies. I attended the Cap[tain] on Shore, as likewise did a Mr Mather from the *Bedford*, a friend of Cap[tain] Walker's & appointed as secretary to Cap[tain] McK[enzie] by the Senior Officer.

The Governor received us with much politeness, and entertained us with a very good dinner, but expressed his conviction that the Viceroy could not, until he received orders to that effect from Spain, venture to permit a free trade with the English; & wished Cap[tain] M[acKenzie]. to defer going to Buenos Ayres until a Frigate daily expected to arrive with proper instructions should appear. Our negociators do not appear to have sufficiently considered the relative situation of a colony with the mother country, & believing that this settlement is but slightly attached to Spain, & eager for independence they have, in my mind, been incautious in not observing that the present crisis has overturned all party distinctions, animating every Spaniard with the sole wish of resisting the common

---

105. Francisco Xavier de Elío was a Spanish officer. He commanded the forces defeated by Pack outside Colônia do Sacramento on 9 June and a section of Liniers's forces in Buenos Aires. He became governor of Montevideo after the withdrawal of the British in August 1807 and led the rebellion against Liniers's authority. In 1811 he became the last Spanish viceroy of La Plata with his capital in Montevideo.

enemy, & have consequently repeatedly pressed the Governor of Monte Vedeo to furnish them with a sketch of such terms as he deemed proper now to grant to the English in return// for assistance offered. The Governor replies that he is in want of nothing; that the English may be assured of being received as friends, but that he has no powers to grant any favours beyond assistance to such vessels as may put in for refreshments; nor can he permit trade until authorized. A vessel, however, was to be provided to convey Cap[tain] McK[enzie] to Buenos Ayres on the 10th· but on the 9th at night a small Schooner arrived from Rio Janeiro bringing dispatches from S[ir] Sydney Smith & in her Cap[tain] McK. immediately proceeded, giving me a passage in the vessel which the Governor was to send alongside the frigate the next day, and in which he intended to return.

SPANISH SETTLEMENTS IN THE RÍO DE LA PLATA

Early on the morning of the 10th I went on Shore & waited on the Governor to enquire when he would order off the vessel, but learnt that he had already counter-ordered her, in consequence of having heard of Cap[tain] McK[enzie]'s sudden departure, at which indeed he seemed little pleased, & probably did not think himself treated with due respect. On informing him that an Officer of the *Monarch* was to have followed

Cap[tain] McK[enzie] as well as myself he promised me that if we would bring our baggage ashore the next morning, he would find us the means of proceeding to Buenos Ayres the wind being such as not to permit one of the River small craft to come alongside the vessel in quest of us.

The Governor observing that I occupied no efficient[106] situation, advised me not to think of proceeding to Buenos Ayres, without commercial regulations having first taken place, but on// representing that in the event of no open trade being granted, I should still be glad to avail myself of the present favourable opportunity to satisfy my curiosity, he yielded his objections. The Governor is an European, a man of much quickness & intelligence & very Gentlemanly. I have been prevented from profiting by his promise to procure me a conveyance to Buenos-Ayres.

I am writing this on board the *President* 11th Sep[tember] the wind having during the night changed to the Westward, and consequently contrary to my object & so strong as even to prevent my going on Shore, as the three Ships are anchored in the open Road full 7 miles distant from the Shore. Cap[tain] McK[enzie] who led them in, was afraid to approach nearer as the water is known to be shoal, and the two 74 gun ships are the largest which have ever entered the River Plate.

Our situation is so unfavorable that we are at least 2 hours going ashore, & as little sheltered from the wind and sea as if in the midst of the Atlantic, but the Anchorage is good. The ships would be taken nearer shore, but the time of their stay is not expected to be so long, as to compensate the trouble & risk moving them. As I suppose the Officer of the *Monarch* will not now be sent, I shall of course be left to provide myself a passage in the first vessel which will probably be as soon as the weather will permit.

On the first day of landing I attended Cap[tain] McKenzie round the fortifications// of this City. They have been greatly increased since the late seige, particularly by a well built bastion close to the waters edge, where the breach at which Sir S. Achmuty's army[107] stormed the town, & where

---

106. He may mean 'official'.

107. Sir Samuel Auchmuty (1756–1822) was a loyalist officer born in New York. He had been with Beresford in Egypt and commanded the forces sent to the Río de la Plata to reinforce Beresford. He captured Montevideo on 3 February 1807. In 1811 he commanded the British forces that conquered Java and was subsequently appointed commander-in-chief in Ireland. See Introduction.

so many brave men fell, was made.[108] The bastion is circular & calculated both to prevent a landing among the Rocks to the West of it before the town & (which it is thought would last year have been the easiest mode of attack) to present additional annoyance to any who may be inclined to make a breach in the same place as before from the land. The citadel is by no means contemptible, and though the Walls of the whole place are not, except at particular points, of much apparent strength, & do not present an appearance at all comparable to the works at Portsmouth, they are mounted with good artillery, mostly brass & very well kept. The Arsenals contain a good supply of Ordnance stores.

I have been greatly sorry to see numbers of Englishmen wearing the Spanish uniform.[109] I have not had opportunity to ascertain satisfactorily the actual number, & therefore hope that 2000, the number I have been told are in Garrison here, & in quarters at Buenos Ayres, greatly exceeds the truth. They have been tempted by the large wages given, which amount to 16 Dollars a month, to a private a very large allowance in a country where the necessaries of life are cheaper than in almost any other. They are mostly very fine men, & have the grace to show some embarrassment at facing the English Officers.

108. For details of the assault on Montevideo see Ian Fletcher, *The Waters of Oblivion*, Spellmount (Stroud, 2006) pp.41–60.
109. Soldiers of Beresford's and Whitelocke's army who, after the surrender, preferred to enlist with the Spanish. McKinnon reports an incident in 1809 of a British sailor being assaulted and wounded by 'three of Whitelocke's Irish deserters'. National Archives (Kew) FO 72 90 Alex McKinnon to Canning , Buenos Aires 2 November 1809, The view of Montevideo is from a water colour in the John Carter Brown Library.

To the West of the town is a very commodious harbour, sheltered from the West// wind by a hill, which I suppose may be between 200 and 250 feet high, & which is the largest eminence here & gives name to the town, & has on its summit a signal station for ships in the offing. The harbour is oval & has 2 rivulets of good water running into it from the River. The town itself affords some shelter to the E[ast] being built on a small slope. The bottom of the harbour is composed [of] such very soft mud that, though on sounding in the deepest part the lead only gives 3 ½ fathoms, vessels drawing more than that depth may enter at high tide without receiving any damage & large merchantmen do lay in water of less depth than their draught, bedding themselves at low water into the mud.

The landing place is within the Eastward point of the harbours mouth, quite in still water. The streets are built at right angles of good width, with foot-paving & posts between the path & the horse-way in some; but they are exceedingly muddy in the middle, & as nearly all the houses are built in hollow squares the windows opening behind or within & presenting blank walls to the streets, intermixed with cottages & small yards bounded by old brick walls, the aspect is very mean, & brings continually to my mind the seige; although there is only one part of the place which suffered in the least from it. In external appearance this place does not equal Rio de Janeiro, but many of the houses seem better inside than those of that City. The rooms are numerous and of good// dimensions, most of the houses being only one story high, & many having only the ground-floor; having nearly all flat terrassed roofs with parapets & two or three of the highest, which are 2 stories high, having look-out Towers erected above the roof from which the whole city, the roads of the adjacent country for several miles round may be seen.

I brought an introduction to a Gen[tleman] inhabiting one of the last mentioned class of houses, Don Francis Juanico.[110] He has always been a great favorer of the English & voluntarily gave up his house to Admiral

---

110. Don Francisco Juanico was a merchant who began trading with Brazil and the United States after 1780. He dealt in Brazilian products, tobacco, slaves, sugar and textiles. (I am indebted to Fabricio Prado for this information.)

Stirling.[111] He is a merchant. It is but justice that I mention the manner of his hospitality, being some what similar to what I have known usual among the more liberal Portuguese, and seemingly fairly indicative of the general temper of the merchants here. When I presented him my letter, I told him that I expected to proceed to Buenos Ayres immediately; he observed that my absence would deprive him of any opportunity of entertaining me, but he wished me to inform my friends on board the Frigate that when they came into the city he should be glad to see them to dine or sleep in his house. When I had left him he sent after me to the Governor's two letters of introduction addressed to residents at Buenos Ayres.

Having remaind longer than I expected here, I have had an opportunity of knowing it was his intention I should take his civilities to the letter, & having once informed me that his family dine at half past one he expects to find me at table every day if I am in town disengaged. The officers on shore from the several ships// have expressed themselves equally well placed [pleased?] with the hospitality they have met with, though mostly without introduction. The many enquiries made of me respecting persons who were here last year, indicate a partiality to the English & at present every body wears a cockade with the initials of Ferdinand the Seventh, the ground blue and red, intending by those colours to express the union betwixt England & Spain.[112] The Ladies embroider them & give them away. There is very little resemblance between the Ladies here & at Rio de Janeiro. Many of them are handsome, they all seem lively, and are neat, nay somewhat elegant in their dress, which is all in the English fashion; & appear to have paid much more attention than the others to the cultivation of their heads. Very few however, talk any language but their own, but their talents are so much more alert than their neighbours, that I find my Spanish of 10 days old much better understood, (and their own phrases repeated & varied to my comprehension according as they

---

111. Admiral Sir Charles Sterling (1760–1833) commanded the ships which brought Auchmuty's army to Montevideo. He replaced Sir Home Popham in command of the naval forces. He served in the War of 1812 and in 1814, was court-martialled for misconduct and retired on half pay.

112. Ferdinand VII became king of Spain on the abdication of his father Carlos IV in March 1808. He was lured to France and also forced to abdicate, being replaced by Joseph Bonaparte. The risings in Spain, which took place in May, were in the name of Ferdinand as legitimate king.

perceive me hunting, as it were for their meaning) than was my Portuguese which I had been studying two months at the time I quitted Rio de Janeiro. They are not tall but light & elegant in figure. The men whom I have hitherto met with are well informed & desirous of information.

At the Governor's house I found the Officers greedy in listening to anything I had to communicate relative to the management & discipline of our Ships of War & regulations of our service, conducting// their enquiries with great judgment & expressing their admiration of the *Bedford* for the very same points which I have heard our great naval officers, giving her the preference to most of the Ships on the station. In fact the difference between them & the Portuguese as to the rationality of the opinions they broach, & the manner in which a contrary opinion is received, was in my eye quite conspicuous. I am informed that most of the English manufactured goods introduced last year are already in consumption, & that such a scarcity of most articles is felt as will insure in all probability good profits to the first shippers of goods, should the trade be opened. It proves the consumption of the interior to be very great, & furnishes a slight criterion from which to judge, both of the number & wealth of the Spanish colonists in this quarter of the Globe.

The Cathedral Church of Monte Video[113] is a large brick building conspicuous at a great distance, & serving as a good mark to Ships steering for the City. It has a dome near the Centre & two towers, not exactly alike, over the entrance, the body a Parallellogram, inducing the belief that the Architect had seen a plan of St Peters & St Pauls. The inside is in a style of very great neatness, & would in any city be thought a handsome church, differing intirely from the gawdy style of the Portuguese Churches at Madeira & Rio Janeiro, resembling more the simple elegance of our// best English specimens of Church decoration. The church is not yet quite finished, but wants nothing in the interior except pavement which is now of square tiles.

I have now to notice a considerable nuisance, arising from great carelessness & want of proper regulation. The Cattle are mostly

---

113. The Catedral Metropolitana de Montevideo was begun in 1724.

slaughtered by the beach close by the wall to the East of the town & the remains left to putrify, causing the stench perceptable for a mile when you happen to be to leeward of it as I have experienced even in a boat with so much salt water intervening.

From what I have already seen of Monte Video, I am induced to prefer a residence in Rio de Janeiro, to one in this country. It is true the advantages of climate & society seem on the side of the river Plate, but after all, Spanish Society may certainly be seen to greater advantage in Spain & healthy climates may be found nearer home than in 34th degree of S. Latitude. The country on its banks is an intire flat, & I anticipate that it can present little which would not with less cost of time be learned from books & the conversation of those who have been here. At Rio de Janeiro, on the contrary, no description can convey to any reader a just idea of the beautiful & inexhaustible variety in the animated & inanimate works of nature. They must be seen to be judged of, & would exhaust fifty lives without draining the sources of curiosity dry. I should much regret to be condemned to// pass my life near either of these provinces, & therefore my preference must be understood to apply to a temporary stay for the purpose of obtaining new ideas & again returning to Europe with such information as is not to be obtained within its limits.

It may very well happen that I shall alter my opinion when, by some stay at Buenos Ayres, I have had an opportunity of seeing things more nearly so that, though I have often regretted that the continuity of my notes has been much broken in upon by unavoidable interruptions, my friends who read them may well be glad to have been saved from the perplexity naturally arising in notes regularly taken, by the sentiments committed to paper to-day being contradicted by those of to morrow.//

Page 82 ends half way down

Monte Video

Sep[tember] 12th.

The wind moderating I closed the former sheets of my remarks & leaving them in the *President* in order to secure their transmission to Rio de Janeiro & to England, I quitted the Frigate with my baggage, the wind being still fresh & the Sea so rough that it was entirely owing to the Skill of a Lieutenant who took the trouble of steering the boat himself that we arrived dry ashore. I have now to mention what came under my observation there during my stay until 25th Sep[tember] at the hazard of repeating what I have already said in the Sheets closed up.

The country in the neighbourhood of this city is so unvaried, that having once rode out & viewed it from two or three different elevations, I found little inducement again to stir beyond its walls, as the horses are taken so little care of that in general it required more whipping and spurring than I found myself at all disposed to apply, to make them move at any tolerable pace, with the continual unpleasant knowledge that you are forcing your horse not only beyond his will, but to his manifest hurt. Indeed one sight of the country suffices to convey as correct an Idea as can be attained without journeying to a distance in the Interior, as in every direction it presents open downs covered with a fine verdant pasture (generally trefoil) swarming with herds of cattle; & in particular spots, where tufts of thistles offer cover for them, great abundance of Partridges of the common species, but remarkably large & strong, flying quicker & consequently much more difficult to// shoot than those in England. The rivulets which run into the bay contain numerous wild ducks & other aquatic birds, & snipes on the borders; & on the open downs are many plovers, which however, the people will not eat in the persuasion that they live on Carrion, which is not the case, & many of them were taken on board the Ships of War & proved very good.

On one occasion, shooting near some osier beds, I dislodged a number of large dogs somewhat resembling Mastiffs. The immense number of oxen killed as I have said solely for the hides &c, affords plenty of subsistence to these animals, which consequently increase greatly, and run about wild in great numbers. Farther from the city the brown Ostrich[114] is very common & large flocks were seen by the Officers of the different Ships of War who rode to the distance of 8 or 10 miles. The river S[anta] Lucia[115] falls into the "La Plata" about 20 miles to the West of M[onte] V[ideo] & from its vicinity all the wood used as fuel in that city is brought in Carts, this as well as every other article requiring human labour to bring it to market is very dear.

For all purposes of carriage here & at Buenos Ayres & throu'out the interior of the Vice-royalty of La Plata, a large, high two-wheeled Cart is used, superior to that of Rio de Janeiro, as the Axle-tree does not move with the wheels. It consists of a platform of solid wood with sides of perpendicular stakes crossed again with osiers, or thongs of dried hides,// and is open at each end, but those used for distant carriage are tilted, the covering being made of dried hides. These latter are drawn by 4 or 6 oxen yoked, and the fore most pairs connected with the pole of the wagon by long thongs of dried hides. These animals are driven with a goad by a man in a Waggon the goad being loosely suspended from the roof of the tilt in Slings, in the manner of the ancient battering ram, the necessary length of the pole being much too great for it to be wielded by hand. The Carts used in the towns are mostly drawn by horses: these animals being fastened merely to the end of the pole by a thong attached to the saddle girth, & their bodies are brought very nearly in contact with the pole. The driver rides the near side one. Very few people in Monte Video keep carriages. Those they have resemble distantly English coaches or chariots, but are very roughly made & negligently kept, always dirty & in condition inferior to the average of London hackney coaches.

There are no white domestics either in [Monte] V[ideo] or B[uenos] A[ires] but the quantity of negroes is by no means so striking as in Rio de Janeiro[116], as in the country they have very little agriculture & no

114. The Rhea (pterocnemia pennata).
115. The Santa Lucía river is the main source of water for Montevideo and is the main river in southern Uruguay. It forms a delta where it enters the Río de la Plata.
116. About a quarter of the population were slaves.

plantations of sugar or coffee neither are they used, as in Brazil, as beasts of burden. Though the lower class of inhabitants here will not engage themselves as domestic servants, they occupy many of the employments which in Brazil// are solely fulfilled by negroes. The carts I have mentioned belong to them & are driven by the owners & the care of the herds of pastured horses and oxen, or to speak more correctly, the catching the one species and slaughtering the other, is the work of the white colonist.

In Monte Video the numbers of Friars is small, not exceeding 30 or 40, and there is no convent of Nuns. The articles of commerce more immediately belonging to M[onte] V[ideo] consist in tallow, hides, horns, salted tongues & some furs especially the Tyger's skin (spotted).[117] The price of these varies from 4 Piastres or Dollars to 6 & many of them are large & are of great beauty. I measured 2 taken at hazard & found that from the tip of the nose, to the insertion of the tail they exceeded six feet by some inches, & suppose the excess above six feet may be allowed for the stretching of the Skin in order to dry it, which is performed in the same manner as with Ox hides, by pinning it to the ground the inner side upwards, with pegs inserted through holes cut for them in the edges. These animals abound throughout Paraguay & in the Pampas to the W[est] of B[uenos] Ayres, & in the Portuguese Provinces most southern, from whence through the settlement of St Pedro de Rio Grande,[118] many skins are sent to Rio de Janeiro. They sometimes are killed very near to Monte Video.

From a Gentleman resident at M[onte] V[ideo] I obtained a short notice concerning Rio Grande, & the country between it// and Monte Video. He disembarked some merchandize at Rio G[rande] and transported it in Waggons to M[onte] V[ideo]. The country about Rio Grande is flat & marshy, affording vast quantities of cattle but the settlement is very poor, & so situated as to be very greatly annoyed by sand. From Rio Grande to S[anta] Teresa, on the boundaries between Spain & Portugal he found no settlement, but from thence to M[onte]

117. Presumably the ocelot (Leopardus pardalis) though these animals do not reach the size Kinder describes.
118. Rio Grande de São Pedro, the southernmost major port in Brazil, was founded in 1737.

V[ideo] was enabled each night to procure some lodgment. The journey occupied 14 days, he being obliged to accompany his caravan, but might easily be performed in six. He saw numberless cattle, some tygers, serpents of various descriptions, deer, & many other wild animals. He computed the distance he travelled at about 140 leagues, S[anta] Theresa being situated about midway. The first part of the country is well diversified with hill & dale & wood, and throughout the whole the country was perfectly passable.

During my stay at Monte V[ideo] I rode out to visit the country seat of my hospitable friend Francis Juanico, having heard it represented as the best in the country adjacent and well worth seeing.

My disappointment was considerable to find a place large enough it is true, but without taste, neatness, convenience, or tolerable furniture. The rooms in general are on a Par with a farm-house kitchen in England, brick-floors, white-washed walls, with the flat roof apparent consisting of a range of rafters supporting a flooring of square thick tiles, (which description may serve for the roofs of all houses here, except that the better rooms are ceiled within with planks painted or white-washed & corniced// and all the windows looking in one direction. The Garden was neatly kept with a pleasant copse at the bottom, bordering a rivulet & an orangery, in other words, a double row of orange trees which are not common near Monte V[ideo].

The Town [of Montevideo] is built on a Peninsula, and has 2 Gates only leading into the country, that opening to the Eastward leads immediately toward a large establishment for slaughtering Oxen and drying their Skins, & no sooner have you hastened to get away from this, than you arrive at a plot of Ground where the carcases of these miserable animals are stretched in hundreds, perhaps thousands a prey to the seagulls, which flock there in great numbers, the hides, & fat, & tongues being solely taken away, for as to the horns, such a number of Oxen are killed that beyond a certain quantity the horns are left.

If you go out at the other gate the scene is but little improved, as all the horses for hire are kept close outside the walls tethered ten or twelve together in circular pens, & a more miserable set of hacks were never seen in one spot. Here you chuse your horse, or if you are nice about y[our] saddle you have him sent into the City for an English one, as they are sufficiently common here. For my part I rode on the saddle of the country, which is composed of 2 or 3 pieces of thick leather, & a large piece of blue woollen rug, all strapped up on a saddle tree, (in some measure adapted to the back of a horse) with straps of dried hide pared thin. Your horse is bridled with a strong curb, the reins being of plaited thongs resembling an English coach-whip & one end left very long in order to serve as// a whip, in the same manner as the bridles of light dragoons in England. Thus equipped, you pay a dollar for your ride, & should you chance to like your horse may probably buy him for 2. I found the sort of saddle I have described sufficiently easy.

But to return within the Walls. The state of society here is extremely monotonous. The theatre is open twice a week, and every body attends it, every man of property having a box for his family & a seat or two in the Pitt (as he is a connoisseur) to approach nearer to the Actors. On the evenings, the party to which I might be said to belong, always took a turn or two about the ramparts, divided each time into the same subdivisions, & after taking a Cup of Chocolate at the same coffee house, met again at the house of a Merchant who always held himself ready to give us a cup of Tea. Here, as well as at every other interval, we played at drafts. The only interesting personage I met in these parties was the old General who commanded the Spanish troops in the battle fought against Sir S.Achmuty prior to the storming of the town – his name de Croq[119], but he is a Spaniard. He is about 72 years of age, and by no means differing materially from any other man of his years. The Spaniards all ridicule the Idea of such a man being sent out to fight Sir S. Achmuty & efforts were made to prevent him, but he was senior & obstinate. During the battle he held his snuff box in his hand when// a Cannon ball shot off the left side of his hat. He nevertheless took his snuff very composedly, because (as I ventured to suppose) he was probably not immediately aware of what had occurred. Be that as it may, he certainly showed firmness enough to entitle him to great praise on that account.

119. General Bernardo Lecoq.

As to drafts, I became so tired of seeing this game perpetually, that I exerted myself to teach three or four of them to play back-gammon & having accomplished that object, I attempted Chess & left some very deeply engaged in that Game at my departure, & cannot but take great merit to myself on the score of public spirit in thus varying the amusements of this very dull place. During my stay there I had every reason to be grateful for the attention shewn to me personally & the estimation in which it is obvious my countrymen are held in this City. Repeated enquiries were made of me respecting very many of the individuals of our nation who were at Monte V[ideo] while it was in our possession, as well Mercantile Men as Naval & Military. Sir S. Achmuty is respected by all in the highest possible degree. The good order he preserved in his army & the precautions he took effectually to prevent any of those evils so greatly to be feared in a city taken by storm have endeared his name to every Spaniard & to use the words of one of them, "They all loved him as though he had actually been a Spanish General".

They greatly blame Whitelocke[120] for the disorders said to have been committed by his troops during the attack upon// B[uenos] A[ires] & many say that Sir S. Achmuty would have taken the city with half the number of men the other was defeated & not have suffered the same excesses to be committed; but national vanity makes the very same men commit the manifest absurdity of exculpating Whitelocke on account of the Gallant and as they say, insurmountable resistance offered him.

The Governor Don Xavier Eleo, who was at Buenos Ayres the whole time & to whom the people of Monte Vedio attribute the greatest part of the success, has delivered to Cap[tain] Lee of the *Monarch* (Senior officer here) his testimony in favour of General Whitelocke, in order that it may be made any use of in England in any way that can be made of any advantage or consolation to him.[121] What this memorial consists of I know not, but I was myself the medium of a conversation between Governor

---

120. General John Whitelocke (1757–1833) commanded the British forces sent to recapture Buenos Aires in 1807. His failed attack led to the surrender of his army and the evacuation of Montevideo captured earlier in the year. On returning to Britain he was court-martialled and dismissed from the army. See Introduction.

121. The court martial verdict against Whitelocke, handed down 24 March 1808, declared that he be 'cashiered, and declared unfit, and unworthy to serve His Majesty in any military capacity whatever.'

Elio & Cap[tain] Lee in which the former expressed himself in terms I have mentioned & indeed stronger in consequence of my asking at Cap[tain] Lee's request if he would give his permission to a Copy of it being shewn to General Brownrigg[122] who is by marriage connected to Whitelocke. But notwithstanding that, the Spaniards shake their heads & say it is extremely severe that he should be deprived of all his honours & declared incapable & *unworthy* to serve his Majesty in future, & set up partial defences for him by declaring that others deserved worse of their country than he did; some being inveterate against Gower[123], some against Crawford[124], & nearly all against Pack.[125] Let not my friends suppose that Whitelocke has suffered unjustly. Having read his trial in the most authen[tic]// form & being now on the spot (B[uenos] A[ires]) where I can collect and compare the opinions of the inhabitants both with each other & with the actual state of the forces here, & the localities of the place, the case appears to me so plain that freely stating that I have received none of the advantages of a Military Education I feel notwithstanding perfectly competent to declare that nothing short of a most culpable want of every qualification necessary to form a commander, could have occasioned the failure of the Expedition W[hitelocke] commanded. Indeed, so very unfit was his conduct for the place he occupied, that his name had gone here before him with such odium as was sufficient in itself to raise every soul in arms against him, while that of Sir S. Achmuty would probably have induced surrender without the expence of a single cannon ball.

Among other errors which Whitelocke has attempted to disseminate in England is this, viz that the People of Buenos Ayres have a particular hatred

122. Sir Robert Brownrigg (1759–1833) was military secretary to the Duke of York, served with Sir Samuel Auchmuty at Montevideo and in 1813 became Governor of Ceylon. He and General Whitelocke married sisters, the daughters of William Lewis of Jamaica.

123. Major-General John Leveson-Gower, who was Whitelocke's second-in-command. Later served with Wellington in the Peninsular War

124. Brigadier (later major-general) Robert Craufurd (1764–1812) had been the first choice to command the army sent to Buenos Aires. He was, however, superseded by Whitelocke. After Whitelocke's court martial he was appointed to command the Light Division in Spain under Moore and gained an almost legendary reputation as a field commander. He was killed at the siege of Ciudad Rodrigo in 1812.

125. Major-General Sir Denis Pack (1772–1823) accompanied Beresford to Buenos Aires in 1806, escaped with him to the British feet and joined Sir Samuel Auchmuty. He became an officer in the Portuguese army under Beresford and commanded a brigade at Waterloo. In 1816 he married Beresford's half sister Elizabeth Louise.

& aversion, not merely temporary, but as it were constitutional and hereditary, independent of all casual circumstances, against Englishmen. Now it is true enough, that these people are extremely fickle & that in the best of times they have an inward inclination always to insult a stranger, so that hitherto the condition of all foreigners here has been precarious and unpleasant at best, the reasons for which are to be found in the laws, which so far from protecting strangers enable the party in power whenever they choose, to put them in force to seize & imprison the person of any stranger found in the place. The people naturally have no respect for those who by//[126] not having licences from the Viceroy (which of course are not granted to the subjects of countries at War with Spain) subject themselves to such risks, accounting them smugglers & men of no respectability. But if they have any respect for the individuals of one nation more than for those of another, it is certainly in favour of the English. They all say that the English character is much more similar to their own, than is the light & fickle temper of the French, many proofs of their dislike of whom have been given long prior to the present motives of disgust. As to the Portuguese every body knows the extreme rancorous hatred borne them by the Spaniards. Nevertheless, they are addmitted among them to trade (but not to mix much in society) & to establish themselves, because being accounted by the nation the only true Catholics, I may almost say the only Christians besides themselves, the laws of Spain grant them that advantage, in consequence of which, though hated infinitely more than any other strangers, they do not suffer the same inconvenience. Terms are scarcely strong enough to express the contempt these people entertain for the Portuguese: Dogs are in much higher estimation.

But to return to Monte V[ideo]. One evening there, I was surprized by repeated cries of "Vive Elio". Vive el Rey. I found on enquiry that they were caused by the arrival of a new governor named Michelina, a Cap[tain] in the Navy sent by Liniers to replace Elio.[127] The people did

---

126. Two pages of the MS are numbered 92.
127. Juan Ángel Michelena (1774–1831) commanded various Spanish vessels in the Río de la Plata during the British invasion. He was a supporter of Liniers, who sent him of 20 September to replace Elío as governor of Montevideo

not chuse to part with Elio, & Michelina who entered the town at eight o'clock in the evening, was glad at 3 in the morning// to embark in a boat in the bay (at the great risk of being drowned, for it blew a very violent Pampero[128]) in order to cross a corner of it and return by land (as he came) to B[uenos] A[ires] fearing he should lose his life if he retreated by the gate and was perceived by the populace. The cause of this attempt to displace Elio was as follows. The Abdication of Charles 4th of the Crown of Spain in favour of Ferdinand 7th being known at Monte V[ideo] preparations were made for celebrating his coronation there. On the eve of that ceremony an emissary of Bonoparte[129] arrived & took occasion to recommend to the Governor to postpone it for a short time untill he received further advices from Spain. Elio demanded why, on which the emissary told him that, prior to his departure from Europe, Ferdinand 7th had again abdicated the throne & that Joseph Bonaparte was king to the great joy of all Spain, throughout the whole of which tranquillity prevailed.

Elio rejoined, that so far on that account from defferring the celebration of the festival proposed, he wished that all was ready that he might proclaim Ferdinand 7th that very evening, being determined not to acknowledge any other king. Ferdinand was accordingly proclaimed, and the emissary proceeded by the first opportunity to Buenos Ayres. After he had remained for some time in this City, & no further advises had been received from Europe, public curiosity being very much alive to know what was the purport of his mission & the actual state of affairs, a

---

128. A violent wind coming off the pampas which could create very rough conditions in the river. In 1799 a particularly violent pampero destroyed forty vessels anchored off Montevideo. John Luccock gives his experience of one. 'We observed an appearance to windward, which we took for a small water-spout, rapidly approaching. It was actually the surface of the water, lashed into spray by "the Demon of the coming blast", ... We were instantly on our beam-ends, the lee-guns, taffrail, and boom in the water, and the sea making a thorough breach over the ship; the people having no other means of securing themselves than by clinging to the first firm thing they could seize... After a pause of a few moments the wind burst through the sails with the noise of thunder, and frittered them into small shreds, which fell to leeward like flakes of snow.' Luccock, *Notes on Rio de Janeiro and the southern parts of Brazil...*, pp.146–7.

129. This was the Marquis de Sassenay who arrived August 1808. Sassenay brought with him a proclamation part of which read '...The dynasty has changed, but the monarchy still lives. You should honour and defend that part of it which is entrusted to your care, and prevent such a magnificent monarchy from losing a single one of its precious possessions... The bond uniting France to Spain will become useful to the American colonies after it opens a vaster field to their commerce.' Quoted in W. S. Robertson, 'The Juntas of 1808 and the Spanish Colonies', *English Historical Review*, 21 (1916) p.575.

proclamation[130] appeared addressed to the People & forwarded circularly to all the Governors within the// Viceroyalty recommending patience and unanimity of opinion, apologizing in some measure for aparent want of confidence in not sooner communicating respecting the state of affairs & the intelligence brought by the Emissary (who is expressly alluded to) & observing that in the absence of fuller advices it was resolved to proclaim Ferdinand 7th which was accordingly ordered everywhere to be done, informing the People of the Congress which was pending at Bayonne[131] & placing in terms very little equivocal the destinies of Spain in the will of the mighty genius who governs Europe: it recommends them to wait with patience the fate of the northern [mother?] country & to be determined by it. The Viceroy speaks throughout this paper which is signed in his name. It is very loosely & insiduously worded, & I regret that I have not by me a copy to translate, but believe I have given its general sense very equitably.

When Elio received this circular, he returned to Liniers a very harsh reply (which I have not seen) inferring a falling off from his allegiance due to the family of Spain & declaring that he would be at war with any nation, province, city or individual whomsoever whom should swerve from their duty to Ferdinand 7th.

Liniers returned for answer, that the proclamation was not his act, but that of the Cabildo assembly, & in the meanwhile news of the real state of affairs arriving other proclamations in every respect coinciding in sentiment with those published in Spain have been circulated from B[uenos] A[ires]. In consequence of his offence Elio was recalled to B[uenos] A[ires] under the pretence however// of his presence being necessary in order to be a member of a junta to be formed according to the general orders of the supreme junta of Seville[132] of the principal men

---

130. *Circular que el Excmo Senor Virey dirigio el 17 de Agosto de este ano a todos los Gobernadores y Xefes de las Provincias, baxo el titulo de reservada.*
131. Congress of Bayonne: this refers to the meeting at Bayonne between Napoleon and Carlos IV and Ferdinand VII which followed the uprising at Aranjuez in March 1808. At this meeting Carlos IV abdicated in favour of Joseph Bonaparte.
132. This is a reference to the Junta of Seville which claimed sovereignty over Spain's colonial possessions. It was superseded by the Junta Central which was established on 25 September 1808.

in each province or Colony. Elio remained at M[onte] Vedeo, & in consequence Michelina was dispatched and entered that City unexpectedly on the day of bustle which I have mentioned.

His first step on entering the City was to go in person to the Commanders of the different Military Corps, requiring them to act under his orders. Then he entered the fort, and after the usual salutations told Elio that he came to replace him & that he ceased to be Governor, not however shewing any commission. Elio observed that he knew nothing of him in that capacity, when the other rejoined, that he would cause him to know him. Elio on that, shortly & contemptuously answered – as "you indeed give me cause to know you". Or some terms to that effect. M[ichelina] therefore produced a Pistol & requiring Elio to surrender himself a prisoner in the name of the King. E[lio] turned the Pistol aside, & M[ichelina] was thrown, either by E[lio] or by his brother-in-law who was said to be present. However, he quitted the fort, & having caused the Cabildo to be assembled produced to them his commission & required them to acknowledge him as Governor which they complied with, but declined taking any steps to execute his commission, declaring themselves ready to obey him, but observing that they who were at the time assembled & clamouring in the square outside, he was therefore obliged to fly as I have related. The next morning, an open Cabildo[133] was held attended by 20 deputies from the people & it was resolved that Elio should remain// & that no further orders from B[uenos] A[ires] should be obeyed in M[onte] V[ideo]. The Governor at the breaking up of the Cabildo communicated to the people his intention of remaining among them & was drawn back by them in triumph to his residence, & as the carriage returned to the Cathedral door for his Lady who was at Mass, she likewise experienced the same mark of popular favour. After this, no further tumult occurred in Monte V[ideo] during my stay there, nor indeed was it likely as every body there seems of one mind in this affair.

Don Xavier Elio came from Spain during the time of our expeditions as commander of the Interior on the N[orth] bank of the river Plate. The

---

133. A Cabildo Abierto was an open meeting of leading citizens.

governor of Monte Video being sent prisoner to England[134], Elio was appointed by the Viceroy as governor on the evacuation of the place by the English & was confirmed by F[erdinand] 7th before he went to Bayonne. The Viceroys of de la Plata enjoy the privilege of appointing to vacancies within their provinces subject to the approbation of the King, which, once granted, they cannot change the appointment or displace an officer without alledging charges against him on which to bring him to trial. On this ground Elio stands, & few Englishmen when they have the case before them, but will wish him fortunately through this species of mutiny against his superior officer. The Cabildo are here supposed to be representatives of the people. That of Monte V[ideo] consists, I believe, of nine. They get out every year to chuse their successors.//

The jealousies between Monte Video & Buenos A[ires] are so great, that it is quite sufficient that Elio is popular in M[onte] V[ideo] to cause the people in B[uenos] A[ires] to side with their Viceroy. Prior to Sir S. Achmuty's attacks on M[onte] V[ideo], deputies were sent to B[uenos] A[ires] anticipating that attack & begging assistance. These deputies were ignominiously forced to fly, & the people of Monte V[ideo] consequently felt a superior gust in returning in the person of Michelina the insults their deputies felt at B[uenos] A[ires]. Attempts have here been made to restrain nature, & to make this city the Port & the residence of M[onte] V[ideo] in order to transfer the Seat of government to that City.

Therefore though most of the individuals in each city have friends in the other, & every week's Courier brings letters from almost all of them, they being very active letter-writers, still in all public matters the utmost dissension prevails, & is fomented among the mob.

At M[onte] V[ideo] I had the good fortune to see a very violent Pampero, the hardest that has blown for the space of 2 years. Coming direct from the S[outh] it raised so much Sea in the harbour as to render it much worse than the offing, & to endanger every Ship at Anchor there. Fortunately none were lost – a small brig belonging to my friend Franico [sic][135] parted 3 Cables, but

134. The governor was Pascual Ruiz Huidobro (1752–1813), a Spanish naval officer who had been appointed governor of Montevideo in 1803. He was sent as a prisoner of war to Britain along with 600 of his men.
135. i.e. Francisco Juanico.

luckily the gale moderated before the 4th gave way. It blew about 24 hours,// the sky being clear at intervals, but generally hazy, though not much overcast. This storm, the first I have ever seen, by no means equalled my ideas of the sublimity & terror of a Storm at Sea.[136] No doubt any boat must have perished in it but I only rejoice at being out of the Frigate, because I knew the motion could not fail to make me sick. In fact, I am convinced that the Idea of these commotions of the elements raised in us by Poets & other exagerations greatly exceeds the reality but at the same time I must allow that these waves which, seen from an elevated situation on shore scarcely seem to ruffle the surface, are found very troublesome if you are passing through them in a light boat, having several times experienced in it. My stay in M[onte] V[ideo] was from 8th to 25 Sep[tember].

The wind was so unfavorable for several days after [the departure] of Cap[tain] Mc Kenzie for Buenos Aires that I could not follow him [soon] enough to hope to find him there. I consequently determined to wait his return, not chusing to visit that City, except under the protection of his mission, until I had heard that permission was granted me. Cap[tain] M[cKenzie] on his return informed me that though for want of sufficient authority from Spain, no commercial regulations could take place at present, all was as friendly as could be desired & that the Viceroy gave me permission to go there & stay as long as I choose to satisfy// my curiosity. Two Spanish Gentlemen accompanied him from Buenos Aires and next day sett sail with him in the *President* to Rio de Janeiro, as Envoys from the Viceroy to Admiral Sir S[idney] Smyth. Accordingly having obtained a pasport from Gov[ernor] Elio, previous to the arrival & flight of Michelina, I embarked at 10 o'Clock on the 25th Sep[tember] f[o]r Buenos Aires.

The means of transferring yourself from Monte Video to Buenos Aires are extremely disagreeable. The preferable manner I am inclined to believe is to pass to Colonia del Sacramento[137] (on the N[orth] Bank of the River Plate, immediately opposite to Buenos Aires) by land, leaving only 8

---

136. This could be a specific reference to J.M.W. Turner's famous paintings Snowstorm and Shipwreck, both of which were exhibited in 1805.

137. Colonia del Sacramento, situated on the north bank of the Río de la Plata, was originally a Portuguese settlement called Colônia do Sacramento. It was founded in 1680 and became a major port through which contraband entered the Spanish territories. It was fought over continuously between Spain and Portugal, finally passing into the control of the independent republic of Uruguay in 1828. See Introduction.

leagues of water to be passed: the breadth of this mighty River at this City. Regular changes of horses are provided for those who chuse to adopt this method. The distance is supposed 40 leagues & may be passed over without much difficulty in 22 hours which, of course, it is necessary to divide by sleeping one night upon the road for which there is no further convenience than such as the meanest hovel can afford. The horse too, on which you will be mounted, may probably some of them never have been backed[138] before, & though you may be a skilful horseman, the danger of being thrown is not to be despised.

On the other hand, if you prefer passing by water to encountering these difficulties, the only means are such as I availd myself of considering that it would require more attendants, horses & trouble to carry my trunks & Cot by land & not liking to risk the// loss of them by separating myself from them. The vessels which trade between Buenos Aires & Monte Video are Launches or Balandras,[139] cutter rigged and drawing about 4 feet [of] water carrying from 40 to 80 Tons. That in which I embarked had a small Cabin astern containing just room enough for three people to sleep in. I remained upon deck during day light until being complètely exhausted by sea-sickness I turn[ed] into the Cabin & passed the night on one of the Matresses in my Clothes, expecting to be overwhelmed with vermin, but on opening my eyes in the morning I found to my great consolation that the beams were very clean and that I had distressed myself with very little cause on that account. I eat nothing except a very little bread, during my voyage. Indeed, to have eaten would have required a very vigorous apetite notwithstanding that the good old Patrono or Captain had provided, as he thought, very nobly for his guest.

At supper the cloth was spread (consisting of a circular piece of ox's hide) on the deck. On this was placed a leathern bucket full of bits of sea-buiscuit (the fresh loaf being given to me who was seated in the boat), a large piece of stick, with half a dozen roasted sausages stuck into the end of it, it having been used as a toasting fork, & a pail full of pieces of boiled beef in

138. Ridden.
139. A one-masted sailing boat.

the water it had been cooked in, which I think I observed to be taken out of the River so soon after we left Monte Video that it must have contained many saline particles useful in corning the beef a little. For the convenience of eating this several cockle shells were produced together with one knife// & one spoon which latter was of mixed metal notwithstanding that this is the land of Plate.[140]

Luckily I was on board this vessel not quite 24 hours. It frequently happens that, owing to contrary winds, they are a week or a fortnight in passing up in which case most of the time is passed at Anchor in the open River & if it blows strongly, the waves here are so short & embarressing, & the construction of the vessels so favorable to perpetual motion, that the strongest stomachs cannot endure it, and Men of iron who in the longest voyages have not known sea-sickness have here suffered so much as to endanger their lives. On arriving near Buenos Aires, if there is not water enough to enter the River Chuelo,[141] the launch is brought to Anchor directly opposite to the town. The Patrono sounding the depth continually found water sufficient to pass over the bar, which I was glad of because it blew a stiff gale from the N[orth] & raised such a Sea as must have prevented my getting my baggage dry ashore, had we anchored opposite the town. Rubbing the bottom a little occasionally we passed over the bar, & arrived very speedily at anchor in perfectly white water not a hundred yards from the embouchure of the River which is not above 60 feet wide, the ground about the entrance very marshy, & growing many willows & osiers which as the water was very high were dipping their branches into it. I transferred my baggage into a Cart, & paying 9 dollars for my passage proceeded towards the City, but soon found// myself obliged to mount the Cart along with it as the only road for Carts into the City is along the beach which was perfectly overflowed, & in many places full of holes, immersing our vehicles up to the Axle tree & putting us in imminent danger of being overturned, as a precaution against which a Man was mounted on a horse attached by a long thong to the end of a Pole, that if the road was found impassable by that horse we might by cutting the thong escape a total wreck.

---

140. This comment can be translated 'one spoon which latter was of some alloy notwithstanding that this is the land of silver.'
141. The River Chuelo enters the Río de la Plata 3 miles below Buenos Aires. Beresford had to clear a Spanish force from the opposite bank before being able to enter the city on 27 June 1806.

There is a foot path 100 yards further inland, but I could not avail myself of it because of my baggage which obliged me to enter Buenos Aires in this manner. I had just begun to feel the want of a servant, having the day before I quitted Rio Janeiro discharged one I brought there from England[142], deeming it better to be absolutely without, than to put up with the negligence of a very bad one & had had no time to enquire for another.

Being informed that there were no Inns here, or any house of entertainment where I could put up, I descended from my Cart as soon as it had passed the water & directing it to drive to Don Thomas An[thony] Romera's[143] accompanied it there. That Gentleman, as soon as he had read a letter I brought him from an English Merchant, who during the time of General Beresford has experienced the hospitality of his house, ordered my baggage to be unladen & appointed me a room in his house. As by continuing to state at length what I observe in the City, I should subject myself to the error, which I fear I have in some instances run into, of stating as general circumstances which only appertain to individual objects, I shall till a longer residence// enables me to speak with more confidence, confine myself to what may probably be supplied at once to be matter for record. On the 29th I was introduced to the Viceroy general Liniers by his Aid de Camp Don Francisco Diaz de Arenas (who, as well as myself is an inmate in Don T. A. Romera's house).

The Viceroy very readily comprehended, what I have found it very difficult to instill into people both here & in Monte Video viz. that without having actually any business on hand, I am come to look about

---

142. There is no reference to this servant in the account of the voyage to Madeira and Rio.
143. Don Tomás Antonio Romero was known as the most influential merchant in Buenos Aires. He imported slaves from the Indian Ocean and contraband tobacco from Brazil. In 1801 the *Marianna*, a ship owned by him, was discovered to be engaged in contraband. The viceroy tried unsuccessfully to obtain Romero's conviction. See Cooney, 'Oceanic Commerce and Platine Merchants, 1796–1806', p.520 and especially Susan Migden Socolow, *The Bureaucrats of Buenos Aires, 1769–1810: Amor al Real Servicio*, Duke University Press (Durham and London, 1987) pp.236–43.
The View of Buenos Aires is from a water colour in the John Carter Brown Library

me & to acquire information. I had been told by several that it would be necessary that I should assume some distinct character which embarrassed one somewhat as it would have compelled me to enter into an explanation at length to his Excellency; as had I represented myself as a Merchant I should at once have subjected myself to be told that the regulations of the Government did not permit my being here in such a Capacity & should have been supposed to be a smuggler & had I avoided intirely the Mercantile character & represented myself as coming solely to look about me, then in case that the regulations hereafter encourage me to form an establishment I should have been liable to the imputation of practising deceit on the Viceroy.

Cap[tain] McKenzie had however explained to him my object, & his Aid de Camp still further; therefore he contented himself with observing that if he could afford me any facilities he should be very happy to do so, that under the present circumstances he was peculiarly happy to see me there as an Englishman, and after some// other polite things said of Cap[tain] McKenzie & some to myself, I took my leave, having returned my thanks to the General for the kind expressions he was pleased to use towards me, & expressed as well as I was able the pleasure which in common with every other Englishman I felt at the close alliance subsisting between Spain & England. I was introduced to him in an Antichamber as he was returning from Mass and we both remained standing during the short time I was there, he passing to his closet at the same time that I quitted the Room.

I had deemed it necessary to pay my respects to the Viceroy, both because of what Cap[tain] Mackenzie had said of me, as also to obtain the highest possible sanction of public authority for my safe residence here, having before explained the uneasy situation of foreigners not so circumstanced. I am therefore at present the only stranger whose residence here is so acknowledged except some few French Emigrants, who have been here since the commencement of the revolution & are become subjects of Spain. The Viceroy is a tall good-looking man of a cheerful countenance, but with a quik [quiet?] and indistinct voice. He had on his uniform of

General when I saw him. His elder brother, the Count de Liniers is a Major-general in the service & is thought a man of more talent than the Viceroy.[144] Everybody here is perfectly well satisfied, that the tales circulated in London as to his being a pastry-cook in Madrid, are void of foundation, as I know that Sir S[idney] Smith has made use of all the means he possesses (which are considerable) to obtain// correct information as to the family of the Viceroy & as the result, he is convinced that he is of an ancient family in France, the title of which, as I have said, his elder brother now assumes.

The house I am in here differs very little from what I have described as the style of building at Monte V[ideo] but is in some respects preferable.[145] It presents a large front to the street, the gate being in the centre, & all the rooms in front only communicating with the street. These apartments are lett off, by the occupier of the house to divers Tradesmen, at about 12 dollars p[er] month each and as there are 4 of them, and as he pays a hundred dollars for the whole tenement, his nett rent is 52 dollars p[er] month, very cheap for such a house in this City. The right hand side of the quadrangle contains a dining room & the study of Don Josef Maria Romera, the son of Don Tho[mas] & holding the lucrative situation of Treasurer to the Kingdom of La Plata, by which he is prohibited from Commerce.[146] The left hand side is occupied by the Porter, the principal clerk of Don Tho[mas] & myself who am in the room occupied by Colonel Campbell[147], during Beresfords Expidition. The Center is occupied by the Chamber & office of Don Thomas & the chamber of his daughter-in-law.

There is another Story over the Center, which contains a very handsome drawing room, & anteroom superbly furnished & Carpetted

---

144. Count Santiago Luis Enrique de Liniers established himself as a trader in Buenos Aires in 1790. He came under suspicion of being sympathetic to the French Revolution when he translated a pamphlet about events in France and when some Frenchmen who had met in his house were arrested as conspirators. See Caillet-Bois, 'The Río de la Plata and the French Revolution', in Humphreys and Lynch, *The Origins of the Latin American Revolutions, 1808–1826*, pp.94–105.

145. The custom of Buenos Aires merchants letting out rooms in their houses, which they also used as offices is discussed in Susan Migden Socolow, *The Merchants of Buenos Aires 1778–1810*, Cambridge University Press (Cambridge, 1978) pp.63–4.

146. José María Romero was active in supporting his father's enterprises and in undermining the influence of his father's enemies. See discussion of his role in the viceregal administration in Socolow, *The Bureaucrats of Buenos Aires, 1769–1810: Amor al Real Servicio*, pp.242–3.

147. He was, in fact, major in the 71st Regiment of Foot.

with Skins of the Sorrellios[148] or Skunk, the Guanaco[149], & a particular species of hare, as well as one square// of Ostrich skins remarkably neat & handsome. The other 3 sides of the Quadrangle have flat roofs, accessible by the same staircase which leads to the Drawing-room. The chamber of the Lady is likewise well-furnished as is Don Josef's study or office but in all the rest of the house is the most complete want of all manner of European conveniences. Behind the Center of the Quadrangle is another containing Warehouses, Clerks apartments, & stables, kitchen, &c &c lodgments for Negroes. In almost every apartment here is a striking want as well of cleanliness as of convenience. That I occupy bears all the marks of not having been swept for some weeks. The chairs are somewhat worse than English Kitchen Chairs & the rest of the furniture consists of 2 large presses roughly made of ordinary wood, a massy oaken Table, with a desk & Ink stands on it, the room being used in the day time by one of the Clerks, as an Office. I am furnished with a stand on which I use my own Cot, & by good fortune have with me a wash hand stand, brought from England for use on Ship board.

I am however, just as well lodged as my host, except that he has a separate room for his Office. All our apartments open into the Yard, which is very ample being about [*blank*] feet square & is paved with Marble (in alternate squares of black & veined) brought from Genoa, & has a Cistern of very excellent water in the middle. I pass my time as follows. As soon as I rise a Negro brings me my breakfast (for all the family breakfast// separately) which having taken at my leisure, I generally remain in my apartment writing or reading the whole forenoon, except visiting Don Tho[mas] & Donna Francisca each for a few minutes and walking out to make a Call or two. We dine at two, & the moment Dinner is over, all rise, the family to make the Siesta & myself to take Coffee at a Coffee-house & walk a few miles after it returning to the house at about four. Don Fr[ancisco] de Arenas, & myself again sally forth to pass the evening at various houses.

---

148. *Zorrillo*, a skunk.
149. A Guanaco is a llama.

I always return early enough to pass an hour with the only Lady we have in this house, in whose chamber I uniformly meet another (the same) & occasionally some Gents, friends of the family. After that I see no more of the family, each supping in his own Apartment, while a very handsome supper is served up to Arenas, myself, & one of the Clerks in the Dining-room. All that part of the family arrangement that comes under the inspection of the Lady is better arranged than I have seen in a foriegn family, the utmost nicety being apparent in the dining-room and the dishes so brought to the table as to leave no fears as to the negligence or dirtiness of the Cooks. The Negroes are much the most regular & best instructed of any I have seen, & she lamented much to me on one occasion, the impossibility of here having European servants observing that the Negroes gave her incredible trouble.

My evenings passed in company with the 2 Ladies I have mentioned are much the most agreeable part of my time, & as they// both possessed much information respecting the state of these colonies, & entertain Ideas very liberal both of Government & of Religion, I may add the most instructive. Donna Francisca Sorrelea [150] smokes cigars & has a lap dog, but these two vices apart, is as neat & nice a woman as any English Lady. She takes out her cigars with equal indifference, whether in her friend's Chamber, or in the Viceroy's drawing room, having acquired this habit at Ascension [151], where she resided many years, her husband being then Gov[ernor] of Paraguay. The Ladies of Paraguay universally smoak. These two Ladies are about 30 years of age, frank and aimiable in their conversation, & though they speak no language but their own they speak that with great elegance & what is of more consequence to me, with that distinctness & variety of expression that renders it very easy to understand them.

---

150. María Francisca de Sarratea, daughter of Martín de Sarratea and Tomasa de Altolaguirre. Her sister had married Santiago de Liniers. She was the wife of Lázaro de Rivera y Espinosa who had been Intendant of Paraguay 1796–1806.
151. Asunción, the capital of Paraguay. Its complete name is Nuestra Señora Santa Maria de la Asunción. The first settlement there was made in 1537.

Buenos Ayres, Octo[ber] 2:

I have hitherto not quitted the city, except for a very short distance on
the side of the Plaza del Tauros. The impossibility of obtaining a servant,
& the dislike I have to buying a slave[152] prevents my buying horses. It
would indeed, be possible to hire them, but then I must ride alone not
having yet seen any one who rides out for his pleasure. The horses here are
generally much better taken care of than at Monte V[ideo], in short, none
of the miserable wretches I saw there are to be seen here. On the contrary
I see very many in excellent order, though ridden by the// lower class of
people. The Plaza del Tauros, the fort, and the line of Convents &
Churches which are situate[d] in the street next parallel with the shore, has
been so often mentioned (& likewise a plan is laid down of them in
Whitelock[e]'s tryal) that it is become needless for me to describe them.
I will only therefore observe that the insides of all I have hitherto entered
resemble each other in plan very exactly, being the same as the Church of
Monte V[ideo] viz: a nave of circular Arches with 2 side [a]isles &
transepts of the same & a dome in the middle the whole adorned with
doric pilasters, & all the walls of the side [a]isles in the compartments
which are opposite to the open Arches of the Nave contain each an Altar
or Painting together with a profusion of Gilt Pillars and Entab[l]atures, &
a blaze of riches surrounding the principal altar in the Choir, as well as
those in the transepts. From what I see here, I am apprehensive that all the
neatness I praised in Monte V[ideo] will soon vanish by being covered
with similar trumpery. However these Churches are still superior to those
at Rio de Janeiro, demonstrating somewhat more taste & less gaudiness
in the distribution of the ornaments, with equal riches.

And here, while speaking of Churches, I cannot avoid expressing my
aprobation of the manner in which R[oman] Catholics attend divine
service. The women always dress themselves on purpose in black, in a
particular fashion, free from ornament, but neat. The whole body of the
Church is open, & only a few benches along the nave, & slaves// and

---

152. The 'reluctance' of the British in South America to buy slaves is discussed in Louise Guenther, *British Merchants in nineteenth century Brazil,* Centre for Brazilian Studies (Oxford, 2004).

freemen, poor and rich choosing themselves places to kneel in, the women of condition solely indulging themselves with a piece of Carpet brought & spread for them by the domestic who attends them. The present viceroy holds his place only, "ad interim"[153] & in consequence receives only 20,000 Dollars per Annum, so long while a Viceroy "in propriedad," viz. one appointed with a patent to hold the place four years, & not displaceable except for complaints of Malversation in his office, receives double that sum. But they have likewise a profit arising out of a certain share of seized contraband goods. The last Viceroy was likewise only "ad interim". When the King appoints a Viceroy, a sealed letter is given, which he brings with him to his Government, to be opened in case of his discease. In it are 3 names of Persons appointed to succeed him "ad interim", until another shall arrive from Spain. When the Viceroy Pino[154] died, the Marquis del Sobremonte[155] was the third mentioned in the letter then opened by the Audiencia, but as the first was dead, & the second absent, he succeeded to the Viceroyalty.[156]

The Marquis had led a miserable life ever since the invasion of the country by General Beresford. He was then struck with the general panic, & fled without even seeing the enemy. Nevertheless, those who then participated in his fears, & acted the same dastardly part, have circulated the cry, that he is a Traitor. He lives at a few leagues distant from the City, in most perfect retirement, molested// by the reproaches made by his nearest connections for his pusillamity [sic] which has reduced them so low. In England I have heard it supposed, that General Beresford's easy entry arose from his being favoured by the inclinations of the People, desirous to better their condition from a Change of Government.[157] The truth is, that having had no communication with Europe for a very long

153. Santiago de Liniers was sworn in as viceroy 'ad interim' on 16 May 1808.
154. Joaquín del Pino y Rozas, viceroy (1801–1804).
155. Rafael de Sobremonte, Marqués de Sobremonte (1745–1827). Born in 1745, he had followed a military career in Spain and America until he was appointed first secretary to the viceroyalty in 1779. In 1783 he was appointed Intendant of Córdoba, a position which he filled with distinction until 1797 when he became inspector-general of the royal forces in the viceroyalty. He was appointed viceroy in 1804.
156. José Fernando Abascal y Sousa, Marqués of Concordia was the second named.
157. For a discussion of Beresford's capture of the city see Introduction.

period prior to his arrival, they had sunk into a state of perfect apathy as to affairs from without, & never having seen an enemy, had no conception of what it was. When the Gen[eral] landed, no attempts were made to oppose him, or even to reconnoitre his Army, nothing further being known than the reports of the Country people, or what is much the same thing, the exagerations of a body of men on horseback, whom they are pleased to call Cavalry, who went out the second day to oppose his passage over a marsh which lay in his road, and in which he lost his Cannon.[158] These men fled at the first discharge, & though not a man was hurt, swore that the bullets rained upon them, that there were six thousand of the Enemy, all Grenadiers as big as Patagonians, observing in terms of complete surprize, that they had brought horses with them, having seen 4 or 5 on which the General & his Staff were mounted. The Spanish horsemen might be 2000 in number, but not one of them could be brought to face the English, flying into the country in all directions.

An American Gentleman[159] who furnished me with part of these particulars was at a country house, situated a little to the S[outh] of the City. //He saw one of the horsemen gallop by his window, after the action, at full speed, of whom he learnt afterwards that he kept his way with all possible expedition till he got to Cordova[160], 400 miles into the Interior. The following morning this American went in a Chaise with his host, a Spaniard of respectability, to the E[ast] of the City, to an eminence, from which the approach of the English might be seen. Arrived at the W[est] end of the street, next parellel with the river, they saw the Army of Infantry just ready to sally from the City. It extended from the Fort to the end of the street, and occupied the whole width of the street, being at a rough calculation at least 3000 men. It was headed by a Col[onel] who was a

158. The combat at Reduction, 26 June 1806.
159. This was presumably William Pius White, better known as Guillerme Pio White. He was born in Boston in 1770 and became a slaver and contraband trader. In Mauritius he had dealings with the Périchon family and arrived in Buenos Aires in 1797 at the same time as Mrs O'Gorman (La Périchona) who became Liniers's mistress. White was an active contraband trader working with Bernardino Rivadavia and maintaining a friendship with Liniers. He provided information for Whitelocke, who used his house as the army's headquarters. He was imprisoned as a spy but freed on the orders of Liniers. He died in 1842.
160. Córdoba, founded in 1573, is situated 440 miles from Buenos Aires. It is the capital of Córdoba province. Sobremonte was Intendant there 1783–97.

friend of the two Gents I have mentioned. Can a more decided proof of the non-existence of all Military propriety be given, than to say, that this Col[onel] halted his Column merely to have a Gossip with these two men in a Gig? He told them that the Viceroy had ordered him out to occupy the entrances into the City but that it was only sacrificing the lives of the men, as resistance was of no use. Just then a horseman arrived to report the advance of the English, adding some nonsense about the Caps of the Grenadiers & their regular encampment in tents the night before, & their ferocious appearance, at which our 2 Spaniards shook their heads, & agreed it was all over with them, the one turning about his Gig to return home, & the other recommencing his march.

The 2 forces did not come in contact that day, the British// having to march some distance, but the next morning, according to the watch of my American friend, they kept up a very brisk fire for 17 minutes, in which hardly anyone was hurt, & which need not have continued beyond the first discharge, but that General Beresford, with a prudence that does him honour, deemed it necessary, [to] clear very completely the hedges, being apprehensive of an Ambuscade.[161] But after a few discharges all appearance of an Enemy vanished, & the General advanced to the entrance of the City where he halted for a few minutes. It is thought, that being able from the spot to see the immense length of some of the streets & size of the buildings, number of Churches &c he hesitated whether with so small a force, to enter a City so populous. However he soon entered, & continuing his march strait along the street now named "de Liniers" without seeing anybody, he arrived at the fort & took immediate possession of the quarters of the Viceroy who had fled to make room for him. His Army was exceedingly exhausted, having eat[en] very little since they quitted the Ships, & entered the town covered with the mud of the Marsh through which they had travelled two days before.

The defeated Spaniards were seen skulking about for 2 or 3 days, in the outskirts of the town, peeping out from the hedges, with their muskets in their hands, in perpetual fear that the English were at their heels, but

---

161. A reference to the fight at the crossing of the Chuelo.

not being pursued they returned quietly to their habitations. In course of time, when the number of the English became known, & it was seen that they were no bigger than other men, every one became ashamed of his former pusillanimous conduct// & probably to fear punishment for having yielded so scandalously to so small a force, if ever, at a peace, the Colony was again given up to Spain; & consequently when the present Viceroy attempted to retake the place, he was joined by numbers sufficient to ensure success, though I have heard many Spaniards say, that had Gen[eral] B[eresford] possessed the talents of a Politician as well as those of a General, he might have kept it until the arrival of succours.[162] He & his Officers are generally liked here. It is a common observation that to his invasion is owing the present freedom of the Country from a state of foreign subjection. If 6000 men had been sent here at first, not only B[uenos] A[ires] might have been preserved, but a sufficient force have been detached to take possession of such parts in Peru as would have secured the obedience of that Viceroyalty where, besides that the colonists are not in the least warlike, a very considerable party might have been formed in favor of the Invaders among the inhabitants of Cuzco, & of other places which have already made several efforts to change the form of Government, & probably among the Indians.[163]

Such is the opinion of many Spaniards best qualified to judge. I cannot but think that the Army of Whitelocke would now be sufficient for all these objects. At the present moment, when the people are under the influence of the emotions which the present crisis produces, perhaps such a force might not be sufficient, but if ever the Colony is again governed by the Mother-country according to laws which check her prosperity as heretofore, the experiment would certainly succeed.

The evidence given on the trial of Whitelocke// gives so plenary an account of what passed on the day of attack that I can add little or nothing to it. All agree however, in the brutality & incapacity of this man. After the capitulation, he was invited to dine in the fort with Liniers, who

---

162. This point is discussed in the Introduction.
163. Cuzco was the old Inca capital of Peru. This may be a reference to the revolt of José Gabriel Tupac Amaru in 1780.

likewise invited the Staff of both Armies. On entering the fort, he observed the Spanish Officers collected together, who as at present owing to the great scarcity of European manufactures, were probably very ill clothed. He expressed his surprise to a Mr O'Reilly who was in conversation with him at his being invited to dine with all these blackguards. He probably knew that he was not understood. I have seen several Officers that were stationed near the Church of Santo Domingo, at the time Crawford capitulated. They all agree that he might have withdrawn his Column along the beach, or even have joined other detachments by the street with little loss. If I may judge from the manner in which the Officer who received his sword related the transaction to me, that officer thinks his conduct on that occasion very pusillanimous.[164]

The Commandant of the Grenadiers of Liniers[165] told me that Colonel Crawford addressed himself to him, enquiring in terms of great anxiety if he was safe from personal danger. This took place in the confusion that ensued immediately on the surrender of his Brigade, when the Mob entered the Church & were pillaging the Soldiers of their Caps, of muskets & bayonets in the utmost confusion. That officer answered that [he] would be responsible for the B[r]igadier's safety, & offered him his Arm//protected by which he escaped from the Mob. He expressed his gratitude to that officer in lively terms, giving him an address & invitation to his house in case of his coming to London. The Commandant expressed to me his opinion that Crawford was a man of the most attainments of any in this expedition, but I observed that though he probably did not intend that I should draw any inferences discreditable to the bravery of that officer from what he related to me, he abstained from any opinion on that head, or as to his military talents. This commandant of Grenadiers is the most of a soldier of any I have seen here. He is from Spain & received his Education in a College in Madrid. I consequently think his opinion may be triumphantly quoted against those who say that the Soldiers of Whitelocke's Army and the officers generally did not do

164. See Introduction.
165. Juan Florencio Terrada, who introduced freemasonry to Buenos Aires.

their duty. He gives his testamony decidedly in favour of both, especially of the officers & refers the ill success of the attack entirely to the badness of the plan & the incapacity of the General.

One more observation, before I have done with Colonel Crawford. I have heard many Spaniards condemn in the strongest terms, the very great impropriety of signing the Paper presented to him by Liniers after he was taken Prisoner. It is but justice to myself to say that these observasions were made gratuitously, as I have never directed my enquiries to such points as tended to inculpate any officer.

The strongest attestation to their bravery & general good conduct is the number of them, who fell on that unfortunate day. It was the custom of the antients upon such occasions to demand// a truce for the express purpose of burying the dead, but in these civilized times no regard, as far as I can learn was paid to that object by the English General, although he made a truce for other purposes, of which it is probable he might have availed himself. It was consequently left to the people, who performed it according to their convenience, in some instances leaving it undone. General Liniers paid to the memory of Col[onel] Kington[166] who died of his wounds after the attack, the respect due to a brave Officer, by causing a Pyramidal Monument to be erected over him, outside the walls of the building formerly the College of the Jesuits - the only remembrance left upon the spot of any officer that fell here.

The College of the Jesuits demonstrates by its extent the riches and influence of that society here. It occupied the whole superficies of a Quadra[167] & a considerable part of an adjacent Quadra is covered by buildings formerly the barracks of the numerous slaves employed by the Jesuits in the cultivation of their possessions in the vicinity. This last is at present the barracks of the only regiment of regular troops here, while in the College are the quarters of one of the new raised regiments called the Patricios.[168] Emediately after the

---

166. Colonel Peter Kington (1777–1807) commanded the dismounted 6th Dragoon Guards and 9th Light Dragoons in Whitelocke's attack on Buenos Aires. He was killed in action during the British attack on the city on 5 July1807.
167. The city was laid out in a grid pattern and a quadra is one square of the grid.
168. The Patricios was a regiment of Creoles commanded by Cornélio de Saavedra. It played a crucial role in defeating the coup attempted by the Cabildo on 1 January 1809.

expulsion of the Jesuits, a College for the education of the Youth of the place was established in their buildings, & though General Beresford was in urgent want of quarters for his officers, for which purpose it was suggested to him to occupy this building, of course he preferred any other expedient, as soon as he was informed that it was employed in education. But after the expulsion of the English, the enlightened// Cadre [?] of this City has thought that the Genius of the Creoles[169] is sufficient without the help of tutorage & has consequently turned out the Collegians to make room for the troops, thereby overthrowing the only place of education in the City, unless the day schools where the Children of the Slaves mix indiscriminately with those of their Masters can be called such.

This town is built in squares of equal dimensions each side being about 350 feet. The Ground to a great distance round the City is laid out in the same manner, being enclosed by hedges of Juna. This word is the Spanish name for the Indian fig, or Cactus-Apuntia of Lin[aeus][170], but the plant to which it is here applied resembles in some degree that which in Madeira I have heard called by the English, the prickley Pear. Within these enclosures, in most directions all is cultivated ground, supplying the City with fruit, vegetables & flowers. Open spots are left on each side of the city for Corralles[171], i.e. places for slaughtering Oxen, where the same disgusting sights I have described at M[onte] V[ideo] again annoy you, but a little better arranged & regulated. At a distance of a league from the fort to the W[est] of the City, on the bank of the Rio Chuelo is Barracas[172], which is a collection of warehouses belonging to Merchants of this City for the produce of the Country which the peasants bring there for sale, & for the loading & unloading of the River craft, which as I have before said, come up there when there is water enough to pass the Bar, at the mouth of the Chuelo. Barracas properly signifies a store for hides with which, indeed they are principally// occupied. Each consists of an ample area, surrounded by a wall & sheds or warehouses for the Workmen. All

169. Creole is the term used for a Spaniard born in South America.
170. Opuntia or prickly pear. One species is the *Opuntia ficus-indica*.
171. It was at the Coralle del Miserere on the east side of the city that Liniers was defeated by General Gower on 1 July.
172. A barraca is a hut or shack and the term is also used for a shantytown.

is arranged with propriety, & great attention paid to preserving the merchandize in the most saleable state. The productions of the country which may at this time be procured for exportation, are as follows.[173]

Ox hides	Do points of
D° dressed	Do Chapas*
Horse d°	Tallow
Otter skins i.e. nutria[174]	Copper in bars
Chinchilla Skins	Wool of vicuna
Swans D°	Do sheep
Tigers D°	Flower [flour?]
Deer D°	Wheat
Horse Hair	Peruvian bark
Horns	

*Chapas are the longer part of the Horn flattened out for Combs &c &c &c.

To this List is to be added the precious Metals, & many sorts of wool not here mentioned, & if ever a proper degree of commercial activity is admitted into these provinces, many other articles not now attended to for want of purchasers will come into the Market. The productions of Paraguay are very valuable & various, although as far as I can learn the Agriculture of that province, as well as the advancement of the natives towards civilization, have been more than stagnant since the expulsion of the Jesuits.[175] At present indeed, some of the furs I have mentioned are not to be met with in this City// the last brought having sold so as not to pay the hunters for their trouble, but the revival of an export trade will soon bring matters to their former state & already the hopes of it have produced some effect.

---

173. Lists of exports and their volume for the years 1796 and 1810 are included in Woodbine Parish's 'Report on the Trade of the River Plate' (FO 354/8) printed in Humphreys, *British Consular Reports on the Trade and Politics of Latin America 1824–1826*, pp28–62. The 1810 list includes ox-hides, horse hides, tallow, vicuña wool, common wool, horns, copper, bark, flour, horse hair, skins of chinchilla and nutria, and silver bullion.

174. Nutria is the coypu (*myocaster*).

175. The expulsion of the Jesuits followed the transfer of mission territory to Portugal in 1750. The order itself was abolished in Portugal in 1759 and Spain in 1767.

The Corralles in the neighbourhood of the city are chiefly employed in slaughtering such Cattle only as are for the consumption of the inhabitants, the Tallow & hides for exportation being mostly brought from Estancias[176] or farms in the Interior. 6,548 head of Oxen were slaughtered for the consumption of B[uenos] A[ires] in Sep[tember] last past. Among other taxes impose[d] lately in consequence of the invasions of the Country, is one of 4 Rials a head on Oxen killed for the use of the Inhabitants.

A public Market for Beef is appointed near the fort, where the whole is exposed for sale in a neat and commodious manner, except indeed as to the cutting up of which they have no notion according to English Ideas. In the Barracas I have observed that the natives of the country (I mean the Indians) are employed as labourers. I have frequently endeavoured [to] ascertain why they are not employed in the City as domestic Servants. I am told that they do not understand the language & that they are stupid & that they only come out of the Country in gangs of 8 or 10 together & will never engage themselves without the whole gang or at least half of it is hired.

These reasons are not satisfactory to me. Certainly the new negroes do not understand Spanish, & if any opinion// of their intellects can be formed from their appearance they are much more stupid than the Indians. The third reason seems of more weight, but when it is considered that in every family who live respectably 8 or 10 Slaves are kept that objection is much lessened, because it is hardly supposeable that all the Indians would quit the service of their master together if they were well used, as in general I think the Slaves here are. In Peru the domestic servants are all, or nearly all Indians, the Spaniards having been obliged to employ them, not being able to procure negroes.

October 25th. The experience of a month has much lowered the expectations which with regard to society I brought into this City. I have found that those with whom I have had intercourse, concluding that my arrangements for business were settled with the Gentleman in whose house I am, & consequently that they had little hopes of gaining by me, have been but little attentive. Likewise of the numbers whom I have seen & conversed

---

176. Estancia is the term used for a cattle ranch.

with during my residence in this house, from the Count de Liniers to the Clerks who may have occasionally eat[en] a Sunday's dinner here, not one has ever invited me to his house. But they have been principally Merchants, & consequently influenced by the reasons I have above given.

Having before experienced the politeness of Military Men I should hope better of these here, but here they nearly are all commercial men. My society therefore, consists of such few Spaniards as I brought letters of recommendation to, & who in consequence are always polite when they see me; & such Americans as have amidst all manner of inconveniences, been allured by the profits of contraband to reside here. From these latter I am assailed with perpetual complaints of the total want of good faith, honor or even common honesty here, from those who compose the Cabildo downwards; & as all the Spaniards privately abuse one another I am enabled by collating & comparing evidence, to ascertain in some measure the truth of my information, which to a lamentable extent I am obliged to acquiesce in.

It appears very plainly, that the confidence which the Americans have been obliged to repose in them, has been in almost every instance abused. The trade being from beginning to end contraband, it has been in almost every instance necessary to make complete transfers of property into Spanish hands in order to protect it, & the law being silent in behalf of the stranger, the merchant has been able to remain with the proceeds of sales. The system of smuggling is so organized here that it is nearly a certainty that any vessel permitted to remain in harbour a week, clears her cargo, even though the Viceroy should dispatch his principal officers abroad to watch it. The profit to the Officers is so great that Spanish integrity cannot withstand it. There is one, & only one Merchant here, to whose integrity all// give testimony. As for the rest, foreigners establish it as a rule, that no consignment quits the hands of a Spanish Merchant here without his contriving at least to clear 25 p[er] cent upon it if he does not detain the whole, & as numbers have built splendid houses, & started up rich men suddenly, having been known to have had only 5 or 6 consignments, such a calculation seems but too probable.

In consequence, every Merchant here is a decided enemy to the establishment of free trade, & to Englishmen being permitted to settle as

Merchants. They see therein the downfall of these rich profits for which they cannot hope honestly to compensate themselves. To such a pitch has this risen, that the Cabildo would have virtually deposed the Viceroy, in order that they might establish such regulations as suit their interests; but the Soldiery & the people are generally with him and the party of the Cabildo was crushed last week by the seizure and imprisonment of some officers who had demonstrated dispositions in its favor. The Viceroy waits for authority from Spain before he conceives himself authorized in the least to relax from the laws, but he is known as the friend of an open Commerce, & the people who suffer in their purses & in their personal convenience by the Monopoly, which is the consequence of consignments being limmitted to Spanish merchants, will all be glad if the English are permitted to// establish themselves. I am aware that my friends will look upon my information as very suspicious if I suffer them to remain in the belief that it is grounded only on the authority of American contraband traders. Those are people in whom I have myself no confidence, but I have heard the same facts concerning individual Spaniards related by different men in such a manner, as effectually to corroborate each other, & the suspicious conduct of the Spanish Merchants towards me, & opinions which in the warmth of argument I have been able to extract from them have confirmed my belief.

Mixed society of both sexes seems little known here. In this very house a splendid dinner was given on St Francis's day[177], the Lady being named Francesca, at which no other Lady attended, & I am told it is not usual to see more females at Table. I hear of dances, but apprehend they are mostly confined to the inferior classes. Public amusements seem to be confined to the single one of walking to the Convent called the Recoleta[178] on days of festival. This is a Convent of the Order of St Francis, the term Recoleta, expressing such as are obliged by the rules of this establishment to observe monastic discipline more rigidly than usual. It is situated on the bank of the River, about a league to the W[est] of the City. The ground

177. The feast of St Francis is 4 October.
178. Now a suburb of Buenos Aires, this was the area around the Franciscan Convento de los Recoletos Descalzos.

on which it stands is a little more elevated above the bank of the River, than the surrounding country, & the immediate neighbourhood being well planned & cultivated makes it the pleasantest spot near this City.//

In front of the Convent is an open space, with a battery overlooking the river & a few oak trees disposed over it, and here on the festivals of certain Saints booths of hides are erected, & eatables (dulces) offered for sale very much in the manner of the meanest species of country fairs in England. The Avenues leading into this area are guarded by Centinels to prevent persons on horseback not Military Officers from entring, and a numerous horse patrole keeps watch within to crush quarrels & riots.

On such occasions, if the weather is favorable, every vehicle in B[uenos] A[ires] is driven towards the Recoleta (as carriages are permitted to enter) and only on these occasions are very good horses to be seen. But the whole is a most paltry exhibition. There are not six Carriages in Buenos A[ires] fit to compare with a handsome London Hackney Coach. In *all* but *one* Mules are driven. About a fortnight ago at one of these festivals, a baker started with 2 new Carriages, one of which is a neat English chariot, to which he harnessed a pair of horses. This, & another belonging to the Viceroy, are the only ones in this City, except indeed, a Chariot belonging to my friend D[ona] Franc[esca] which, as it is very much admired here, may serve to convey an idea of the taste of the people. I conclude it to have belonged to a Sherif of London recently, being painted gaily in the pannels with Glass sides which are very much liked here, every one ardently desiring to see, & to be seen. This Chariot, as well as most others has a box for the Coachman which is never used, all driving post, with probably a tall black postilion with a huge cocked hat. The single men upon these occasions put on// their handsomest uniforms, & mount their horses of Chile richly caparisoned with velvet embroidered with Silver & pace slowly to the scene of action with the dignity of my Lord Mayor [*illegible*] proclamations of peace. But as Carts are permitted on the road leading to the Recol[e]ta, which is likewise covered with swarms of the Country people & of Slaves mounted on horses of all descriptions, it is a scene of the most vulgar confusion & of real danger to all whose nerves are not strong & who are not good horsemen (as the Countrymen are the greatest brutes under the sun, & make no scruple of riding against any body whom they do not think likely to knock them off their horses) & the Dust is much more insufferable than that of the Drive in the Hyde Park on a Sunday in June.

Towards evening all decent people retire, the Countrymen get to gaming & consequently to quarrelling & I apprehend the night seldom or [n]ever ends without murder. On the only occasion on which I busied my self particularly to enquire what had taken place during the night I learnt that 4 had been murdered. A word of abuse is sufficient. He who first becomes enraged, draws out his knife & stabs his neighbour & probably sits upon the body to fix the bets he may have layed with others. I must observe that this account is solely furnish[ed] me by Spaniards. I take it to be the natural temper & manners of these people without exception of Classes.

Though certainly not the advocate of duelists, I have found myself obliged to become in some measure the Apologist of the practice// in some instances wherein it has been mentioned as horrible in the English & unworthy of civilized nations. On such occasions I have been forced to alledge cases in which from the nature of the insult offered, it was not fit matter for a Court of justice & to ask if by constant submission in such circumstances men of real honor are for the future to subject themselves to the caprice of every blackguard who in the knowledge that he shall not suffer for it has meaness to offer an unprovoked insult. – O, no, by no means! What then? Kill him instantly! Thus every man becomes judge & executioner in his own case, & is constitutionally (if I may so say) an Assassin.

I am now therefore determined that if by any chance I ever become a member of the Parliament of Great Britain, that as far as boxing is concerned, I will be a strenuous Windhamite[179], & zealously oppose every

179. William Windham (1750–1810), Secretary for War and the Colonies under William Pitt and again in 1806–7 in Grenville's ministry. The comment of Kinder refers to a speech made by Windham in support of a Bill to Prevent Bull-baiting and Bull-running on 24 May 1802. In this speech he said: 'To horse-racing he was himself personally no more an enemy than he was to boxing—though in making this observation he was far from meaning to disparage boxing so far, as to put them on an equal footing, or to insinuate that so poor, mean, and wretched an amusement as the one, was at all to vie in importance with the other, which was connected with ideas of personal merit, and individual dignity.' Thomas Amyot ed., *Speeches in Parliament of the Right Honourable William Windham to which is prefixed some account of his life*, 3 vols, Longman, Hurst, Rees, Orme and Brown (London, 1812) p.348.

enactment that has the least tendency to make John Bull lay aside his honest love of "fair play" & follow the example of these savages in venting the passions inseparable from Man by the lurking vilany of the Stiletto.

If the murder[er] falls at once into the hands of the Civil Officers he is certainly hanged for the crime; but for one who suffers, to escape. In trifles likewise, as well as in things of greater moment, the police here is much neglected. The streets are covered with dust in large quantities, & carcases of animals are left to rot every where. Such however is the drying quality of the air, that in a few days all putrescent particles are absorbed & the sight alone is offended by such objects. There are regulations// in existence for the better ordering of such matters, but the present Viceroy is a man most culpably careless in the administration of his duties, so inactive that all his inferiors neglect their duty, & so easy & good natured that all his enemies escape punishment & every one else can obtain from him what ever they chuse to ask.

When the king of Spain conferred on him the dignity he holds, he wrote to him in terms strictly descriptive of the fact to say that he was not fit for the office. The fiscal who wrote the proclamation I have before mentioned, probably thought he was adapting it to the sentiments of the Viceroy in the sentences to which I have alluded & Liniers signed it when presented, thinking no doubt it was as well to leave his determinations in an ambiguous state until the fate of Spain became decided when, if such are the sentiments of the people, he would, for the sake of avoiding additional commotions, submit to the orders of Bonaparte & probably his national vanity would be gratified by so doing. But certainly he does not possess the Spirit of Ambition & intrigue so prominent in Frenchmen of the present day & so far I think from being likely actively to promote the subjection of this colony to France, in case Spain is subjugated, that if the people remain in the same sentiments they now so loudly profess, I doubt not that, as he is a Soldier of great courage, he would again lead them against the invader. The honours which, in consequence of a contrary conduct, he might hope to reap in France, & the advantages or pleasure of returning there, could be but little use to him. He has been here 24 years or more, has once married here, & his children are now under the care of his// wife's sisters, with whom, as well as with many other families & individuals here he is on terms of the strictest intimacy.[180]

As to Elio, the Governor of Mon[te] V[ideo] I now think that the part he has taken has probably been with a view of making his loyalty evident in Spain & so obtaining promotion (perhaps the Viceroyalty) in case of success against France in Europe or, in the Contrary event, to obtain a rich reward for delivering over the left bank of the River Plate to the Princess Charlotte, wife of the Prince of Brasil[181], who will then be the nearest representation of the Royal family of Spain. After the answer he wrote to the Viceroy, he was summoned here not to be a member of a junta as I before supposed, but distinctly to give an account of his conduct & such summons was not only sent by Liniers, but by the Sen[or] Gorgonache[182] who had just then arrived from Spain as an emissary from the Junta Suprema[183], with unprecedented powers such as gave him a control over all the Viceroys & Governors in the Country. G[orgonache] was well convinced of the motives which actuated the 2 individuals, & issued the summons for Elio's attendance & departed for Peru, but E[lio] instead of obeying has involved G[orgonache] in the charges of treachery circulated against the Viceroy. This conduct is so much the worse, as by coming he would at the most have only lost his employ, for such is the character of the Viceroy & the inactivity of his Government that it is next to certain that should E[lio] arrive in the City to-morrow he would suffer no molestation from the government, or at most a temporary arrest.

Not content with disowning the supreme power, it has been attempted to make all// swear allegiance to the Cabildo or Junta of Monte Video, & in consequence numbers have quitted the place & yesterday arrived here

180. This is a reference to the suspicions in some quarters that Liniers, as a Frenchman, might turn out to be sympathetic to Napoleon and the Bonapartist regime in Spain. See Introduction.
181. The Infanta Carlota Joaquina was wife of the Portuguese prince regent, Dom João. She was the sister of Ferdinand VII of Spain and, after her brother was detained by Napoleon and forced to abdicate, she planned to claim the regency over the Spanish overseas possessions.
182. José Manuel de Goyeneche (1776–1846) was sent as envoy by the Central Junta in Seville to proclaim Ferdinand VII. Later he became commander of the royal forces in Peru.
183. The Central Junta (Junta Suprema) was established in Seville on 25 September 1808 to bring together in one body the provincial juntas that had sprung up following the May insurrection in Spain.

all the marine officers near 50 in number.[184] Liniers has probably thought that the arrival of intelligence would set all right, & has consequently contented himself with summoning particular individuals. The Courier has regularly gone between the 2 Cities, but the Governor of Monte V[ideo] has had the impudence to withhold documents necessary for the prosecution of a rebel suit now pending & which have been written for by the law officers in the customary manner. The reason is because the suit in question is on the part of White (a [*illegible*] whose name appears in Whitelocke's trial) against some of Elio's abettors in Monte V[ideo] in the bad effect such an example may have on many parts of Peru, known to be ready to take fire at the least application of stimulus.

The horses here all appear to have originated from the same stock, but there is a vast difference in the value. A horse imported from Chile, black, & taught to pace with stateliness & temper will sometimes sell for 1000 Piastres.[185] These horses are truly beautiful animals, & so temperate, notwithstanding their high condition & the little exercise they have, that a man may approach close to a bench full of Ladies, & converse as long as he pleases, without the least risk of his horse's stirring, or giving cause for fear. Some of the best horses of this province are educated in the same manner & I am not aware of any difference except in the price.

The next class of horses, & in fact the most valuable, are such as have been selected for their beauty from the herds in the Country, have// been well fed, & taught to pace. The amble they learn, is so easy, that a man may ride day after day without the least fatigue & they are swift beside, going from 6 miles an hour to 10. Such horses may be bought from 20 Piastres to 30. Among the horses, the most excellent trotting horse in good condition, would be esteemed high priced at 20 Piastres in the City. I mean here to speak of such an one as you might be tempted to buy from seeing him frequently about the streets, & knowing (to use the phrase of

---

184. Elío had refused to accept the legitimacy of the Seville Central Junta and had, instead, formed a provincial Junta in Montevideo. 'There is no doubt that the decisive manner in which Elío defended his threatened authority was a determining factor in the growth of dissidence in the Banda Oriental.' Halperin-Donghi, *Politics, Economics and Society in Argentina in the Revolutionary period*, p.139.

185. The piastre was another name for the peso which was the South American equivalent of the Spanish silver dollar of 8 reales.

a Jockey) that he had meat in him. If his Master did not tell you he would not sell him at all, he would not certainly ask above 20 Piastres; if you are at any of the Estancia's in the Country at a few leagues distant & want a horse to come home on, it is probable that for a silk handkerchief you may have any you fix your eye upon & may very likely get an excellent horse in very good condition but of course only Grass fed. The Creoles never or seldom trouble themselves about keeping horses up for the purpose of riding.

In every instance there is a large Corrall where a quantity of horses are kept for the use of the Estancia, & when from over-riding or want of food a horse becomes unfit for use he is turned loose, the Lazo[186] men keeping the Corrall constantly supplied. Lazo signifies, noose, the horses being caught by a man riding after them until he has a convenient opportunity of throwing a running noose either round the neck or the legs which they manage with the greatest dexterity. Therefore, when a Creole wants a horse, he enters the Corrall nooses the first he likes, if refractory ties his legs, puts on the Saddle & gets astride the animal probably lying on the ground after which somebody casts// the horse loose & away they go. The Creole then probably rides his horse for 2 or 3 days without giving him anything to eat, & when he can go no longer turns him loose & again supplies himself as before. These then [men?] they say are never thrown, & I have seen children ride in the outskirts of the City in such a manner, as makes me give credit to it, but I wish to see some of the feats of horsemanship of which I have heard frequent mention before I insert them here.

There is little peculiar in the dress of the people of these Countries, only that they use neither caps, hats, or bonnets, covering their heads when walking with their triangular Mantles the two long corners of which hang down in front. The men universally wear boots & Panteloons. Many wear great Coats (the common English coat being introduced only of late years) & the more genteel, elastic hats. The Countrymen wear jackets, over which when cold they use the Poncho, an Indian dress manufactured

186. Lassoo.

in the Country & consisting merely of a well wrought cotton cloth about 9 feet long by 4 feet wide, fringed & striped with broad stripes of red & blue wove into the texture, with a slit lengthways in the center to put the head in. When not wearing it, they coil it round them in the Saddle. It is a very convenient riding dress sheltering the body perfectly, at the same time leaving the arms & legs at liberty, & many Ponchos are so well worn as to turn away rain. In winter time they tie up their heads in a white handkerchief leaving one end to hang down behind, & put on their hats over it.

I forgot to mention, that notwithstanding the Creoles ride so well, there is seldom any elegance in the manner of their sitting their horses.// They all use stirrups extremely long, extending their legs forward & sideways to a great distance from the Saddle, turning out their toes so much, that a regiment of them would take up at least half as much more room as well drilled Europeans. That they sit their horses so well notwithstanding this bad habit is merely the result of the incessant practice which they all have from their infancy. The saddles & bridles are the same as at M[onte] V[ideo] only that the bridles are plentifully laden with silver in those parts which are on the horse's head, which I did much observe in that City.

By Creole, is meant every person born in the country, without exception as to his Parentage. The natives of old Spain affect great contempt for the Creoles with very little foundation as I suspect that a considerable number of the Spaniards here have quitted their Country to escape their creditors, or for motives but little superior. However they intermarry & live in society together, though the Military men of any rank, & the Officers of the Royal revenue are all sent from Spain.

The keepers of Estancias & others resident out of the City, are all Creoles, & to them I have generally hitherto meant to apply the term of reproach. Living in the country which produces [for] them, with little labour, all they think necessary, & under a Government, which instead of stimulating them to industry, has hitherto sedulously prevented them gaining by it if so inclined, their tempers become revengeful & malignant & consequently their bodily & mental activity finds vent in broils & murders. Reading forms a very inconsiderable part of the amusement of this people. Good Spanish works are very difficult to be met// with. Those who are disposed to read generally understand French, & consequently procure only French books. The few booksellers shops there are very little frequented & contain hardly anything but dust-covered divinity. In this respect B[uenos] A[ires] is much behind Rio de Janeiro.

Here is only one Printing office called "de los Ninos Expositos"[187] because the owner is obliged to pay a certain sum yearly – 1500 Piastres to the Foundling Hospital. A license to establish another would I apprehend be difficult to obtain, & consequently printing is dear & the profits of this office considerable from the number of proclamations & Gazettes published whenever news arrives from Europe or from Rio de Janeiro.

There are here, as at M[onte] V[ideo], Billiard tables in all the coffee-houses, which are miserable places for anything beyond Tea, Coffee, Dulces ie light pastry, barley sugar &c, a good dinner much less a good bed being very difficult to obtain in this City. There is one place for playing at Pilotto[188], a game to which the Biscayans are particularly addicted, & which is violent exercise & requires strength and activity. It is a species of Tennis in which the Ball is only required to touch the wall from the hand of him who first rises it, after which it is kept up from one end of the yard to the other, that side losing, in whose ground it is stopped after falling. They play with the hand, some using Gloves faced with very thick leather. They generally play high, for 50 P[esos] or more each sett; the game occupying about an hour, & each side consisting generally of 4 men. The Pilloto Grand is always attended by people of all conditions.

Having in a former Sheet said that the Town is built in Squares// I feel it is necessary to explain lest my friends (as I did from reading Whitelocke's tryal) should adopt a wrong Idea. The Spanish term is Quadra, which signifies here & in Peru a mass of buildings, equilateral of given dimensions. As these Quadras are all the same size, & correctly laid out, all the Streets in this City run completely thro' it in all directions. In the

---

187. The Imprenta de Niños Expósitos (literally the press of the foundling children) was indeed the name of the official printer in Buenos Aires. The contract to establish this press was granted to a Portuguese José de Silva e Aguiar in 1780. The first imprints from this press appeared in 1781.
188. Pelota (pilote in Basque).

South part 2 or 3 Quadras are left unoccupied, but near the river the only open Square is the Plaza Mayor, bounded on the E[ast] by private houses & shops, on the W[est] by the Cathedral & a large Corral for horses occupied as quarters for different regiments, and on the N[orth] by the Recova or market ie a long range of shops with flat roofs, surrounded with a covered walk, faced all round with Arches of Roman Architecture having a Center more elevated, & correspondent with a carriageway through it. The roof is inclosed with Ballustrades of Iron. This building, as well as all the houses, is built of bricks plastered white, the Churches being the only buildings where the base bricks are suffered to meet the eye. The area of the Plaza Mayor is the space of one Quadra & the width of 2 streets ie about 140 y[ar]ds Square, and the Recova compleatly occupies one side. On the N[orth] of the Recova is another space occupied on the side next the River by the Fort, which is the residence of the Viceroy, & bounded on E[ast] & W[est] by old ill-looking buildings, the area being used as a market place. The Plaza Mayor is quite centrical, the City extending along the bank of the River to an equal distance E[ast] & W[est]. Among the places of amusement in this City, I should not have omitted the Plaza del Tauros[189]// – it is a circular amphitheatre built of wood, now falling to decay & never used. Likewise there is no theatre at present open, my friends informing me that the Taxes levied for the defence of the Country & still more the distress of many private families from the loss of their relatives in battle, have occasioned the present stagnation of Amusement.

The humane English Amusement of Cock-fighting is in estimation here, & English cocks are highly prized here. I have heard nothing of Bull-baiting.

The manufactories here are the following. Hats made of the fur of the Nutria, or Otter. They are not ill made. They are strong and soft, and last longer than those of European manufacture, but they do not succeed in dying a good black, & consequently might prefer such as are brown. They cost about 14 dollars each round Hat or 32 each elastic Hat. Boots & shoes are tolerably made here by the English deserters from Whitelocke's Army.

---

189. This was the site of the only major success of the British army during Whitelocke's attack on the city. The British captured the Plaza de Toros and took a thousand prisoners there.

They were before supplied by Spanish workmen at half the price they now pay, which [is] 14 Piastres for a Pair of Hessian boots[190], or 2 1/2 [for a] pair of Shoes, which latter is little worn, are less attended to & ill-made. In the Interior, they manufacture the Poncho of which I have made mention, and some other coarse cloth but only in the quantity necessary to supply their wants, never having recourse to their own manufacture when they can obtain European articles, which, if obtainable, scarcely cost so much as those of the country & are better liked. Now a yard of English superfine broad Cloth costs 14 Piastres & consequently with other materials & making a coat costs 40 or 45 [piastres] - & a pair of Silk hose for women, with Lace worked Clocks, will sell for 20 Piastres. At Potosi[191]// which from its distance from the Sea, & the difficulty of access & the abundance of money I suppose to be the dearest place in the world, as to European manufactures, in the last war a Coat cost 70 Piastres, & silk stockings sold for 50 Piastres a pair. The women here are exceedingly expensive & fickle in their dress, changing oftener than Ladies who in London can in a moment procure at small expence whatever they wish for. They particularly attend to their feet, always going abroad in silk shoes & stockings, which must oftener serve them only a single time, as they never wear them after they have contracted any dirt, & not knowing how to restore the colour given them by the maker.

January 3rd 1809

The disgusts which I mentioned as subsisting between the Cabildo & the Viceroy have come to a crisis, & having on the 1st of this month materially endangered the tranquillity of this City are now terminating in a complete victory for Liniers, where power seems infinitely stronger than at any former period. The Viceroy having, as I before mentioned, seized some officers known as adherents of the Cabildo, crushed for the time any open revolt, but the Cabildantes have been continually plotting his overthrow, & the 1st January has been long expected by those well informed as a time of popular commotion.

---

190. Hessian boots were knee length boots with a low heel. Originally designed for military use, they had become popular with civilians by the end of the eighteenth century.
191. The silver mining town in modern Bolivia.

The members of the late Cabildo are all Spaniards except one, the Alcalde of the first vote being Don Martin Alsager[192], a man of vast intrigue, known by a most decided hatred of all strangers, viewing them as interfering with the priviledges of Spaniards in commercial affairs, & persecuting them by confiscation,// imprisonment & every vexation in his power. The same hatred he likewise extended to the Creoles, so far as to declare that at the last election, he having the preceding year occupied a seat in the Cabildo, that he would not again be a member if any Creole were admitted. The natives of old Spain are all of the same party, entertaining, to a man, the same illiberality towards every one who can possibly interfere with their gains, nay more, thinking it impossible that any one can gain, without their experiencing a consequent loss. Had these men succeeded, I doubt not, from what I have heard many of them utter as their sentiments, that every stranger would immediately have been imprisoned, & probably many of the principal Creoles & from experience, the temper of the troops is so well known that all now congratulate one another on seeing their houses safe from pillage & their families from insult.

The 2nd party consists of Liniers & those personal adherents who, deriving profit from the commercial advantages by winking at & even favouring contraband, or protection from their enemies by his power, find their prosperity attached to his, but these men are not sufficient to sustain him, but for the aggregation of the third party which is the entire body of Creoles, who finding him equally with themselves hated by the Spaniards &, not as yet knowing the extent of their own force here, supported his case solely with the hope of crushing the common enemy & gaining one step towards independence, & likewise because they do not know where else to look for a head.

192. Don Martín de Álzaga (1755–1812) was born in Spain. A merchant and founder member of the Consulado in 1794, he organised the insurrection against Beresford and summoned the *cabildo abierto* which removed Sobremonte from office. He played a major role in La Defensa and in the capitulation of Whitelocke and led the failed coup against Liniers on 1 January 1809 after which he was sent into exile to Patagonia. He then supported the replacement of Cisneros by a Junta on 25 May 1810. Accused of plotting against the Primer Triunvirato, he was tried and executed on 6 July 1812. According to Kinder, 'Alsager himself [was] supposed to have gained near 300,000 dollars, by the facilities his situation at the head of the municipality afforded him, for the introduction of contraband.'

The objections to Liniers, among all the rational people, is his attachment to a French Lady,// married here to one O'Gorman, who is now in Chili enjoying himself upon some appointment given him there by Liniers, while she & her brothers, in the name of the Viceroy govern the Viceroyalty.[193] Liniers himself is perfectly careless of money, so much so that were he to die now his children would be left utterly destitute; but on the other hand he grants every favour & extricates out of every difficulty in the face of law & of justice, those who are interceded for by Mrs O'Gorman, whose favour it needs much money though very little delicacy in the application, to purchase. White [?][194] who is extremely odious here, especially among the Spaniards, was rescued from Elio who held him in close imprisonment many months after the English evacuated M[onte] V[ideo] by the express command of Liniers at her request, W[hite] being supposed to have gratified her with presents to the amount of at least 30,000 dollars, & in consequence up to the present time he enjoys commercial advantages beyond every other man here.

Her brothers would any where be looked upon with contempt, as rising from their sister's disgrace, but are besides men of known meanness; notwithstanding which Liniers last week had the imprudence to marry his eldest daughter to one of them in spite of the remonstrances of his brother the Count, the whole of his late wife's family[1195], his confessor & every person of worth who has sufficient intimacy with him to venture to express their minds. In addition to the pernicious influence of this family, he is naturally careless & inconsequent, &// it may be also doubted whether he possesses any other good qualities more than great good nature & humanity, together with some courage, & openness of disposition. The attempt of the Cabildo to depose him, was invited by 2 or 3 favorable

---

193. Marie Anne Périchon de Vandeuil, known in Buenos Aires as 'La Périchona', was the daughter of a French official in Ile de France (Mauritius). She married Thomas O'Gorman, who had been an officer in an Irish regiment in French service. O'Gorman and his wife's family established themselves in Buenos Aires in 1797. As a contraband trader O'Gorman had commercial dealings with Tomás Antonio Romero and in 1806 left his family to organise shipments to the west coast of South America. It was then that La Périchona became mistress of Liniers.

194. The name is not clearly legible in the manuscript.

195. Liniers first married Juana de Menviel, who died in 1790. In 1791 he married in Buenos Aires Maria Martina Sarratea Altolaguirre, daughter of Martín de Sarratea, who died in 1805. A daughter, Maria del Carmen was born in July 1792. She married Captain J.B. Périchon de Vandeuil in 1808.

circumstances – the marriage of his daughter with Cap[tain] Perechon disgusted every body & was besides contrary to law, which expressly prohibits any servant of the king in these Colonies to marry himself or his children without the king's consent, declaring that any Viceroy so acting shall by the act itself be dismissed & enjoining the officers of Royal Revenues not to pay his salary.

The arrival here of the late Governor of M[onte] V[ideo] Don Ruez Huidobro[196] who is said formerly to have received a commission from Charles IV to succeed the Marquis del Sobremonte in the viceroyalty, though it probably was never the intention of the Cabildo to employ him, furnished them a stalking Horse to allure some of the people, as he is said to have lent himself to their plans, as well as Molina, a Brigadier who arrived in the *Flora* frigate[197] from Cadiz, with a Commission to pass to Peru as Commandante of the Port of Calloa.[198]

The Cabildo goes out of office with the year, electing its successors subject to the approval of the Viceroy. The only ground for expecting a popular commotion exactly on the day of election, was that the Creoles were determined to have a Cabildo composed of at least a majority of Creoles, a measure never to be expected, unless by intimidating the Cabildantes to elect such a one by the appearance of force, or by inducing the Viceroy to cancel their// election & name others. However, the Cabildantes relying on their strength, or rather with a want of calculation which manifests their want of abilities, sent on the evening of the 31st D[ecember] a message to the Audiencia requesting to know to whom they were to apply to confirm their successors, as the Viceroy had vacated his office in consequence of the marriage of his daughter.[199]

This tribunal being composed of a set of cautious men, determined to abide by the strongest & probably anticipating the preponderance of Liniers,

---

196. Ruiz Huidobro had been appointed viceroy by the Junta of Gallicia but this appointment had been rendered ineffective by the powers of this Junta having been taken over by the Central Junta in September.
197. HMS *Flora* was a 36–gun frigate launched in 1780 and wrecked in 1809.
198. Callao is the main port of Peru.
199. This was not the first time the Cabildo had acted in this way. In January 1807 Sobremonte had refused to confirm the elections with the result that the Cabildo had appealed to the Audiencia, which did confirm them. See Lynch, *Spanish Colonial Administration, 1782–1810*, p.235.

returned no answer; the disposition of the members, as well as of the Ministers of the Royal Revenues, is supposed to be congenial with those of the Cabildo and some of them are said to have committed themselves in conversation. On the following morning the Cabildo met to proceed to the business of the election & about 11 o'clock the great square was filled with people & occupied all sides & at the entrances by the 3 Corps in the interests of the Cabildo, viz. the Catalans, Biscayans & Gallegos.[200] The great bell was also rung to excite alarm & draw together the populace & the generale beaten [sic].

The Catalans were quartered in a house in the Square, & the Andalusians next door & they being the only Corps containing any number of Spaniards not under arms, an application was made by the commander of the Catalans that they should decide themselves & turn out on behalf of the Cabildo, but the Commander of the Andaluses[201] contented himself with observing, that there was no enemy on the ground & consequently he would remain till he was wanted, probably// either doubting his Corps, which contains at least half its number of Creoles, or distrustful of the success of all their efforts. At the same time some of the members of the Cabildo harangued the populace, who immediately hallowed out "Long live Ferdinand 7th & the Cabildo and down with the Frenchmen". These cries continued till towards two o'clock, several emissaries being sent from the Catalans, to the quarters of the Provincial Artillery to request Guns, & lastly threatening to come & take them, when two Cannon were brought, & pointed down the streets in which they were expected to appear & the whole vicinity terrified with the momentary expectation of a battle. At last the Patricios[202] were ordered from their quarters, & marched to those of the artillery, escorting the cannon back to their own quarters.

About two o'clock a violent shower of rain came on & dispersed the populace, the three forementioned regiments remaining formed in the

200. These were three new regiments recruited among the Spanish in the city whose names indicated the provinces of origin of the men. The Catalanes were commanded by José Alaguer Reynal, the Asturianos y Vizcainos (Biscayans) by Prudencio Murguiondo and the Gallegos by Pedro Antonio Cerviño. The Asturianos y Vizcainos were financed by Martín de Álzaga.

201. The Andaluces were commanded by José Merelo.

202. The Legion Patricia, always known as the Patricios, was commanded by Cornelio de Saavedra and was by far the largest military unit in the new army.

square, & now beginning to fire on such of the opposite party as happened to enter the Square & shew themselves at the entrances. In the meantime Liniers, alarmed at the ascendance the Cabildantes had obtained, instantly acceded to the new members named by them, & they having left their Hall of meeting were assembled in the fort, where they represented to the Viceroy that the people were discontented with the present form of Government & required, after the example of the provinces of old Spain & in pursuance of the instructions of the Junta of Seville, to be governed by a Junta, offering him the presidency with a Salary of 20000 dollars// p[er] annum the same which he now receives. He had consented to this arrangement, when the Colonel of the Patricios[203], accompanied by the Commandantes of the other Creole corps entered the Room with a file of Soldiers with fixed Bayonets, & striking the table with his drawn sword swore he would kill any body who dared to talk of a Junta.[204]

The Bishop[205] rose in extreme panic & embracing him, begged he would mention the form of government, testifying their instant submission to his pleasure in the most abject manner. Saavedra declared his determination to uphold the present government, & addressing himself to Liniers told him, that the Cabildo had been grossly imposing upon him, that the wish of the people was quite contrary to their report, requesting him to go into the Square & satisfy himself of the truth of his statement & content the people with assurances of his again governing them. They entered the Square, by that time in complete possession of the Patricios, the Biscayans, Catalans & Gallegoes having dispersed & fled immediately they perceived the cannon of their opponents. The cannon were then planted in front of the Recova, pointed towards the Town house & the Square was again full of people (the shower having ended) who now greeted Liniers with uninterrupted "Vivas". After this, no shots were

---

203. Cornelio de Saavedra was born in Potosí in 1761. He had been president of the Cabildo in 1801 and was appointed by Liniers to command the Patricio regiment in 1806. He later became president of the first Junta in 1810 and died in 1829.

204. The complexity of the political alignments made people take up contrary positions. The Cabildo, made up largely of Spaniards who want to maintain the old colonial system, called for a Junta, while the Creoles who wanted greater autonomy defended the authority of the viceroy.

205. The Bishop was Benito Lué Riega (1753–1812). He was appointed Bishop of Buenos Aires in 1802.

fired, the Patricios having, not only uninterrupted possession of the Square, but of the quarters of all their adversaries, from whence they took the arms they held, thus virtually disbanding them. In the course of the day near fifty people were wounded by the random shots of the Biscayans &c whose object// seemed to be the spreading of universal terror & confusion as the people wounded were not in regimentals & they never ventured to show the face of resistance to their opponents, except one small party who discharged their muskets harmlessly & instantly rounded the next corner in complete confusion.

Thus concluded the events of the day, an order being issued to illuminate the City, the troops remaining under Arms in the Square, & in the fort Centinels being posted at all the Avenues leading thereto at every turning for the distance of several Quadras, where indeed they yet remain (Jan[uary] 16) challenging every body that passes after night-fall. Neither were the troops or Garrison, withdrawn till the 8th instant. The members of the Cabildo together with several of their adherents remained under arrest in the fort till the third instant when Ascalger[206], San[to] Caloma[207], Villa Nueva[208], with Reynalis[209] commandante of the Gallicians & Neira a rich ship owner very active in behalf of the party, were embarked on board one of the small vessels of war in the Port & in 2 or 3 days more commenced their voyage for an unknown destination[210], their families having first obtained permission to send them beds & provisions for a long voyage.

The other Cabildantes were released, the evidence instantly procured against them, not appearing deeply to involve them in the conspiracy, but many others were arrested & depositions are every day taken by commissioners appointed for the purpose, who immediately order the

---

206. Presumably Martín de Álzaga.
207. Don Gaspar de Santa Coloma (1742–1815) was one of the leading Spanish merchants in Buenos Aires. Martín de Álzaga had started out as his clerk. A bitter opponent of contraband traders and of Liniers, who he believed was a supporter of opening the trade of the Río de la Plata, he supported Álzaga and the Cabildo financially and politically. See the lengthy discussion of his career, based on his letters, in Socolow, *The Merchants of Buenos Aires, 1778–1810*, pp.151–166
208. Attorney to the Cabildo.
209. José Olaguer Reynal was commander of the Catalanes, not the Gallegos.
210. They were sent south to exile in Patagonia but were later released by naval vessels from Montevideo sent by Elío.

confinement of such as they conceive implicated who remain according to the Caprice of those who guard them perhaps incommunicable, & some even with double irons on their legs. No regular// process has yet been formed even against those who have been embarked & sent away, some conceiving that they are ordered to Spain for sentence, others that sentence will be given against them here & their goods confiscated, which latter seems a very likely means & may in part be said to have taken place already, though under the mask of a forced loan, as Liniers having, by the information of a Slave, learnt of a large sum of money concealed in Villa Nueva's house, sent for his son in law & demanded a loan of 100,000 dollars & on the other's protesting he had no money in the house, ordered a party of pioneers to search for it, who discovered in a hole in the center of the reservoir upwards of 230,000 dollars of Gold & silver which has already been given out in payment to some of the troops.

It is calculated that a confiscation of the property of the five embarked, will produce two millions of Dollars & I cannot avoid expressing my sentiments that many others have bought their escape by large presents to influencial individuals. Papers are said to have been seized indicating the plans of the revolutionists, who contemplated a complete change in most of the departments of Governments & revenue, especially a removal of all the present officers of customs, together with an Instant embarkation of all the foreigners which must have been attended with confiscation of property to such as have outstanding debts, or indeed every species of property which they cannot instantly remove. These plans are rendered probable by the known sentiments of the party which indeed// I heard several express in the course of the morning of the 1st instant, while they flattered themselves with complete success & by the spirit of monopoly, known as the first spring of all their movements, which alone, & not the service of the king, was the motive for wishing a change in the Customs-house department, intending to introduce such as would countenance them, but suppress the contraband proceedings of all those who are not of their party. It is true, that a more venal set of men than the present cannot be found, but then they are not sufficiently exclusive in their favors, but still no patriotism can be a moment supposed in favour of the revolutionists, because they are all known as great smugglers, Alsager himself being supposed to have gained near 300,000 dollars, by the facilities his situation at the head of the municipality afforded him, for the introduction of contraband.

Now that I am touching on this subject, it will be as well to give an idea of the state of commerce here at this moment. It is well known that the laws of Spain prohibit absolutely, the entry of foreign manufactures in foreign Ships, but they do not presume all the world to be equally well acquainted with their laws, as to make them legally liable to seizure, merely for approaching in search of a market, till warned off & denied admittance although it has frequently happened that Ships have been seized & detained upon suspicion alone, & even now [it] depends more upon the standing of the nation whose flag they bear, or upon the interest of the individuals who speak in their behalf, than upon the law.// This latter assersion is clearly proved by the present circumstances, as there are now 5 British Ships unmolested in harbour, while one Portuguese coming under exactly the same circumstances was brought in for adjudication & her supercargoes have been kept incommunicable on board for 3 weeks, nor would she ever be released but these supercargoes are Englishmen & the property British, Shipped in a Portuguese bottom from a mistaken notion at Rio Janeiro that the Port was open under certain circumstances to vessels under that flag. The other five vessels have all now been here some time. Each requests leave to sell his cargo, & combats the denial he receives & the various orders issued for him to quit the anchorage by pleas of want of repairs & by the interest he has made to support those pleas.

The reasons alledged by the General's favourites against his granting leave to sell are the existing laws, the danger to the commerce of Spain & hurt to the revenue all evidently falsehoods because none of those who alledge them are ignorant that everything gets ashore, but all the individuals from the Viceroy (or at least from Mrs O'Gorman) downwards are aware that though revenue could not but profit greatly from permitting a regular entry, they must necessarily lose the hush-money each either gets or hopes to get. As it is obvious that but a few can enjoy the favors, the murmurs of the discontented ca[u]se the Viceroy, once a week, to send round a general order for the Ships to depart, but immediately each separately makes interest for & obtains an order to grant him a little more time.

Of course they profit by that time, but// the expence of so doing is fully equal to the circular duties viz: 33 ½ [per cent] as they have to arrange with the Commandante of the Vessels in the harbour, with the Cap[tain] of the Port, with the Cap[tain] of the Resguardo whose especial business it is to prevent contraband, besides paying the Guards on board the Ships, & ashore, with immence wages to all the boatmen, cartmen, Porters, & every other description of person who must necessarily be privy to the business, added to all [of] which prior arrangements, a prudent smuggler always carries twenty or thirty onza's (72 each) in his pocket to provide against unforeseen incidents.[211] When the expence of bribing all the nest of hornets is considered together with the risk of bad faith in your consignee, at whose mercy you are immediately after having committed yourself by one illegal step, it cannot be wondered that so few have escaped total loss. A former Cap[tain] of the Resguardo at M[onte] V[ideo] (the proper station of that officer) so completely made his office his own, that after having for the first few months pursued the smugglers with such vigour, as to make it evident that nothing could escape him, or go ashore without his consent, was accustomed to undertake the landing (ensuring himself the property) of any cargo on receiving for his own use, the said circular duties & he being able to compound with the other departments at a lower rate than any merchant could, cleared for himself an immense regular profit.

To prevent your vessel being ordered out of harbour, you will likewise have to make a friend of somebody, who has the General's favour, the necessity of which has, in fact, thrown the business of// all the English cargoes now here into the hands of those who personally possess his Ear,

& exactly in proportion to the degree of his favour they enjoy & the confidence the abovementioned officers have in them, does the business get forward, for it cannot be supposed that any of these rascals are such bad calculators as to trust their offices, & perhaps their lives, in the hands of one, whose circumstances they do not know to be such that he cannot denounce them without ruining or deeply prejudicing himself. Accordingly the consignee to one of these cargoes is L[ieutenant] Col[onel] & Aid de Camp to Liniers, but he not being confided in by the other officers, does not proceed so quickly in his business as do two of the others, one of whom is Sarratoa, Brother in Law of Liniers[212], but who never appears in the affair & transacts all by means of an agent versed in these affairs, & the other is a merchant who, formerly being Clerk in Sarratoa's office when Liniers resided in the house, now enjoys his favour, & the facility of arranging [?] with the best.

The remaining two vessels as yet remain unsettled, but are kept in Port by the same sort of interest, those who support them hoping to get the consignment & having mentioned thus the Persons who are at this moment supporters of this commerce, with a view of furnishing an Idea of the extent & formality of the business, it is but justice to say I believe the 2 last mentioned to be faithful to their consigners in all respects. We have likewise a striking proof of the necessity of a cautious conduct in such transactions, as a Cargo is now in the Custom-house which was procured to be landed under pretence of// the Ships repairs requiring to unload, & in the hope that leave to sell might afterwards be more easily be obtained, (probably supposing the trade would speedily be opened by arrangement between the 2 Governments or by the loss of Spain). And the Ship being lost in heaving down[213], the supercargo then made himself sure that the Government would then grant him leave to sell his Cargo, as the old pretences of the Viceroy that he should compromise himself with his superiors by granting any indulgence, seemed now to be superceded by the rights of hospitality towards the subject of a

212. Manuel de Sarratea (1774–1849) played a major role in the early history of Argentina, commanding troops sent to Banda Oriental, acting as ambassador to Brazil and as Foreign Minister in 1816 and governor of Buenos Aires in 1820. Liniers married his sister Martina de Sarratea in 1792.
213. The process of hauling a ship over onto its side to careen it.

friendly power, so situated that the consignees were disgusted by the evident wish of the supercargo to manage the business himself , & diminish their opportunities to profit by him. [And] the officers of the Customs were compromised by the inconsiderate conversation which subjected them to the suspicion of having already favoured him, in consequence of which he has with dificulty obtained leave to send to Rio de Janeiro there to charter a vessel to come here empty for his Cargo, the first orders of the Government being that he should immediately take freight here where none is to be had except for Rio – a place already fully glutted with manufactures, & that freight at immensely high rates.

Under a more cautious conduct, 10,000 [dollars] presented to Mrs O'Gorman, in due form, would certainly have obtained him leave to sell, or if that had failed, by distributing a like sum or somewhat more among the three officers who keep the keys of the Custom-house Warehouses, he might have taken his whole cargo out of the trunks and bales in which it is packed & shipped them again full of bricks or rubbish. Of course with all these difficulties attached// to it in the introduction, the manufacture must come very dear to the purchaser. None of the Capitalists who venture on these speculations (and there are many who alone, & many others who united in partnership for the occasion of 2 or 3 members, can purchase any Cargo of the value of 2 or 3 hundred thousand) will risk their capital without gaining from 50 to 100 P[er] C[ent] & the gains of the shopkeeper are scarcely inferior, so that the whole Colony is sacrificed to the exorbitant gains of a few. Of those who otherwise might be stimulated to industry, finding that they can scarcely hope to acquire good cloathing, or any manufactured goods which come from Europe with the produce of their labour, notwithstanding the high wages given in this Country, resolve not to labour, as with a Saddle a Lassoo, a Knife & a Poncho they are able to meet their little wants as they arise, living always on horseback or in the fields, supplying themselves by the Lassoo with a fresh horse as often as they are displeased with that they have, sleeping in the air or under a hide, eating without even the addition of salt, beef all the year round. Such is the life of a large portion of the lower class, who with due encouragement might be made serviceable in Agriculture, as well as in all those numerous modes of day labour so necessary in a thriving City, but at present are barely to be distinguished from the Indians, the difference between these being in their features, not in their dress or customs.//

London March 1811.

Commercial affairs at Buenos Ayres were managed as I have described till the month of July 1809 except that the system became more methodical and the ingenuity of those concerned in the contraband found out slight varieties in the mode of carrying it on by which they reduced the expence & diminished to [the?] risk. So many cargoes were introduced before general Liniers gave up the Government to his successor that prices were very greatly reduced and a glut was beginning to be felt. In order to give an Idea of the extent to which this contraband trade was carried on, I will subjoin a list of such vessels as arrived in the Port of Buenos Ayres between the 1st of November 1808 and the same date in 1809 and will distinguish by a mark O such as discharged any part of their cargoes by virtue of Licences granted by the Viceroy and paid the duties thereon, and such as to my knowledge were wholly, or nearly so, smuggled ashore, shall be thus indicated, Q.[214]

Hope	£ 30,000	x
Q *Tagus*	20,000	x
Q *Venus*	70,000	x
Q *Princetown*	100,000	x
Q *Fingal*	20,000	
Q *King George*	£10,000	
Q *Lady Gamber* [215]	20,000	x
Mary Anne	10,000	

214. The same list of ships entering the ports of Buenos Aires and Montevideo was provided to the British Government by the acting British Consul Robert Staples in 1812. Kinder and Staples clearly had access to exactly the same information but Staples listed the ships in a different order and Kinder adds information about the status of each ship and how he obtained the information. See National Archives (Kew) FO 72 157, Robert Staples to Castlereagh, 22 June 1812. This is not a complete list as other English ships are recorded in a contemporary list published in Buenos Aires, *El Excmo Senor /virey de Buenos-Ayres a sus habitantes* (1809).

215. Captain William Hart.

Jupiter	20,000	
Spanish Hero	20,000	x
Midas	20,000	
Q *Generous Planter*	15,000	x
Q *Cumberland*	25,000	x
Q *Invention*	70,000	x
Q *Dart*	10,000	
Q *May*	20,000	x
Speedwell	20,000	x
Q *Braganza*	30,000	x
Q *Laurel*	15,000	
O *Kitty*	100,000	x
O *Brothers*	90,000	x
Juliet Seymour	25,000	
O *Levant*	35,000	x
Q *Mercurio*	25,000	x
Mary Ann	10,000	
Q *Higginson*	70,000	x
Q *Richard*	126,000	x
Harmony	25,000	
Superb	20,000	
Griffin	£20,000	
Q *Antelope*	40,000	
	£1,131,000	Sterling

Of the proceedings of those vessels to which I have affixed no mark I have
no certain data, but with respect to the others I had as good information
as the nature of the case would admit, being personally acquainted with
the Supercargoes of most of them as well as with their Spanish consignees,
and could detail was it necessary the means resorted to in most of the
instances when I have marked them as trading by contraband, and several
of the Supercargoes permitted me to take from their invoices the gross
amount of their investments. With respect to the amount of the others, I

obtained it by enquiries through those acquainted with the parties concerned and I believe that I am not wrong above five per Cent of the gross amount. Of these thirty one vessels the seventeen which have crosses X placed after the amount affixed to them were ships averaging at least a burden of 350 Tons each, several of them well manned and armed being originally intended for Voyages round Cape Horn, when [where?] the *Higginson*, *Kitty*, and *Antelope* had actually been, but// when [were?] prevented from trading by the vigilance of the Cruisers from Callao.

The following entered into the Port of Monte Video when they discharged their cargoes by permission of General Elio and paid the circular duties in 33 ¼ P[er] Cent besides considerable gratifications distributed in obtaining permission to discharge.

Admiral Berkeley [216]	£40,000
Earl of Caledon	60,000
Spanish Hero	25,000
Agreable	15,000
Ethelred	100,000
Diamond	
Hound	20,000
Mary [217]	20,000
John Parish	25,000
Maria	30,000
Clarkson	50,000
	£385,000
Amount at Buenos Ayres	£1,131,000
	£1,516,000

---

216. The *Admiral Berkeley* allegedly paid a bribe of 20,000 dollars to land its cargo. See R.A. Humphreys, *Liberation in South America 1806–1827. The Career of James Paroissien*, Athlone Press (London, 1952) p.32.
217. The *Mary* had on board James Paroissien and Miguel de Julián, both political agents working for Carlotta Joaquina. See Humphreys, *Liberation in South America 1806–1827. The Career of James Paroissien*, pp.21 and 28.

Two ships named *Mary Ann* came to Buenos Ayres & the name of the *Spanish Hero* occurs twice because that vessel discharged part of her cargo at Monte Video and part// at Buenos Ayres and I believe by contraband at both ports.[218] Eight vessels were at different times nearly within the same dates lost near the entrance of the River Plata, the cargoes of which would not have been of less value than £280 or £300,000.

Adding to the above Lists, 3 or 4 American vessels which brought cargoes of dry goods, and allowing for the value of the numerous lots of goods introduced in the vessels trading in Slaves or Colonial produce from Rio de Janeiro & Bahia which values I had no means of ascertaining, I should think that the imports into the River Plata, during the year mentioned did not fall short of Two Millions Sterling, nine tenths at least of which was smuggled in & an equal bulk of return produce smuggled out. The outward duties cannot be exactly estimated but, allowing in favor of the Inward cargoes every deduction which favour could procure of the custom-house officers, had they been regularly entered the whole amount of duties paid to the Government could not have been less than 500,000 [dollars?].

I suppose the average return cargo of the vessels given in the list would be worth £10,000 each at the very least, the duty on which would amount to a considerable sum. It will be seen that the value of// the return still greatly falls short of those imported, to compensate which about 1,500,000 Spanish milled Dollars, such as have been restruck in England, were smuggld on which a duty of two per Cent might very easily have been levied had their exportation been permitted as it cost about that sum or rather more to get them on board without accounting anything for the risk which was very small.

This sum of dollars will not appear large but it must be remembered that great part of the silver of the Upper Provinces of this Viceroyalty finds its way to the Coasts of Peru, of which Viceroyalty those provinces formerly made a part[219] and that remittance were from Buenos Ayres to Spain during

---

218. Alex McKinnon sent his first dispatch to Canning on board *Spanish Hero* on 18 December 1809. See National Archives (Kew) FO 72 107, Alex McKinnon to Canning, Buenos Aires, 4 February 1810.
219. The silver mining regions were attached to the viceroyalty of La Plata in 1776.

the same period of about 2,000,000 Dollars in gold & silver. At this period the demand for tallow which the Russian war created in England was quickly to take off all that was made in the Viceroyalty, but the quantity of hides remaining [in the] Warehouses when I came away was immense, the trade not taking off more than the constant supply, while some hundreds of thousands had accumulated during the War which appears to me to have little chance of ever leaving the place.

The surveyor of the Customs, Commandante del// Resguardo, with his dependants had the largest share of the profits of this contraband. The naval officiers commanding the small vessels of war stationed in the port, the Viceroy & Madam O'Gorman would gladly have deprived him of his influence & profit, but each party had two [too] far involved themselves to venture to inculpate him & it was impossible to manage the business without his permission & intervention. In one instance in which his intervention was notorious, General Liniers and his son Don Luis Liniers[220] were very violent in their abuse of this officer and expressed to me the certainty of his degradation, but the matter soon subsided and was heard no more of.

Towards the middle of 1809 the remittances from Peru were stopt, in consequences of expences incurred to suppress a fermentation which the state of affairs in Spain had given rise to in the Upper Provinces; especially La Paz where they have always manifested a spirit of independence & revolt.[221] The Custom house produced nothing & consequently the troops were unpaid & the officiers in the different departments were some quartiers [sic] without having received their salaries. At the same time the market beginning to fall deprived the speculators of their// hopes of great profits & the land holders were dissatisfied with the little incouragement given to the export of their hides which they fancied would have gone off quicker

220. Luis Liniers was born in Spain in 1783, the son of Santiago Liniers's first marriage to Juana Ursula de Menviel. In 1800 he became an officer in the Real Compañía de Guardias Marinas. On the death of his father he succeeded to the posthumous title as second Conde de la Lealtad and returned to Spain.
221. The rising in La Paz followed Liniers's victory over the Cabildo in Buenos Aires. Between May and October 1809 the region was in the control of Creole revolutionaries led by Pedro Domingo Murillo. The rising was eventually suppressed by Nieto and Goyeneche in October. See Lynch, *Spanish Colonial Administration, 1782–1810*, pp.271–3.

through the regular channel, being too bulky & of too little value to be smuggled when any other produce could be obtained to ship.

The English newspapers continually brought unfavourable accounts of affairs in Spain & the Creoles began to think that the opportunity for asserting their freedom was arrived & and were impatient under farther delay. General Liniers himself was under great alarm at this growing discontent, & even once went so far as to express to me his fears of the effect which the news contained in a London paper which I had in my hand might occasion if it transpired & became generally known in the City. He saw his popularity decline, & his family seemed to be in hourly apprehension that a popular commotion might deprive him of his power, & Mrs O'Gorman & her brothers, who knew the popular feeling with respect to themselves, justly feared the subversion of insubordination. As a palliation the General began to think of opening the port to English trade & by that means obtain a revenue which would enable him to pay the troops & the civil departments & thereby secure their adherence. Mrs O'Gorman even// herself abetted the measure & the more readily as the Commandant of the Resguardo had contrived to appropriate the profits of contraband & leave the unpopularity of it principally with the Government, & indeed at this time Mrs O'Gorman's fears began to get the better of her love of money, I will not call it avarice, as she desired it to spend & not to hoard.

When the General had resolved to open the Port & another week would have seen the enactment probably on liberal terms, every body was surprised by the arrival of the aid de Camp of Don Balthzer Hidalgo de Cisneros[222] to announce the landing of that officer at Monte Video with commission from the Supreme Junta to supersede General Liniers as Viceroy.

During the six months since the commencement of 1809 my progress in the Spanish Language & situation had enabled me to extend my connections so far as to pass my time in a more varied manner than before, & to be in the way of obtaining such information respecting the interior of the Spanish colonies in this part of the World as could be got in Buenos Ayres. I had taken

---

222. Baltasar Hidalgo de Cisneros de la Torre (1758–1829) was a Spanish naval officer who had been present at Trafalgar. He was appointed to succeed Liniers in 1809 but was ousted by the May Revolution in 1810 and returned to Spain.

a house jointly with Mr Robert Staples[223] of Belfast where we were enabled
to entertain our acquaintance in a manner which we// fancied bore some
distant resemblance to English propriety, comfort would be too good a
word to use. I had become acquainted with most men of any estimation
in Buenos Ayres & with the viceroy General Liniers, who frequently
honoured me with invitations to dine at the Fort & several times made me
one in his Sunday parties at a small country house about eighteen miles
south of Buenos Ayres belonging to Mrs O'Gorman, where everything
was greatly inferior to a comfortable English farm house, except the
profusion of the table & nothing bespoke the presence of a Viceroy but
the escort of Dragoons which always attended him. I have always
supposed that my having received no invitations from General Liniers for
a considerable time after my first introduction, arose from his
unwillingness to give umbrage to the old Spanish party by noticing any
stranger; but the heads of that party had since been banished by him, &
were thought of only with contempt, while the part the English
Government was taking in the affairs of Spain & the desire of all the
independant party to obtain the protection of the English navy against the
efforts of the French Government of Spain to retain them in their old
colonial dependence, had caused the English Character to be continually//
on the rise in Buenos Ayres ever since my arrival there.

My friend Lieutenant Stow[224] Commanding H.M.Brig *Steady*[225]
requesting me to accompany him to the fort on matters of business
brought me again under the notice of General Liniers & though the
various discussions between him & the Lieutenant, as the then
representative of the British Government, about the English vessels in the

---

223. Robert Ponsonby Staples was the representative in Buenos Aires of Montgomery, Staples & Co and
Staples, McNeile & Co. He was appointed 'consul on the banks of the River Plate' in March 1811 but
the authorities in Buenos Aires refused to acknowledge him. He returned to Buenos Aires in 1813 and
acted unofficially as Consul until 1819 when he was appointed as Consul in Acapulco. His firm
negotiated a loan for the Mexican government, for which he was dismissed by Canning. He later
entered a business partnership with Kinder but the two fell out over the purchase of land in Mexico
(see Introduction). His commercial reports on the Río de la Plata are to be found in National Archives
(Kew) FO 72 157. See entry in Maxine Hanon, *Diccionario de Británicos en Buenos Aires*, M. Hanon
(Buenos Aires, 2005).
224. Lieutenant Arthur Stowe. Promoted captain in 1812, he died of fever aboard his ship *Tamar* in 1820.
225. HMS *Steady* was a 14–gun brig built in 1804.

river & the interests of British subjects embarked & ashore, came ultimately to be carried on almost wholly by me, & obliged me more than once (particularly respecting the detention of a vessel with English property, through the intrigues of White who wanted to purchase her, although she had entered in conformity to the laws) to remark pretty strongly on the injustice of the conduct of the Government of which the General was the head, he never intermitted his politeness to me afterwards. The character I have already given of him appeared pretty correct on a nearer acquaintance. He was of too easy a temper, careless rather than radically unprincipled or extravagant, affectionate to his family & very easily swayed by those around him. His conversation was fluent and lively.// He was certainly not a little vain, but strange as it may seem after the part he has acted I cannot forbear saying that I did not think him very ambitious. He always placed his comfort in sitting down on his Estate with his family around him, & occasionally to divert himself with his dog & gun & he solicited of the king a grant of a large Island in the Parana as the place of his ultimate retirement.

I happened to be in his Company at the Country house above mentioned some months before the arrival of the New Viceroy, when he received dispatches from Spain informing him of his having been elevated to the rank of Nobility[226] [and] of a pension of 5000 Dollars per Ann. Conferred on himself & 1000 dollars per ann[um] on each of his Children for his good services while he had been Viceroy of Buenos Ayres. This ambiguous expression was not noticed either by himself or any one at table. His vanity seemed highly gratified by the honor conferred upon him, but his feelings were certainly most interested in the pensions given to his Children. After Breakfast under the Viranda when no one was present, but the Commandant of the Guard & myself, he again read the dispatch & inferred from the form of expression that a successor had been appointed – although I// watched him narrowly I could not perceive that it made the smallest impression upon him, on the contrary he seemed to feel the satisfaction he expressed to us at the prospect of his being relieved &

---

226. The title was Conde de Buenos Aires. He was awarded the title Conde de la Lealtad posthumously.

employing himself according to his inclinations. He was certainly not insensible to Glory when opportunities offered themselves of acquiring it, although with risk & temporary fatigue, but he was of too easy a temper. I may say too idle, to form & act up to [any] extensive scheme of ambition.

I also became partially acquainted with Don Cornelio Saavedra the present head of the Government of Buenos Ayres & who acted so conspicuous a part on the first of Jan[uary] 1809. This man appears to me likely to hold a good while the influence he possesses as it is founded on military command & he has prudence to attend to his popularity with his soldiers. His talents are not brilliant, but I only saw one individual at Buenos Ayres whose talents appeared to me to be brilliant & he is a Monk, the Superior of the order of Nuestra Señora de los Mercedes.[227] No Education can be obtained at Buenos Ayres. Saavedra's characteristic is caution. He was brought up to the law & from the practice of his profession has learnt to conceal himself// although naturally somewhat dissipated & addicted to gaming.

The person after most conspicuous is Manuel Perez Belgrano[228] of an Italian family, & quite an Italian in character, cautious, artful & intriguing. He would be more than a match for Saavedra was he a military man & as he has obtained the direction of an expedition to Paraguay, it seems probable he will aim at obtaining military influence.[229]

During my more enlarged intercourse with the better informed resident[s] at Buenos Ayres I found that the spirit of independence had pervaded every order except the merchants natives of Spain & the officers in high Civil Employ. Even the Clergy, with the Exception of the Bishop & two or three of the higher dignieties, were much decided revolutionists. Not a Country Curate in the whole Viceroyalty, but is a warm partisan of independence the ideas of which had even broken into

---

227. Nuestra Señora de los Mercedes (Order of the Blessed Virgin Mary of Mercy) was founded in 1218 for the redemption of Christian captives. The convent of La Merced in Buenos Aires was founded in the sixteenth century with a new church being constructed between 1733 and 1779.
228. Manuel Perez Belgrano (1770–1820) was born in Buenos Aires and became a leader of the Creole independence movement. He was secretary of the Consulado de Comercio de Buenos Aires, which was established in 1794. He took part in the campaign to expel the British, was elected to the Junta in May 1810 and commanded the army of the North in 1812–14 and 1816–19.
229. This expedition, which departed in September 1810, was unsuccessful.

the Sanctuary of the bishop's residence whose chaplain [a] Dominican friar greatly esteemed by all who knew him & holding the important office of chief deligate from the tribunal of inquisition at Lima[230] used very frequently to chat with me & advance Doctrines which any Spaniard would have deemed highly inflamatory & treasonable. The Superior of La Merced whose// character was more energetic used to declaim in a still warmer style & talk of the long continued oppressions of Spanish Government with a brilliancy & force of diction & strong expression of countenance which made me frequently think him better fitted to head an army in behalf of his countrymen, than to pace in front of a band of fat & idle friers. This so general spirit in the Clergy I suppose, may be attributed to their being nearly all creoles & consequently finding themselves excluded from the high dignities of the church, or should any of them hope to arrive at a Bishopric, he is a [sic] certain he would be transplanted to the Caracas, or to the farthest part of Mexico, far enough from having any influence among his own countrymen. Doubtless such [an] individual feels with respect to himself as Irish Catholic mothers do for their sons when according to Pet[er] Plymly[231] each thinks that her own little preeminent Paddy could not fail to be Lord Chancellor if the Test Act[232] did not stand in his way.

   Don Pasqual Ruiz Huidobro should not be passed over in silence. He was Governor of Monte Video when it was taken by Sir Samuel Achmuty & went to England as a prisoner of War. When released// he passed over [to] Gallicia & obtained a Frigate to bring him to the River Plata to reclaim the Government, his term in it not being expired, & he was provided with new powers by the Junta of Gallicia making him in addition Comandant of the Marine. He therefore expected to find himself in possession of a Post of consequence & a revenue of 15 or 16,000 dollars per Ann[um]. But on

---

230. The Holy Office of the Inquisition was established in Lima in 1568 and had jurisdiction over the Río de la Plata settlements.

231. Peter Plymley was the pseudonym of Sydney Smith (1771–1845), Canon of St Paul's. Smith was the founder of the *Edinburgh Review* and in 1807 began to publish a series of satirical letters entitled *A Letter on the Subject of the Catholics to my brother Abraham who lives in the Country* on the subject of Catholic Emancipation. In all nine letters were published by the end of 1808.

232. The Test Act, passed in 1672, required holders of public office to take a religious test to demonstrate they were members of the Church of England.

his arrival General Elio would not give up his government to him nor would General Liniers yield the commanding of Marine. He therefore remained in Buenos Ayres with a very small income, & though an officier of superior gradation in the navy to the Viceroy, he being a Vice Admiral & Liniers Rear Admiral without any other influence than what he derived from the attentions of those who wished thereby occasionally to pique Liniers, Huidobro being thought to have solicited & not unlikely to obtain the succession to the Viceroyalty.[233] He is a very polite man, not ill informed & a very great favourer of all that is English, but withal the greatest mixture of formality & puppyism [sic] that can be conceived of. His uniforms were all [made] in London, he had brought out carriages & furniture in the newest style, his Wig I suppose had come from Rosses & was always dressed & powdered with the utmost// regularity & a Lady of my acquaintance once told him she was sure he slept in his pantaloons that he might not derange their fitting by pulling them on & off. With all his formality, His Excellency had quite good temper enough to bear a jibe of this sort. What would have been the case if the Ladies lap-dog had licked the blacking off his boots I cannot tell. He was however an excellent Parade figure & was very conspicuous at all reviews & especially at the Dinner given by General Liniers on S[aint] Fernando's day[234], as well as that which we had the honor to give on the Birth-day of George the third:[235] those two dinners formed epochs in our residence at Buenos Ayres & the favor with which the English were viewed there may be gathered from what occured there, especially at the last mentioned.

General Liniers invited Lieutenant Stow, & four Englishmen who had [come] most within his notice, of whom I was one & treated us with particular attention. The day being unusually rainy when he quitted his Carriage on returning from Mass he sent it for us & placed us very near him at table. The company was composed of the Military and Naval Officers of highest gradation// & of the heads of the civil departments,

233. He had received the nomination to the post of viceroy from the short-lived Junta of Gallicia.
234. St Fernando III, King of Castile (1201–1252).
235. George III's birthday was 4 June.

making in the whole about fifty who sat down to dinner. When the company was seated a salute was unexpectedly fired, the superannuated Brigadier General of Artillery having forgot what he was about & as priming had only been issued for two salutes when the Viceroy gave the health of George the third after having drank that of Ferdinand 7th he was surprised not to hear the intended salute. But instead of being angry at this mistake, he remedied it by keeping us all standing for a minute or two while priming was procured, during which he amused us by being very jocose upon those who had occasioned the blunder & then made us fill to the same toast again. He kept the whole company in high spirits until they removed to the drawing room, where after a little while we had a ludicrous scene enough, for as he had promoted a pretty free circulation of the bottle, the Spaniards who were little accustomed to drink deep began to be exhilarated which was somewhat heightened by the liqueurs they took after their coffee, so that with the exception of four who sat down to cards nothing would serve the rest but dancing about, a mode of diversion somewhat in contrast with// the general gravity of their appearance Admirals, & Generals, Judges & Financiers in swords & laced Coats & big wigs were all in confusion together. The General finding his own head not exempt from the general confusion had prudence enough left to withdraw himself from a diversion so little Viceregal & go to bed & the company soon after retired, & all were at home by half past 8 or 9 o'clock.

At the English dinner nearly the same party attended except the Viceroy. Though we were even given to understand that he as well as the Bishop would deem it a compliment to be asked, they excused themselves on the score of etiquette which does not permit their dinning out except with each other. Although several of us doubted whether so many officers of high rank would accept a invitation to dine in public with a set of individuals having only a residence in the place by connivance, none but the Viceroy & the Bishop hesitated a moment to accept, & all conducted themselves as desirous to make conspicuous their deep sense of the generous conduct of England towards Spain. Salutes were fired from Lieutenant Stows Brig of signals of Rockets being sent up when the toasts

were given which were so intended to be honoured & those Salutes were//
answered from the Fort by the Viceroys orders. The most distinguished
Spaniards in company vied with each other in giving toasts expressive of
their wishes for the perpetual union of the two nations. At last the company
broke up amidst the shouts of a large mob collected in the court yard &
in the street who seemed to partake of the enthusiasm of those within.

A dinner was likewise given on the same occasion by the English at Monte
Video, and though General Elio felt himself obliged by the preestablished
etiquette of his station to decline dining with the party, he joined the[m] after
dinner & promoted as much as possible the vivacity of the meeting.[236]

On again looking over my journal I perceive I have made some few
omissions & among others have neglected to describe the most useful &
creditable establishment in the City, the Hospital. The Friars of the order
Balermitas & familiarly distinguished by the Epithet Barbones from their
wearing their beards dedicate themselves to this charitable object.[237] They
have two hospitals under their care. The principal consists of one large
ward containing about 150 beds & separate wards for contagious disorders
& for Lunatics the whole arranged & managed with as much// propriety,
cleanliness & attention to the wants of the patients as in any hospital in
Europe. The Friars themselves study medicine & surgery & when required
call in the aid of the best reputed medical men in the city. All the menial
offices of the Hospital are performed by the Friars with the help of a very
few nurses. The expences of the Establishment are supplied from the
Estates in the Vicinity of the City which belong to the Order & by the
contributions of the Charitable. This hospital is the Residencia a point
frequently mentioned in Whitelocke's trial.[238] I have to regret not having

---

236. Kinder had either not heard what went on at that dinner or else thought it better not to mention it.
After the dinner, according to Alex McKinnon, 'some of our countrymen began to quarrel with the
Spaniards. Some blows were exchanged. They took the sword from one officer and dragged him down
stairs.' The following day the rowdy British were made to apologise and the incident was officially
forgotten. National Archives (Kew) FO 72 90, Alex McKinnon to Canning, Montevideo 11 June 1809.

237. This is the order of Bethlehemites or Betlemitas (the full name being Orden de los Hermanos de
Nuestra Señora de Bethlehem), founded by Pedro de Betancourt in 1656 which received papal
approval in 1687. The order was dedicated to care of the sick, feeding the poor and teaching children.

238. The wounded from Beresford's army were treated at the hospital of the Residencia. This building was
a major target during Whitelocke's assault on the city and was taken by the British early in the day
with almost no loss.

procured the acquaintance of some individuals of this order, having been informed that many of them had applied themselves to the study of Languages & more than usual at Buenos Ayres to general Literature. To preserve the humility of poverty they occasionally resorted to begging, but the brothers of the orders sent out for that purpose always refused money offered at any houses they applied to & would only fill their wallets with such bread and meat as was offered them.

From time to time troops of Indians belonging to the tribes inhabiting the plains to the South & South West of Buenos Ayres[239] come into the city to// receive the gratifications of a few hundreds of Dollars which the government occasionally distributes among them to preserve them in good humour, & to supply themselves with spurs, bridle bits, Iron Pots, Copper, tools, beads & coarse woollen cloth. In return they bring tiger skins, nutria skins, hare skins, & those of the sorellio or skunk which are beautifully striped in alternate bands of dark brown & white & likewise some few trifles of their own manufacture, as bridle reins [and] lassoos which they pla[i]t with great neatness of strips of dryed hide.

The people with whom they carry on this barter, have provided themselves with premises in the South quarter of the Town, containing each a large yard for the houses, surrounded by an open shed for the Indians & their merchandise. They always bring with them three or four horses each, & sometimes very good horses may be bought of them although generally they are in very miserable condition. I remarked that they never brought with them any women, but such as seemed to [be of] the family of the chief who was generally the tallest & best looking man of the party. The persons & manners of American Indians have been so often described that I shall only observe that I saw among those who entered// Buenos Ayres during my stay some of the most athletic figures I have ever seen & several who must have been 3 or 4 inches above six feet high. [And] here I must recur to the opinion I formerly gave respecting the practicality of employing Indians as domestics having myself hired

239. The following have been recorded as indigenous populations of the Buenos Aires region: Atacama, Avá Guaraní, Diaguita-Calchaquí, Huarpe, Kolla, Mapuche, Rankulche, Toba, Tupí Guaraní, Comechingon.

one (who had been before in the employ of a worthy Italian in whose house I lodged for sometime) to take care of my horses, for which he was singularly adapted, being so strong & so perfect a horseman that he subjected the wildest horses with as little apparent difficulty as if he had had to do with sheep. He was exceedingly civil & attentive & though at first a very slovenly groom, he soon improved. He was from the Missions of Paraguay[240] & though only about 5 [foot] 9 Inches high had an immense breadth of chest & a more muscular figure than I ever remember to have seen except in Indians.

In the Carnival of 1809, Bull fights were exhibited & were afterwards frequently repeated. I went twice to see this brutal amusement. The Bull is first attacked by men called Bandaleros from the weapon they carry which is a dart encircled with a garland of paper-work of various colours much resembling what we sometimes see hanging from the ceiling in a country// Inn to attract the flies. In the midst of this are concealed a multitude of crackers so contrived that they begin to explode as soon as the barbe of the dart is fixed in the loose skin of the Bull's neck an operation requiring no great degree of activity or courage as the men generally take their opportunity when the Bull is close to the retiring places in the sides of the arena. Next comes the Picador who is on horseback armed with a long lance & his business is to assail the Bull with his lance the butt end resting against his shoulders. This must be done when the Bull & the horse are both in motion on nearly parallel lines the horse being some feet in advance on the Bull's left side when the point of the lance entering just before his right shoulder his own efforts to overtake the horse only increase the smart & consequently he draws off. If however the aim is not taken with great exactness & the horse put into a gallop the moment the Bull is wounded, horse & rider are probably overturned & whether so or not, the horse is sure to be gored in the belly & killed. I shall not be further particular, for a sight of this sort once so disgusted me that amidst the plaudits & [ ] of about three thousand people among [whom]

---

240. The area of the former Jesuit missions (*reducciones*), which had been closed in 1767, was known as Misiones. The Indians of that region were Guaraní.

were the Viceroy & Vice Queen Cisneros & all the fashion of the Place, I was obliged to prevent myself from sickness & fainting to get out of sight of it,// & support myself against the back of the Box I was in. The station of the Picadors is not a little exposed on such occasions more especially as his Boots are made so strong with a view of guarding his legs should the Bull by accident surprise his horse standing at right angles with him, that he can scarce run in them. In Spain when the encouragement is great, plenty are found to run this risk but at Buenos Ayres, the only Picador was a ruffian, who was in prison when the Town was retaken from General Beresford and would certainly have been executed the next day for (as report says) his seventh murder.

The next combatant is Matador or Killer. He is on foot armed with a rapier & has in his left hand a scarlet cloak which he holds before him when the Bull prepares to gore & stepping a little to the right stabs the animal before the near shoulder to the heart. If he misses his aim, his sword probably breaks against the Bull's shoulder & he runs eminent risk of being killed himself. I never saw a Bull killed in this way on the Theatre, there being no Matador during the early exhibitions when I went.

I once saw a Bull saddled & rode in the Theatre. A very wild one was chosen & was immediately noosed// by the Lassoo men & thrown down & his legs tied. The saddle was then put on but it was girthed so very tight & the bull was so incommoded by a strong girth which passed from the front of the saddle over his shoulders & by several straps or cruppers which passed under his tail that he had not perfect freedom of motion. The man mounted as the Bull still lay on the ground and its legs were then set at liberty, but it did not rise until strincilated with the spur when it gave two or three pretty active capers across the Theatre & some perpendicular leaps which must have shook the rider a good [deal], but he held on by straps before & behind the saddle when necessary & on the whole I think I have often been more exposed to the risk of falling from horseback than this rider was. The Bull when it found its efforts unavailing again lay down when the rider dismounted & killed [it] with his knife.

The Buffoon of the Theatre is a Paraguay Indian who occupies a small vault immediately in the center of the Theatre from which he issues by a hole just large enough to admit him & attacks the Bull behind with a stick or a prod & disappears again on its turning about & puts his head out from time to time making all sorts of grimaces. Eight or nine// Bulls are slaughtered at each exhibition & when there is no Matador, the Lassoo men come into the Theatre on horse-back & take them out & kill them outside.

The country in the Vicinity of Buenos Ayres is singularly flat and unpicturesque. It is built on the very nearest spot to the mouth of the river which could be found on its right bank, at all fit for building upon. Immediately on quitting the town to go to the Rio Chialo [Chuelo] which falls into the Plata about two miles below Buenos Ayres you descend an abrupt bank of about 30 feet in perpendicular height from the top of which you perceive an immense level bounded only by the horizon so little above the surface of the River that it is impossible to avoid thinking it has formerly been under water. A very great part of it is marshy as to be scarcely passable in Winter, & offered very great obstacles to the Armies of Beresford & Whitelocke which approached the Town in that direction.[241] Leaving the Town to proceed up the River you have a little more variety. The same bank on which the City is built continues to afford airy situations for country houses built on its summit. It has an agreeable elevation above the River between which & the bank runs a slip of low ground covered with a lively verdure & diversified// by groups of willows & poplars.

The houses are generally very mean, & when considered residencies of the first families of an opulent city & most have no garden or only a kitchen garden ill laid out bounded by the mean hedges. The same appearance continues along the coast for & about four leagues where the Punta de los Olives, a very salient point of land affords a good view of the City, & the shipping at another in the outer & inner Roads. One league beyond the Punta is San Isidro,[242] a very shabby village where many families who have not estates on the coast between it & Buenos Ayres resort in the

---

241. Beresford crossed the Chuelo by sending seamen under fire to seize boats. Whitelocke's army found a ford upstream of the bridge which was being defended in depth by Liniers.
242. A town which today forms a residential suburb of Buenos Aires.

Summer & for the variety of a country life submit to be cooped up in miserable tenements in which they are obliged to sleep three or four in a room in the hottest weather. They contrive to sleep out as much of their time as possible, & the elderly people play at cards perpetually, the young amusing themselves frequently in the evening with dancing. At San Isidro the Islands which divide into numerous branches the whole of the course of the Parana till it receives the Uruguay & forms with it the noble expanse of water called the River Plata begun to be visible hardly rising above the level of the River by which they are frequently inundated. They are covered with wood of// small growth, some few palms rearing their heads over the rest & breaking the uniformity of the outline.

Two leagues beyond San Isidro you again descend to low marshy ground where the little river de las Conchas[243] joins the great stream. Here is a very singular village built in the midst of the trees each house separate from the rest although the ground is divided into plots resembling quadras which are always isolated at high water & the communication must then be kept up by canoes with which each house is provided. I went many times to San Isidro & to Las Conchas to enjoy the diversion of shooting, which can no where be had to better advantage. The species of wild Ducks which line the edge of the River Plata, & swarm in the marshes near it are innumerable, & there are likewise many sorts of Geese, some Swans, Herons Snipes & Plovers. The river is so shallow that I have frequently been walking in it in quest of game, near a mile from the edge on a bottom of fine even sand. One well acquainted with ornithology would find great diversion here & would see many species of aquatic birds which have not yet been very accurately described. I do not think the botanist would be equally successful. There is very little variety in the vegetation here & the mineralogist would be quite [out] of his element, as I never saw a stone on the bank of the River Plata// that had not been brought from a distance.

Having now quitted the City it may be well to make mention of the arrangements for travelling in the interior. There are regular post stations

---

243. Las Conchas was the place where Liniers together with the force he had organised in Montevideo landed on 3 August 1806 before his attack on Buenos Aires.

to Peru, to Chili, & to Paraguay. There are generally only mud huts where a change of horses is to be had at half a rial a league each horse if for the saddle & 1 rial if for draught. It is necessary to be provided with a pass from the Post Office at Buenos Ayres on which your destination is stated & you pay a duty on extracting it equal to one third of the whole amount your postage will come to. It is necessary to have an attendant used to the road who will so order your stages as to bring you at night to places where bread & some small conveniences may be obtained. The post goes once a fortnight to Lima, & Potosi & to Asumpcion & Paraguay, & to Santeigo de Chili.[244]

To give an example of the speed with which they travel, the Chili postman reaches Mendoza[245] a distance of 900 miles in eight days after he leaves Buenos Ayres. He has then to cross the Andes which takes two or three days more. There are two instances of couriers having gone to Lima with astonishing speed, one in 29 the other in 32 days, a computed distance of 1100 leagues, 400 only of which is level ground, the rest exceedingly mountainous.

I shall here give a statement which I obtained from one of the Ministers of the Royal Review [Revenue?] of the amount of it in ordinary years, & of the Expences of the Government.// These statements can only refer to what took place before the viceroyalty of General Liniers as the events that brought him under into power greatly affected both the receipts & the expenditure, & was it practicable, it would be of no use to furnish data applicable only to a time of unusual emergency [and] of extreme maladministration in all matters of finance.

244. Santiago.
245. Mendoza, the main town in the west of Argentina, dates back to 1561.

	Dollars	Reales
To amount of receipts from all sources	4.029.125	5
Expences		
Finance Department	1.145.687	3
War D[ep]t	2.055.084	7
Ecclesiastical D[ep]t	256.999	5
Political D[ep]t	335.121	2
	3.748.893	1
Balance remittable to Spain	280.232	4

The principal sources of revenue are the tribute of the Indians, the Custom House duties, the Tithes duty. The chief expences are the salaries of a most numerous establishment of officers, civil, financial, ecclesiastical, military & naval.

The following is a list of the various military corps subsisting during my residence at Buenos Ayres. They were mostly raised after// Beresfords capture & before the arrival of Whitelocke.[246]

		Men	Commander
Patricios	Creole Corps	1550	Saavedra
Arribenos	D° of the Upper Provinces	500	O Campo
Gallegos		600	Carveña
Miniones	Catalonian	400	Olaquer
Cazadores	Light Infantry	500	Rivadavia
Huzares		150	Nunez
D°		200	Puridon
D°		150	Vives
D°		150	Castes
Dragones	Dragoons	400	Quintana
Pardos	Blacks & Mulattoes	1200	
Grenadiers of Liniers		400	Terrada
Artillery of the Union		600	Llache

---

246. The military establishment from which Kinder's information is derived is given in Appendix A.

Royal Artillery		200	Pizarro
Biscaynos		600	Rezaval
Andaluses		600	Murelo
Montañeses	from Santander	300	Garcia
Carabineiros de Carlos 4		300	Fernandez
Infantry of the Line		200	Merlo
Blandengues[247] Irregular Cavalry		600	Quintana
Indian Artillery		300	Sanchez
		9550	

//The sudden arrival of the new Viceroy could not but produce the greatest sensation. Everybody supposed the French at the gates of Cadiz or perhaps in possession of it, & the flight of the Central Junta from Seville being known, nobody imagined they could have leisure to send a frigate & a Viceroy to a distant colony. The contents of the dispatch, at the reading of which I was present, had not transpired except as far as related to the pension & honors conferred on General Liniers & the nomination of some Officers to posts in the interior, and General Liniers himself seems to have thought very little of the ambiguous notice he had received after he had laid the papers aside. At the same time as the Aid de Camp announced this General's arrival, we learned by post that the inhabitants of Monte Video & especially the Governor had received him with acclamations, notwithstanding that when he landed he had shewn very evident marks of disconfidence in them & want of boldness by the trepidation with which he made his first steps on the pier. As both General Liniers & Governor Elio had dispatched vessels to Spain, each to justify himself & to criminate the other, the people of Monte Video hailed the coming of the new viceroy as a certain sight [sign?] of the triumph of the Governor. Those of Buenos Ayres on the other hand were greatly incensed when// they heard that General Elio was to be removed from his Government of Monte Video, in order to be promoted to the employ of

---

247. The Cuerpo de Blandengues de la Frontera de Buenos Aires was established in 1780 as a frontier force aimed at protection against Indians. A similar force was established in Montevideo in 1794.

Inspector General of the Troops of the Viceroyalty & the procedure of the New Viceroy did not tend to conciliate them.

Instead of proceeding directly to Buenos Ayres, he first sent a very harsh order to all the naval officers who had removed from Monte Vidio to Buenos Ayres by order of General Liniers at the commencement of the disobedience of General Elio, to return by way of Colonia instantly & he himself proceeded to that place having first thrown into it a strong detachment from the Garrison of Monte Video. At the same time he sent General Nieto[248] the new named governor of Monte Video, as governor ad Interim to Buenos Ayres. In addition to all this he gave pretty strong proofs that, although the colonies had been declared integral parts of the Spanish Empire, it was not the intention of those who had named him to depart any more on that account from the old Spanish mode of Governing them for, being waited upon by a deputation of English in Monte Vidio to enquire on what footing their commercial affairs would be placed, he answered that no innovations having been made in the Laws of the Indies he must confine himself to them.//

The consternation was general. The trades people expected the port to be shut & the military, well knowing how jealous the Spaniards have ever been of arms in the hands of the Creoles, expected to be disbanded. The Commanders of the several Corps held frequent counsels & Saavedra & others strongly urged General Liniers to continue at their head & not to obey a requisition he had received from his successor to pass over to Colonia. The suspition which this order produced in him certainly helped to make him waver, but he had lately seen his popularity on the decline, he knew that Frenchmen were generally hated at Buenos Ayres, & he feared that, should the English Government side with Spain, he should not be able to hold up against the first feelings of discontent which a blockade or the threat of an invasion might create in the people. He knew

248. General Vicente Nieto (1769–1810), a Spanish officer who came to Río de la Plata in 1801 holding various offices including controller of the tobacco monopoly and governor of Potosí. He fought under Liniers against the British, returned to Spain where he took part in the rising against the French and returned with viceroy Cisneros. He was sent to suppress the uprising in Chuquisaca in 1809 and was made president of the Audiencia of Charcas and Intendant of La Plata. Defeated by forces from Buenos Aires he was taken prisoner and shot on 15 December 1810.

too that he had contracted some merit in the eyes of Bonaparte from whom he had received the cross of the Legion of Honour & expected, should he be sent to Spain, he would be able to shew that the conduct he had pursued was the most likely to retain the Colony in dependence on Spain & perhaps he might be commissioned at some future period to regain & Govern it for Joseph. I seem to be justified in this suspicion by his subsequent// conduct in raising a party in Cordova against the independant Junta of Buenos Ayres, for I cannot think he really believed that Spain would escape French tyranny; & in case it should, the line of conduct he chose to pursue was the only one that could place him well with the Spanish Government.

Whatever were his motions [motives?] he shrunk from the daring & brilliant part offered him to act & no one else being found who possessed resolution & influence enough to head the independant party, they determined on submission, & in two or three days after General Liniers & the civil Officers had passed over to Colonia to tender their submissions to the new Viceroy, he proceeded to Buenos Ayres, purposely leaving Liniers at Colonia & made his public entry with manifest uneasiness in his deportment & without receiving any determination of public favour. He went first to the Cathedral, during which the remains of the only regiment of the Line stationary at Buenos Ayres which General Liniers, who prefered Creole Troops with officers of his own promoting, had suffered to be reduced gradually to about 200 men, were seen to cross the Square to take possession of the Post which the Granadiers of Liniers yeilded up to them. General Liniers did not return from Colonia for some days, & his arrival was purposely kept a secret but it quickly transpired & he was met on his landing by a// crowd who conducted him triumphantly to a house he had hired near a Fort & several of the military Commanders hastily drew out their corps to do him honor.

Cisneros proceeded with very great caution. He took no measure whatsoever to send the English Ships from the anchorage, but he removed the administration of the Customs & sent the Commandant of the Resguardo to Monte Video, his proper station, naming others in their places whom he could better depend upon, & the dread which he inspired occasioned such vigilance in search of contraband that it became next to impossible to succeed in it. To prevent it was not his object, as he was gaining greatly by seizures. After observing narrowly the temper of the military, he ventured to disband three of the Corps of Hussars & the Light Infantry of Rivadavia, & restored their arms to three Corps which had been deprived of them by Liniers in consequence of the affairs of the 1st of January, viz the Catalonians, Galicians, & Biscayans. This occasioned many murmurs & greatly alarmed the Creoles, but not being resisted he next intimated his intention of putting General Elio in possession of his office of Inspector General. A remonstrance made by all the Commandants in a body extorted from him a promise that this appointment should not take place & he then became embarrassed how to dispose// of General Nieto, as Elio would not vacate his Government without receiving the Inspectorship. A Rebellion in the interior in which the President of Charcas[249] was deposed & put in prison removed this difficulty by enabling him to give Nieto the command of the expedition sent against the insurgents, together with the Presidency of Charcas.

During the whole of this time Cisneros demonstrated the greatest jealousy & dislike of the English, & actually caused an account to be taken of all the strangers resident at Buenos Ayres & commensed by ordering away some Portuguese. His own necessities however compelled him to furnish the greater part of us with just grounds for remaining in Buenos Ayres for he had early begun to be distrest by the very low state of the public treasury& was at last instigated by the numerous representations he received from the Creole Landholders & others to take into consideration the opening of the port. This measure was strongly opposed by the Spanish merchants, but he told them that he must have a loan of 120,000 dollars monthly or be compelled to do it. They canvassed for names to fill up this loan but could not succeed, so that Cisneros after having two or three times prolonged the term he granted them to determine upon it, at

---

249. Ramón García de León y Pizarro (1730–1815), appointed President of the Audiencia of Charcas and Intendant of La Plata in 1796. In May 1809 he was deposed by the Audiencia and held prisoner until freed by Goyeneche in November.

last assembled a council composed of the members of the Royal audience[250]//, of the Finance department, & of some of the Military commanders & two representatives of the Landed Interest, to whose deliberation he submitted the measure.

Their sittings were opened with an address from the Viceroy which was certainly intended to serve likewise as an apology to his principals, the Merchants of Cadiz, for having ventured to think of a measure so contrary to their desires. He commences by stating that when he entered on the Government the approaching ruin of the State appeared to render useless any efforts he might make to remedy the bad state of affairs. That security depended entirely on the treasury which it was impossible to supply by the usual courses; that it was already deep in debt & its credit exhausted; that the state of Peru precluded the hope of remittances thence; that the troops without which he could not answer for the internal quiet of the state, were unpaid, & for the same reason he could not exact of the Public Officers a punctual execution of their duty. You cannot have, it proceeded, a better measure of the difficulties that surround me, than to see me enter upon a provision which is opponent to the Laws prohibitory of foreign commerce, a blind obedience to which I wish should be the particular distinction of my Government.[251] Another argument is drawn from the impossibility of preventing contraband &, after enlarging greatly on the numerous distresses of the Government, the address// concludes with recommending to the consideration of the councils a list of regulations for the admission of Foreign commerce, which were adopted with very slight alterations, observing that at the same time the residence of strangers should be more than ever guarded against & only permitted as far as was absolutely necessary for the dispatch of the business of each of them.

I [was] promised a copy of this curious document which was very well written & one of the most lamentable state papers ever written from one of the members of the council.[252] The regulations as adopted were very unfavourable & in abstract as follows

---

250. Real Audiencia y Chancillería was the highest court in the Spanish judicial system. The judges of the Audiencia also had executive functions. The Audiencia of Buenos Aires was established in 1783.

251. This appears to be a paraphrase of part of the speech.

252. These new trade regulations were announced on 6 November 1809.

1. Permission to enter to be solicited by Spanish Consignees
2. Manifest of Cargo to be presented within 24 hours of ships arrival
3. Ships papers to be deposited in the Secretary of Governments Office
4. Ship subject to usual formalities of the Port
5. Duties to be paid at 15 days, 1 month, 2 months & 3 months in 4 parts.
6. Oil. Wine. Vinegar Brandy not to be admitted
7. The duties to be those called del Circulo in 33 ½ per Cent to be levied by tariff, or by European prices the tariff was defective
8. No Consignee to retail for his Consigner
9. Hides to pay about 40 per Cent one 1 dollar valuation each Ox & 3 rials each Horse hide//
10. These articles pay 20% on the following valuations & the municipal duties

    Tallow - 5$ - *quintal²⁵³ - 100 Hs*
    Sheeps Wool - *12 reals - arroba²⁵⁴ - 25 Hs*
    Vicuna - *Dº - 6 per pound*
    Horse hair - *2$ - arroba*
    Nutria skins - *6 reals dozen*
    Swan & Chinchilla skins - *20 reals dozen*
    Bark - *4. - Lb*
    Copper - *12$ - quintal*
    Tin - *18$ - Dº*
    Horns - *7$ - 1000*
    &C &C &C
11. Wheat. Barley. Vegetables & Fruits *2 % export duty on market prices*
12. Gold & Silver prohibited. *Ships in ballast to come for returns*

No demands springing from illicit transactions to be admitted in any of the tribunals.

This last enactment, though in principal just, was the more remarkable as it is an innovation on the Laws of Spain by which the tribunal del

253. A Spanish quintal is 100 lbs or 46 kilos.
254. An arroba is 25 lbs or 11.5 kilos.

Consulado[255] is appointed to take cognisance rather in the manner of umpire or arbitrator than judge of all commercial disputes & is always silent as to any breaches of the// [law] which may be disclosed in its sittings. The above resolutions dated Nov[ember] 6 1809 were carried into effect in a manner which gave the English another strong proof of the Viceroy's desire to treat them with no appearance of favour. A copy of the resolutions was merely sent to the Director of the Customs for his Government, & they were not printed or published.

Thereupon I caused a meeting to be called to consider of the conduct the English merchants ought to pursue, & represented the danger to which their interests would be exposed should they warehouse their cargoes on the faith of an enactment to the performance of which the government had in no manner pledged itself to us. I was desired to require of the Director of the Customs an official notification of it as deputy for the whole body, & the meeting adjourned till the following morning. I went & was informed that as an Englishman I could not be supplied with what I wanted, but must apply through a Spanish Consignee.

Having stated this at the meeting it was determined to request Lieutenant Ramsay of the *Misletoe*[256] to ask of the Viceroy a communication of the terms upon which British property was expected to be confided to the good faith of the Government. The Viceroy said// that he had no powers to enter into an official communication with Lieutenant Ramsay, but out of his high respect for the character of any British Officer he would communicate to him the regulations, as to an acquaintance between man & man, but not officially. I rejoined by Ramsays directions that if he received the regulations from the hands of his Excellency, he should consider them as sufficiently official for his purposes, which was simply to transmit them to Government, that they might take such measures as seemed good thereon.

In this manner the Port was at length opened, and the market which had begun to be unprofitable soon became ruinous. Affairs continued in a pretty even tenor till the month of March 1810 when I left the River Plate, the old

255. The Consulado de Comercio de Buenos Aires was established in 1794. Manuel Belgrano was its secretary.
256. *Misletoe* was a Royal Navy schooner (8 guns) built in Bermuda in 1808. In 1811 Lieutenant Robert Ramsay, commanding *Misletoe*, broke the blockade of Buenos Aires by Spanish royalist ships.

Spaniards discontented at the opening of the Port which destroyed their profitable monopoly, & the Creoles anxiously hoping for news of the Political death of Spain, which might render the liberation certain.

General Liniers whose presence in Buenos Ayres gave umbrage to his successor was directed to proceed to Spain where it is expected Ex Governors should present themselves to answer any charges which may// be presented against them, or to retire into the interior, Mendoza being appointed for his residence. He preferred the latter expedient, but instead of going to Mendoza, went to Cordova which had been expressly prohibited to him. He was favourably received by the Governor of that place[257] & by the people with whom he made himself very popular & after some stay he purchased on credit a large tract of ground in the vicinity which had formerly been in the hands of the Jesuits. His pension was never punctually remitted to him & he suffered considerable inconvenience for want of money.

Shortly after I quitted Buenos Ayres the certainty of the occupation of Seville by the French & the investment of Cadiz[258] gave spirits to the Creoles, whose dread of Cisneros's talents had decreased as they saw more of him, to assert their independence. Of this circumstance I have very minute details from an intelligent Englishman who remained on the spot – Mr Alexander Greaves.[259] It took place in a very orderly & deliberate manner. The Commanders of the military corps intimated to the Cabildo or municipality that they would support them in demanding the resignation of the Viceroy's powers into their hands while the people should have// time to elect a Junta of Government. The viceroy temporised, on which the Cabildo assembled a meeting of near six

257. Juan Gutiérrez de la Concha (1760–1810) was a military officer who came to the fore during the British invasions of Río de la Plata. In 1806 he led a corps of volunteers against Beresford and was then made commander of the Real Cuerpo de Marina (Marineros). In 1807 he commanded the troops defending the Plaza de Toros where he was cut off and forced to surrender. Appointed Intendant of Córdoba, he attempted to organise royalist opposition to the Buenos Aires junta with Santiago de Liniers. Troops were sent against them and they were executed on 26 August 1810.

258. The Central Junta, faced with insurrection in Seville, abandoned the city on 23 January and formally dissolved itself on 29 January. Before its formal dissolution the Junta appointed a Regency and summoned a Cortes to meet in Cádiz. The siege of Cádiz began on 5 February 1810.

259. The letter at the end of this narrative is presumably the letter of Alexander Greaves on which Kinder based his account. Greaves arrived in the Río de la Plata in 1807. In 1810 he was a member of the committee of British merchants that voted to censure commodore Elliot for upholding the blockade of Buenos Aires. He was one of those who subscribed to the creation of a national library in Buenos Aires in 1810. He returned to England in 1813.

hundred of the principal people of Buenos Ayres, who gave their written votes for the transmission of the Government into the hands of the Cabildo until the Cabildo should elect a Junta of Government to subsist, till a general congress of deputies from all the Provinces of the viceroyalty should meet. Only sixty Spaniards dissented from this measure. Notwithstanding this the Cabildo (who were mostly Spaniards) who had rather been urged to act this revolutionary part by the pressure of the current of popular opinion than by their own inclinations, when they had received from the viceroys hands his staff of office, proceeded to name a Junta of which they appointed him president, continuing to him his salary & honors. A tumultuous meeting of the people let them know their error & they named another Junta entirely to the satisfaction of every Creole, of which Saavedra is president & Commander of the Forces & the other members are known as old adherents to the cause of independence & have the reputation of talents.//

The new Junta began by inviting the provinces in the interior to join in a league with them &, learning that a party was forming against them at Cordova by General Liniers & the governor, they sent a force into the interior in aid of the numerous partisans they knew favoured them there. Cisneros & some others of the Audience having shewn a disposition to excite a revolt, they immediately were shipped off for Spain in a cutter chartered by the Junta for that purpose. The force sent into the interior being successful in dispersing the party of Liniers which separated with the mere rumour of opposition, the Junta then first disgraced themselves by an act of ingratitude & of most unnecessary severity. Notwithstanding that Saavedra & some others of the members had lived on terms of intimacy with General Liniers, (Larrea[260] had experienced his mercy, being implicated in the revolt of January 1 1809 & in consequence then entirely in Liniers's power) & they could not consider him as [any] longer dangerous to them, they caused him// & Conchas the governor of

---

260. Juan Larrea (1782–1847) was a Spaniard and a merchant. He presided over the *Asamblea del Año XIII*, which took the first steps to abolish slavery and ended the Inquisition, the use of torture and titles of nobility.

Cordova[261], & two other persons of note to be shot. Many were disgusted by such unexpected violence, but their Government has since prospered & except the opposition of Monte Video (which city contrived when the last advices came away to uphold the old form of government & to incommode the trade of Buenos Ayres as much as its means permitted) everything has gone as well as they could wish. The Cities of the interior have joined the league & only three members of those necessary to complete the proposed congress are absent. Chili has followed the example, & as soon as the troops which are on the confines of Peru shall make any demonstration in favour of the independants there, that extensive & rich country will probably be revolutionised. Want of funds must soon reduce the Monte Vidians to submission, as the union of the interior provinces causes the produce of the mines of Potosi & La Paz to go to Buenos Ayres.

I shall conclude, subjoining Copies of the documents from which I took the summary of Revenue & Expences stated in a former page.[262]//

Virreynato de Buenos Ayres	Valores
Diezmos y Cobos	338.097.5
3% del oro	20.293.3
Venta y composicion de tierras	3.088.2
Tributos	681.216.3
Almoxarifazgo	132.452.6
Alcabalas	509.152
Extraccion para el comercio de Negros	37.822.7
Cambio de Frutos con Colonias Extrangeras	1.155.1
Derechos de entrada y Salida en España	137.608.1
Impuesto sobre el Aguardente	6.046.5
Novenos Reales	59.524.3

261. Juan Gutiérrez de la Concha.
262. The same table, this time in translation, is included in Robert Staples' report to Lord Castlereagh in 1812. National Archives FO 72 157, 22 June 1812, Robert Staples to Castlereagh.

Quarta capitular de diezmos de Paraguay	5.881.5
Producto de Azogues de Guancavelico	36.375.4
Producto de Papel Sellado	22.712.5
Producto de Cruzada	26.291.3
Imbalidos	31.799.5
Lanzas y medias annatas	10.255.7
Oficios vendibles y renunciables	9.387
Alcances de cuentas	7.013.3
Almacenage	9.738.6
Composiccion de pulperias	26.454.5
Comisos	33.071.2
Portazgo	2.459.6
Derecho de Guias	4.900.1
Producto de la Casa de Moneda	329.325.
Producto del Banco de Rescates	47.373.7
Real Hacienda en comun	73.400.1
Producto de Azogues de Europa	212.313.6
Producto de Naypes	28.476.7
Vacantes Mayores	60.110.4
Vacantes Minors	37.749.5
Mesadas Eclesiasticas	3.696.3
Sisa	151.785.6
Municipal de Guerra	116.231.5
Donativo para la Guerre	463.1
Producto de Bulas de Indulto	7.372.7
Subsidio Eclesiastico	7.500.7
15% sobre manos muertas	6.140.7
Contribucion sobre herencias transversals	502.7
Temporalidades	37.480.7
Renta de Tabacos	419.165.7
Total de Real Hacienda	3.697.549.1

Ramos Agenos

Media Annata Eclesiastica	12.660.7	
Monte pio military	21.922.1	
Monte pio ministros	12.991.4	
Monte Pio Cirujanos	499.7	
Expolios	8.729.4	
Penas de Camara	2214	10.943.4
Redempcion de Cautivos	719.1	
Hospital de Buenos Ayres	7.694.3	
5% de sinodos p^a curas de Mojos		
y Chiquitos	3.916	
3% de seminario	3.890.5	
Censos de Indios	8.143	
Bienes de Defuntos	5.082.7	
Depositos	243.104.5 = 331.576.4	
	Total 4.029.125.5	

Clases de Gastos

Estado de Real Hacienda

Sueldos de Ministros y Empleados	
en el Tribunal de Cuentas	41.114.1
Idem- Caxas reales	75.308.7
Idem - Adm^r de Alcabalas e Resguardos	100.015.1
Id -Subalternos de la Junta superior	850.1
Id - Ministros Jubilados	8.671.4
Id - y Gastos de Cruzada	6.002.3
Id - y Id de Bulas de Indulto	2.902.1
Id- y Id de Tabacos	246.354
Id- y Id de Naypes	26.5
Id- y Id de Temporalidades	10.489.5
Id - y Id de Casa de Moneda	115.480.1
Id - y Id de Banco de Rescates	46.429
Penciones	11.648.1

Entrega de la Tesoreria del
Monte Pio de Ministros 11.380.3
Gastos de Matriculares de Indios 7.166.6
Idem Ordinarios 138.815.1
Idem Extraordinarios 17.118
Redito de Principales a Censo 21.663.1
Devolucciones de Real Hacienda.
Bienes de Defuntos y Depositos 254.933
Aplicado por R^{les} O^{brs} de unos a otros ramos 15.055.1
Sueldos de Mineralogia y Botanice 10.264.1
1.145.607.3

Estado de Guerra
Sueldos de Virrey y Plana Mayor 69.438
Id - Secretaria del Virreynato 10.920.3
Id - Tropa veterana 630.117.1
Id - Oficiales dispersos 2.325
Id - Milicias y sus Asembleas 381.391.3
Id - Invalidos y Retirados 99.163.3
Id - y Gastos de la Marina 384.513.4
Penciones de Viudas y Huerfanas 10.773.1
Hospitales y Medicinas 42.106.3
Gastos de Artilleria y Sala de Armas 22.380.1
Id – Prisioneros Ingleses 1.463.6
Id – Ordinarios 156.491.6
Id – Extraordinarios 200.000.1
2.011.084.7

Estado Eclesiastico
Sinodos de Curas 170.605
Fomento de Nuevas Misiones 22.181.1
Canonigos de Paraguay 9.103.5
Seminario Conciliar 4.389.1

Fiestas dotadas	600
Mercedes Piedosas	27.666
Hospital de Buenos Ayres	8.053.1
Penciones	14.401.5
	256.999.5

Estado Politico

Sueldos de Reales Audiencias	83.421.3
Id – de Presidente de Charcas,	
Governadores y Intendentes	58.166
Id – de Asesores	10.599.5
Id – de Ministros Jubilados	6.797.1
Id – Proto medico	5.480
Premio a los Subdelegados	25.817.1
Manutencio de Prisioneros	10.442.3
Asignacion alimenticia a popladores Europeos	22.575.3
Auxilios a communidades de Indios	7.151.1
Penciones	2.905
Gastos de Secretarias	4.290.3
Id – Establicim^{to} de Rio Negro y	
Punto Deseado	30.058.2
Id – Islas Malvinas	26.307.6
Id – Ordinarios	32.723.5
Id – Extraordinarios	3.445.1
Sueldos a Ministros transeantes	5.000
	335.121.2

Resuinca

Estado de Real Hacienda	1.145.607.3
Estado de Guerra	2.011.084.7
Estado Eclesiastico	256.999.5
Estado Politico	335.121.2
	3.748.893.1

Comparacion

Entrada	4.029.125.5
Salida	3.740.893.1
Remisible a la metropole	280.232.4

Buenos Ayres[263]

25th May 1810

So few opportunities of sending letters to Rio de Janeiro have offered since you left, that since the departure of Mr Wylie, I have looked in vain for means of continuing the correspondence which your letter from Monte Vidio laid the foundation of. I should have written to you by that Gentleman but the notice which I had of his being about to proceed to Rio was so short, that it did not give me sufficient time to do so. This unavoidable delay, however unsatisfactory in some respects it may have been to both of us, will I think have served to make this commencement of my Epistolary communications to you, more interesting than it otherwise probably could have been, as the protraction of it till now has brought it to a period which has given birth to events that it will be highly gratifying to you to hear of.//

Within these few days the People of this Capital have laid the corner stone of the temple of South American Independence, in a manner that in my opinion, does them the greatest credit. The origin, or more immediate beginning, of this important event, with the actual consequences of it, I will now relate to you & all those circumstances that have attended it, to which I myself have been a witness. On the 14th of the present month, the *Misletoe* Schooner arrived from Rio de Janeiro, and brought us Intelligence of the entrance of the French into Andalusia, of their subsequent occupation of Seville, and of their preparations to attack Cadiz. We learnt at the same time that the People of Seville had, prior to the entrance of the

---

263. The author of this letter appears to be Alexander Greaves, who is referred to by Kinder as his informant.

French there, declared the Central Junta traitors; had arrested several of its Members, and had elected a Junta upon the plan of the former Provincial Junta of that Capital. This news as you may suppose spread immediately through the Town, and caused a very great sensation among all ranks of people. The// two following days passed however in perfect tranquillity and without any indications on the part of the Americans, of an intention to make any changes in the then existing government, although they were making the most active exertions in secret, to unite all the persons of their own class in one grand, and combined plan for their security, and of that of the interior, in the event of the total loss of Spain. On the third day, which was Friday, fresh intelligence was received by the post from Monte Vidio, & from Spain itself, [and] completely confirmed all the accounts given in the English Newspapers, of the disasterous state of the Patriotic Cause. The ferment among the people now rose much higher and it soon became evident, that they had come to a determination to remove the old Authorities. The Viceroy, unable to conceal the truth from the people, had in the mean time, published in part the news he had received, but without giving it in full, and adding to his paper, a note in which he declared that he did not pretend to warrant the truth of the accounts which, as he said, he had thought it proper// to make known for the information of the people. These however were just as well informed on the subject as himself, and did not suffer themselves to be lulled into security by the frivolous means which were employed to quiet them. On Friday evening and Saturday, the Americans in numerous Assemblies, and in the Coffee Houses, began to talk in a tone, and with a freedom, respecting the present state of affairs, and the steps it was proper to take, in consequence of the late events in Spain, which made it evident, that they were all agreed with regard to the plan of conduct to be adopted, and that they were confident of their means of carrying it into effect.

By this time it appears that all the corps after some trifling disputes, had come to the resolution of supporting the Cabildo in a demand which it was agreed upon, should be made by them, of the viceroy, to resign his powers into their hands, until the people should elect a Junta of Government.

While the business remained unsettled, Pedro Andres Grania, whom you may remember to be a famous Intriguer, and who it was said was brought over to the cause of the Carlota[264], pretended to make a shew of a determination// to support the Viceroy in the possession of his authority. Soon finding that in this he would be left alone, he presently changed his plan, and came over to the strongest party.

Things being thus arranged, Dr Leyra[265], the Syndico Procurador[266] of the city, was deputed on the Saturday, to wait on the Viceroy and to inform him that the People required him to resign his staff of Office into the hands of the Cabildo. This at first the viceroy opposed, desiring to be permitted to consult the Audiencia on the subject, and intimating that it was necessary for them to take the opinion of the other viceroys and Governors of the Provinces, before he [Dr Leyra] could consent to any delay of this nature in a matter which required such prompt determination, and [he] gave the Viceroy to understand that the People were resolved on the point, and therefore nothing but evil could result from his opposition to it. On this the Viceroy consented to the measure, and requested Dr Leyra to draw him up a Proclamation conformable to the spirit he had just stated. This Dr // Leyra did, and brought the Proclamation to the Viceroy, who immediately shewed it to the Oidas[267], who prevailed on him to alter it, and to insert in it some observations very little agreeing with what the people required. When the proclamation was published, the alterations were immediately discovered and the people became so irritated by this double dealing of the viceroy, that they immediately determined to oblige him to submit to their plan.

With these sentiments the Commanders of Corps accompanied by some of the persons who had been most active in the business presented themselves to the viceroy on the Sunday Evening, and required of him to

264. Infanta Carlotta Joaquina, wife of the Prince Regent of Portugal Dom João who was trying to claim the regency in America on behalf of her brother Ferdinand VII.
265. This is Julián de Leyva (1749–1818). A lawyer and supporter of Martín de Álzaga, he had been involved in the failed coup of 1 January 1809. He devised the plan for Cisneros to be president of the Junta. Exiled to Catamarca after the revolution, he was elected deputy for Córdoba in 1812.
266. The Síndico or Procurador General was chosen annually to represent the 'needs and grievance of the community before the Cabildo'. See Lynch, *Spanish Colonial Administration*, p.308.
267. Oidores, judges of the Audiencia.

give up his authority to the Cabildo. This he consented to do on the morrow and in this state the affair remained till then. This same night the viceroy held another consultation, as I understand, with the Fiscals[268] and I have also been told, with Dr Juan Vargas[269], by whom he was persuaded to oppose the delivery of his authority on the ensuing morning. Accordingly on the Monday he alledged the propriety of his first consulting with the provinces of the// Viceroyalty, before he resigned his command in the way required of him. The leaders of the people seeing this, determined to bring the viceroy to submit, and at the same time to prevent any violence or disorder in the doing of it.

They therefore directed the Cabildo to give notice to the Viceroy that it was their wish, as the representatives of the people, to hold a meeting of the inhabitants to consider what was to be done in the present state of affairs. To this communication the Viceroy answered in terms of acquiescence and the Cabildo immediately invited by note about five or six hundred[270], as I have been informed, of the principal inhabitants of the place to meet on the Tuesday the 22nd at 9 o'clock in the morning. At the time appointed, the persons invited assembled together, forming a numerous meeting, of how many I do not know, consisting of all orders of respectable persons. The Bishop, Deputies of the Convents, Deputies for the secular Clergy, Lawyers, Military, Merchants, Landholders, assisted, as did also Huidobro and the Oidores as citizens.

When the object of the meeting was publically declared, some debating took place as to the propriety, or necessity of it. The Bishop gave it as his opinion that the Meeting was premature as the whole of Spain was not yet subjugated by the // enemy, and with the view to sustain the Viceroy's authority, asserted that as long as one individual of the Central Junta remained that in him was concentrated all the authority of that body, and that consequently the Viceroy, whose power was conferred by them, ought legally to have the same existence as that authority so situated.

---

270. The actual number was 450, of whom 200 did not attend.
268. Fiscales were prosecuting attorneys attached to the Audiencia.
269. Juan Jacinto de Vargas was private secretary to Cisneros and undertook a secret mission to Montevideo to get support for the viceroy.

This monstrous opinion was instantly, & successfully combated by Dr Casteli[271], who shewed in a clear and impressive manner that it was a fact not to be doubted that the Central Junta had been overthrown by the people of Seville, who had put many of it members in arrest, as traitors, and that the remainder had constituted a Regency of five persons, to whom they had pretended to delegate the authority confided in them by the Nation.

The non-existance of the Central Junta being thus shewn by their own confession, and act, Casteli proved that even in the height of their power, they were without any right, or faculty, to make over that authority which the nation had conferred upon them, to any other person, or body of persons whatever, and that therefore their doing so at all, and more particularly under circumstances which had brought upon them the accusation of treason, so far from being a legal act, was a positive offence against the people. He thus shewed the Regency, so called, to have no founded claim whatever to the obedience of the people, and that they being now both without// a Monarch, and without any representative of him, were themselves the depositories of his rights & authorities, & was perfectly at liberty to confer them on whomsoever they would in trust for him, as it was clear that the powers vested in the subaltern members of the former government must themselves have expired with the power which conferred them. The fiscal, Villota[272] followed and pretended to lament that a City that had given so many distinguished proofs of its loyalty, should at last tarnish all its former glories, by thus attempting to overturn its legitimate authorities.

This Gentleman was answered by an advocate of the name of Pasos[273], a Man of acknowledged probity, and ability, who shewed that the people

---

271. Juan José Castelli (1764–1812) was born in Buenos Aires and was first cousin of Manuel Belgrano. He was a lawyer and founder member of the Sociedad Patriótica Literaria y Económica. In 1806 tried to persuade Beresford to declare Río de la Plata independent. He defended James Paroissien at his trial and led the Cabildo in demanding the resignation of the viceroy on 25 May 1810. His speech to the *Cabildo Abierto* 'dará sólida estrutura juridical al movimento emancipador'. He was principally responsible for the execution of Santiago de Liniers and his associates in Córdoba.

272. Manuel Genaro de Villota (b. 1787 in Spain). At the *Cabildo Abierto* he argued that an assembly in the capital could not speak for the whole country. Sent back to Spain with Cisneros, he was subsequently appointed to the Audiencia of Lima.

273. Juan José Paso (1758–1833) was a professor of philosophy, sent to negotiate with Elío in 1811. He was a member of the First Triumvirate and the Second Triumvirate between 1811 and 1814. He participated in the *Asamblea del año XIII* and went to Chile to try to persuade the Chileans to join the Union.

of Buenos Ayres were perfectly justified in what they did, and that the present steps which they were taking were not those of a violent interruption on their part of the established order of Government, but merely entered upon in the legal assumption, and exercise of their natural rights which, circumstances that they had not the slightest control over, had given them the priviledge to exert actively, in that way which they might judge most for their interest.

As no one attempted to oppose the patriotic orators, the assembly proceeded to the Business for which they were met, which they were then// informed by the Cabildo was to consider and decide upon these two propositions: whether owing to the actual situation of the Spanish monarchy the Viceroy should be required to resign his authority, and if so into whose hands it should be committed. After some discussion it was determined that these questions should be decided by the majority of votes, each person giving his note [vote?] in writing with his signature affixed, and that so given in to the Cabildo, their Notary, should read it aloud to the whole assembly: This point settled they proceeded to the voting, which occupied them till twelve o'clock the same night.

On the following day the proceedings were examined by the Cabildo, when it appeared that the Bishop and almost all the Europeans to the number of something more than sixty, had voted for the continuance of the Viceroy in his situation as such, some with two associates, and some with four consisting of members, either of the Audiencia, or the Cabildo, or of some of the most respectable of the inhabitants. It appeared on the contrary, that the whole remainder of the assembly, which made a very large majority, consisting principally of Americans, had voted that the viceroy should most absolutely resign all his power and authority// into the hands of the Cabildo, in whom it should be vested until this body, under the instruction of the people, should appoint a Junta of Government in which was to reside the supreme authority of the district of Buenos Ayres, to be exercised by them, in the name and for the benefit of Ferdinand the 7th until a Congress or general meeting of deputies from the whole of the Provinces of Spanish America, should as far as those chose to concur in the measure, have assembled together, and have determined what form of Government it was most for the interest of the whole body to adopt.

Among these last were Huidobro and a few old Spaniards. When this result of the voting was made public, it excited a great sensation of satisfaction and joy among the Americans, and produced quite the contrary effect on the European Americans. The Cabildo thus invested by the assembly with the authority to require of the viceroy the resignation of his command into their hands, published a notice to those who had given their votes the preceding day, to assemble again at 3 o'clock on that Evening, to sign again their respective votes, which were to be by that// time extended in a register to serve as a memorial of the present, as well as a foundation of all their future proceedings.

At 3 o'clock the assembly met at the Sala Capitular, according to appointment, and the Cabildo by deputation, went to the Fort and received the Viceroy's resignation, and his staff of Office, and returned to their Hall, invested with the power, and received with the honors of the Captain General of the district.

With these proceedings the day closed and the Cabildo made known by public proclamation the resignation of the viceroy, and their actual possession, as their representatives, of the supreme authority. During all these proceedings the utmost order and tranquillity was maintained throughout the City; not a single act of violence that I have heard of was committed, nor even an insult offered by an American to an European. The only instance of a contrary conduct on the part of the people, that I am acquainted with, was in the case of the Vargas. This man was considered, and I believe with great reason, to have been the // cause of the opposition of the viceroy to the wishes of the people, and he is even said to have advised him to take measures of extreme rigour, and severity against their leaders. Irritated at this, some high spirited, and audacious young men, laid a plan to seize him, and to inflict a whipping on him as a person who had presumed to give advice in matters which he did not understand. The leaders however who had made it a principle to avoid by every means possible, disorder and riot, & who were determined that as far as they could have influence, no European should in the slightest manner be insulted, resolved to defeat this project, which they did by sending some persons to Vargas, to inform him that if he did not leave the Town within a certain time that he would be arrested. This unfortunate Ahitophel[274] did not want this counsel to be repeated. He took immediate advantage of it, & made his retreat, and thus saved himself from the school boy discipline which had been prepared for him. It is said that in company with several marine officers he passed over to Monte Video, where he is likely to meet with no better reception than here, as the spirit of freedom is not less general in that town than// in this.

The Europeans dissatisfied with the preponderance which their American Bretheren were about to take in the government of these countries, and vexed that their endeavours to maintain the viceroy in power, had failed, made another effort to regain their lost ascendancy. On the night of the evening in which he resigned, & on the following morning, they employed their influence with the Cabildo so successfully, that they prevailed upon them to form the Junta of government immediately, and to place the viceroy at the head of it. This accordingly was done on the day of the 24th so suddenly that the people had no notice of it whatever, until it was made public, & that they were told that the Junta was to consist of five persons, viz. the late viceroy, President, & Saavedra, Casteli, one Dr Sola[275] a Clergyman & one Inchauregui a Merchant member.[276] That the affair might be finished without delay, and not to give the people time to think, a proclamation was issued in the evening, informing the people what had been done. In this proclamation however they put the finishing stroke to that act of folly which they had already committed in bringing in the viceroy contrary to the wishes of the people, as in it they still// styled him viceroy, and continued to him his salary, his privileges, his immunities, & viceregal distinctions as such, so that in fact what they had done, was

---

274. Ahitophel was a counsellor of King David and deserted him to support the rebellion of Absalom. When Absalom's rebellion failed he committed suicide.
275. Juan Nepomuceno Solá (1751–1819), a priest born in Buenos Aires.
276. José Santos de Incháurregui, a merchant born in Spain, took part in the *Cabildo Abierto* on 14 August 1806 which made Liniers commandant. He supported the move on 22 May to make Cisneros head of the Junta.

neither more nor less than following the opinion, & vote of the Europeans, who were the minority, that the Viceroy should be continued in his situation, with two or four associates.

When the people heard the proclamation they were in the highest degree irritated, and more especially when they learnt, that the late Viceroy had expressed himself highly discontented, that the command of the arms was not to be committed to him, as this according to the new arrangements, was to be given to Saavedra. In consequence of this, the ferment among the people, and troops became general & arose to a most alarming height, and resolution was taken among them not to accept of the government appointed by the Cabildo.

On the morning of the 25th accordingly, a considerable number of people assembled in the great square & demanded to speak with the Cabildo. On this summons a deputation of that body came to the balcony, and enquired what it was the people// required. Those below answered, that in the name of the people they came to inform them that the body in general were highly dissatisfied with what had [been] done. That the nomination of the late Viceroy to the Presidency was against their inclination, and against what had been determined in the general assembly of the 22nd and that therefore they were resolved that the whole government should be formed anew. The Cabildo who were by this time made sensible of the folly, to say no worse, of their conduct, & who were now informed that the sentiment of the armed force, and of the great body of the people were the same as those expressed by those in the square, expressed their willingness to conform to what was required of them, and immediately informed the late Viceroy that he could not act as President for the reasons which had been communicated to them.

Immediately after this another Junta was formed, & announced by proclamation to the people who admitted it// with every sign of satisfaction and confidence. This Junta consists of Dr Cornelio Saavedra President & Commander of the forces. Dr Casteli, Colonel Ascueraga[277], Rev[erend] Dr

---

277. Miguel de Azcuénaga (1754–1833), son of one of the richest merchants of Buenos Aires and connected by marriage with Gaspar de Santa Coloma and the Basavilabaso family. As a soldier he took part in the conquest of Sacramento in 1777. He was a supporter of Moreno in the *Cabildo Abierto*. Briefly exiled in 1811, he became governor of Buenos Aires and head of the new Republic in 1818.

Alberti[278], Dr Manuel Belgrano, Dr Larrea & Dr Mathew[279]. These two last are Catalonians, men of respectability and information.

The Secretaries are Dr Mareano Mareno[280] & Dr Pasos, both Advocates. The whole affair may now be considered as arranged, for although the Europeans are highly dissatisfied w[ith] it, yet they are conscious that they are too weak of themselves to make any successful opposition to it. What has been most remarkable in the whole of this important change of government, has been the tranquillity which has been maintained by those who have brought it about, and the nobleness and generosity of spirit with which they have conducted// themselves throughout. The Europeans conscious of the many motives, which they have given their American bretheren to complain of them, conscious of their own evil intentions with regard to those over whom they have so long usurped an unlawful ascendancy, & fearful that the opposition which they had discovered on the day of the assembly to the wishes of the Americans, an opposition evidently arising not from any consideration of duty, but from motives of rivalry and party spirit, might have irritated the minds of those who had now gaind the ascendancy, they have lived in inquietude and alarm, throughout the time that this affair has been in agitation. The event has however proved that their fears were only the effect of the over bad designs & the suspicions which these raised up in their minds, for not one single individual among them, has suffered either in his person, or property in the slightest degree.//

On the part of Americans, nothing is heard but expressions of the most earnest desires that the Europeans would look upon them as brothers, and would unite sincerely with them in the general good. This conduct on the part of the natives is the more commendable, as they have the whole of the force in their hands, and as they have not wanted provocations in the

278. Manuel Alberti (1763–1811), born in Buenos Aires and a supporter of Moreno.
279. Domingo Matheu (1765–1831), born in Spain, was involved in the plot of 1 January 1809 but avoided arrest. As a Spaniard, he was excluded from the new government and was put in charge of the production of armaments.
280. Mariano Moreno (1778–1811). A supporter of Martín de Álzaga, he was involved in the failed coup of 1 January 1809 and became first secretary of the Junta formed on 25 May 1810. One of those responsible for the execution of Liniers, he died on a diplomatic mission to Britain.

conduct of the Europeans, to make them feel in their turn the vexations which they have so long made the Americans to suffer.

The views of these people, you will know, are directed farther than they at present choose openly to shew; as in their present arrangement they profess to consider, and have regard to both the immediate & remote interests of Ferdinand, & his successors. With respect to this point therefore I will not extend my remarks as you are just as well acquainted with the subject as myself.

Appendix A

Estado del ejército de la Capital en Octubre de 1806

Real Cuerpo de marina	J.Gutierrez de la Concha	482
Real Cuerpo de artilleria	José Maria Pizarro	219
Fijo de Buenos Aires	José Piris	167
Dragones de Buenos Aires	Florencio Nuñez	196
Blandengues de Buenos Aires	Estévan Hernandez	147
Blandengues de Montevideo	Benito Chain	118

ARTILLERIA

Milicias Provinciales	José Maria Pizarro	100
Union	Gerardo Esteves	395
Indios, Morenos y pardos	Francisco Agustini	426
Maestranza	Rivera Indarte	221

INFANTERIA

Granaderos	Juan Florencio Terrada	107
Legion Patricia	Cornelio de Saavedra	1359
Asturianos y vizcainos	Prudencio Murguiondo	446
Cazadores correantinos	N. Murguiondo	84
Montañeses	José de la Oyuela	231
Gallegos	Pedro Antonio Cerviño	510
Andaluces	José Merelo	431
Catalanes	José Olaguer Reynal	583
Arribeños	Pio de Gama	435
Indios, morenos y pardos	José Ramon Baudriz	352

CABALLERIA

1er Escuadron de Húsares	Juan Martín Pueyrredon	203
2er Escuadron de Húsares	Lucas Vivas	186
3er Escuadron de Húsares	Pedro Ramon Nuñez	181
Cazadores	Luis Fernandez	219
Migueletes	Alejos Castex	193
Carabineros de Carlos IV	Benito Rivadavia	190
Escuadron de labradores	Antonio Luciano Ballesteros	332
Escolta del General		71

RESUMEN

Marina	482	
Artilleria		
Veterana	219	
Milicia	1142	1361
Infanteria		
Veterana	167	
Milicia	4538	4705
Caballeria		
Veterana	461	
Milicia	1575	2036
Total:	8584 plazas	

Source: Ignacio Núñez, *Noticias Históricas de la República Argentina* (Buenos Aires, 1857)

Appendix B

British Library Add Mss 40538

Thomas Kinder to Sir Robert Peel
1 Regent Place East, Regent Square
5 January 1844

Sir,

I had the honour to address you a letter on 21 January 1843 to state to you that my complaints made to Her Majesty's Secretary of State for Foreign Affairs of wrong done me by the authorities of Mexico had been disregarded and to request for reasons then set forth that you would be pleased to bring forward some measure which may provide that the cases of those who have to complain of wrong done them in foreign parts may be fairly and openly investigated by a Committee of Her Majesty's Privy Council or by some other competent judicial authority.

You did me the honor to reply by your note dated 24th January in which you express your confidence that if any just complaint was preferred to the Foreign Office and the case was one which properly admitted of the interference of the Secretary of State it would not be disregarded by the Earl of Aberdeen.

While such confidence on your part, Sir, is highly honourable to the Earl of Aberdeen I am sure you will be ready to admit that it is very desirable that those whose interests depend on the good pleasure of the noble Earl should participate in it. For my own part I lament my inability (which I had then already been made conscious of) to partake therein. Nevertheless I renewed my applications for protection out of respect for your opinion and I have abstained from again bringing the subject before you, from unwillingness to encroach upon your time. But if I don't greatly err, not only is my case, when considered in its operation upon the fortunes of many others, and in the consequences to which the neglect of it has given rise, one of considerable importance, but the general question it involves concerning the expediency of affording to those who suffer wrong in foreign countries a better means of obtaining redress than that which the usual arrangements of the Foreign Office furnish, is of a nature that you may well deem worthy of your attentive consideration. And surely if the confidence you are pleased to express in the administration of that department by the Earl of Aberdeen be well founded the opportunity to make the desired alteration may be deemed favourable, as it may be considered that such alterations should be motived rather by the general expediency of circumstances than by the defective administration of any Minister.

A letter from Viscount Canning dated December 8th 1841 had already at the date of your above mentioned note made known to me the determinations of the Earl of Aberdeen upon my case in terms that left no room for any confidence in their justice or prudence. My renewed applications since the period have confirmed the impression already made upon my mind. It may perhaps be urged that I am not a fit judge in my own case. But nothing has hitherto occurred in my intercourse with the rest of the world, to lead me to infer that it has pleased Providence to deprive me of the use of reason and to cause me to confound the principles of justice and fair dealing in matters requiring merely the use of common sense, being of a plain and easily intelligible nature.

If this is not the case, there is little room for me to fear that I may be in the wrong when I assert that my case is one which properly admits of the interference of the Secretary of State and that though it may not have been disregarded by the Earl of Aberdeen, who has bestowed much attention upon it, it is evident enough that his Lordship's attention has been given to discover plausible arguments by which to gloss over his refusal to interfere, unjustly arbitrarily and partially and without exhibiting any substantial grounds for such refusal, by which I mean any such grounds as can satisfy the minds of men of plain sense and just feeling that he is justified in what he has done.

Allow me to apologise for this expression of my opinion. Unless convinced that the conduct of that department to which I have had occasion to apply for redress [has] been unjust and partial, I should be very wrong to take up the time of the Premier with my complaints. Could my claims have been fairly and openly agreed before any judicial authority capable of deciding upon them upon proper evidence, you, Sir, would have been spared the trouble of this correspondence. But as in despotick governments, access to the Sovereign is often regarded as the only means of obtaining redress of grievances, so as relates to the Foreign Office, the proceedings of which partake of the manner of the most arbitrary rule, it is natural when those proceedings are characterised by more than usual want of candour and equity that recourse should be had to such other quarter as may be most likely to afford attention and procure redress.

But though I do not hesitate thus to express my opinion on a line of conduct which inflicts upon me and upon many other persons great loss and detriments I cannot desire that you, Sir, should adopt those opinions without investigation. In order to enable you to make it, I take the liberty to send herewith copies of my correspondence with the Foreign Office since the commencement of your administration. I have at your service should you desire to have them also copies of my correspondence with Mr Pakenham and Viscount Palmerston but I am unwilling to trouble you with them now, conceiving that what I now send is sufficient to show that I have good cause to complain and have been very unjustly and partially treated.

Confident that you will not approve of the conduct observed towards me I think it proper that you should have the opportunity of becoming acquainted with many circumstances relating to it, of which it appears probable that you are either wholly without knowledge or not accurately informed. When the conduct of an affair gives rise to the finding of a true bill of indictment against an Ambassador and to the interference of a judge to impede the due course of justice in a matter in which that very interference gives palpable testimony of his knowledge of the cogent pressure of the charges brought forward, it can hardly be thought that the circumstances are not worthy the attention of the head of Her Majesty's Government. I have thought it my duty, Sir, to submit them to you. If I am wrong I pray you to excuse the mistake.

Bibliography

Manuscript

National Archives (Kew)

WO 1 162 Sir Samuel Auchmuty to Viceroy or persons professing the supreme authority, Monte Video, 26 February 1807

FO 72 90 Alex McKinnon to Canning, Montevideo, 11 June 1809

FO 72 90 Alex McKinnon to Canning, Buenos Aires, 2 November 1809

FO 72 107 Alex McKinnon to Canning, Buenos Aires, 4 February 1810

FO 72 157 Robert Staples to Castlereagh, 22 June 1812

E 192 5 Robert Staples to General Wavell 10 March 1827; Holdsworth to Kinder 23 June 1826; Kinder to Holdsworth 6 September 1826

British Library

L/MAR/B 141 P Journal of the *Northumberland*

L/MAR/B/141 GG (1) Ledger of *Northumberland*

L/MAR/B/141 GG (2) Receipt book of *Northumberland*

Add Mss 40538 Peel Papers, Thomas Kinder to Sir Robert Peel, 1 Regent Place East, Regent Square, 5 January 1844

Add Mss 40585 f.329 Peel Papers, Thomas Kinder to Sir Robert Peel, 1 Clifton Place, 24 February 1846

Hertfordshire Archives and Local Studies (HALS)

Register of baptisms at St Peter's church St Albans DP 93/1/1–5

University College London

Brougham Papers 44,938 Fanny Kinder to Lord Brougham, St Johns Mews Fulham, 6 February 1833

Brougham Papers 45,923 Thomas Kinder to Lord Brougham, Mexico, 10 June 1833

Brougham Papers 30,655 Thomas Kinder to Lord Brougham, Mexico, 1 October 1834

Brougham Papers 30,656 Observations on Mexico, 22 November 1834

Brougham Papers 4,257 Thomas Kinder to Lord Brougham, Royal Institution, 5 July 1841

Newspapers

Bristol Mercury 12 February 1842

Caledonian Mercury 28 December 1826

Jackson's Oxford Journal 6 March 1802

Morning Chronicle 29 April 1819; 24 May 1819

The Examiner 26 August 1838

The Times 19 December 1821; 22 December 1823; 15 November 1828; 19 November 1828; 2 July and 3 July 1844

Proclamations and Broadsheets

Por Guillermo Carr Beresford, Mayor General, Comandante de las fuerzas de S. M. Britanica, empleadas en la Costa Oriental de la America del Sur, Gobernador de Buenos-Ayres, y todas sus Dependencias. Dated Buenos Aires 19 July 1806

Circular que el Excmo Senor Virey dirigio el 17 de Agosto de este ano a todos los Gobernadores y Xefes de las Provincias, baxo el titulo de reservada. Buenos Aires, 1808

El Excmo Senor/virey de Buenos-Ayres a sus habitantes (1809). List of shipping entering and leaving the ports of the Río de la Plata

Printed Books and Articles

Álzaga, Enrique Williams, *Fuga del General Beresford,* Emece Editores (Buenos Aires, 1965)

Almazan, Bernardo Lozier, *Beresford Gobernador de Buenos Aires,* Galerna (Buenos Aires, 1994)

Amyot, Thomas ed., *Speeches in Parliament of the Right Honourable William Windham to which is prefixed some account of his life,* 3 vols, Longman, Hurst, Rees, Orme and Brown (London, 1812)

Anon, *A Historical Sketch of the Island of Madeira* (London, 1819)

Anon, *An Inquiry into Plans, Progress and Policy of the American Mining Companies,* Murray (London, 1825)

Anon, *Notes on the viceroyalty of La Plata, in South America; with a sketch of the manners and character of the inhabitants, collected during a residence in the city of Monte Video, by a Gentleman recently returned from it,* Stockdale (London, 1808)

Anon, *La Reconquista de Buenos Ayres. Rasgo Encomiastico.* Real Imprenta de los Niños Expósitos (Buenos Ayres, 1806)

Anon, *A Summary Account of the viceroyalty of Buenos-Ayres or, La Plata including its geographical position, climate, aspect of the country natural productions, commerce, government, and State of society and Manners. Extracted from the best authorities.*
R. Dutton (London, 1806)

[Auchmuty, Sir Samuel], *A Narrative of the Operations of a small British Force under the command of Brigadier-General Sir Samuel Auchmuty, employed in the Reduction of Monte Video on the River Plate A.D. 1807,* Written by a "Field Officer on the Staff in South America." Stockdale (London, 1807)

Barrow, John, *A Voyage to Cochinchina in the Years 1792 and 1793*, Cadell and Davies (London, 1806)

Carrera, José Maria Bueno, *La Defensa del Río de la Plata*, Almena (Madrid, 2000)

Cooney, Jerry W., 'Oceanic commerce and Platine Merchants, 1796–1806: the Challenge of War', *The Americas*, 45, 4 (1989) pp.509–524

Costa, Ernestina, *English Invasion of the River Plate*, Kraft (Buenos Aires, 1937)

Cotton, Sir Evan, *East Indiamen*, Blatchworth Press (London, 1949)

Cussans John Edwin, *History of Hertfordshire*, 3 vols., Chatto and Windus (London, 1870–1881), reprinted E.P. Publishing (East Ardsley, 1972)

Cutolo, Vicente Osvaldo ed., *Nuevo Diccionario Biografico Argentino*, Elche (Buenos Aires, 1975)

Dawson, Frank Griffith, *The First Latin American Debt Crisis*, Yale UP (New Haven and London 1990)

English, Henry, *A General Guide to the Companies formed for working Foreign Mines*, Boosey and Sons (London, 1825) pp.93–4

Estala, Pedro de, *Quatro cartas de un Español a un Anglomano en que se manifesta la perfidia del gobierno de la Inglaterra, como pernicioso al genero humano, potencias Europeas, y particularmente á la España*, Buenos Ayres, Real Imprenta de Niños Expósitos, 1807

Fairburn, John, *An authentic and interesting description of the city of Buenos Ayres and the adjacent country; situate on the River Plate on the East Side of South America shewing the Manners, Customs, Produce, and Commerce, of that most important and invaluable Country; including, an account of the Capture of Buenos Ayres, July 2 1806. The whole compiled from the most recent and authentic information and unquestionable authority.* (London, 1806)

Ferns, H.S., 'Britain's Informal Empire in Argentina, 1806–1914', *Past and Present,* 4 (1953) pp. 60–75

Ferns, H.S., *Britain and Argentina in the nineteenth century,* Clarendon Press (Oxford, 1960)

Fletcher, Ian, *The Waters of Oblivion,* Spellmount (Stroud, 2006)

Foster, J., *Alumni Oxoniensis 1715–1886,* 4 vols., Parker (Oxford, 1888)

Francis, John, *The Bank of England. Its times and traditions,* Bankers Magazine (New York, 1862)

Goebel, Dorothy Burne, 'British Trade to the Spanish Colonies, 1796–1823', *The American Historical Review,* 43, 2 (1938) pp.288–320

Grainger, John D., *The Royal Navy in the River Plate 1806–1807,* Scolar Press for the Navy Records Society (Aldershot, 1996)

Gregory, D., 'British Occupations of Madeira during the Wars against Napoleon', *Journal of the Society of Army Research,* 66 (1988) pp.80–96

Guenther, Louise, *British Merchants in nineteenth century Brazil,* Centre for Brazilian Studies (Oxford, 2004)

Halperin-Donghi, Tulio, 'Revolutionary Militarization in Buenos Aires 1806–1815', *Past and Present,* 40 (1968) pp.84–17

Halperin-Donghi, Tulio, *Politics, Economics and Society in Argentina in the Revolutionary period,* Cambridge University Press (Cambridge, 1975)

Hanon, Maxine, *Diccionario de Británicos en Buenos Aires,* M. Hanon (Buenos Aires, 2005)

Heaton, Herbert, 'A Merchant Adventurer in Brazil 1808–1818', *Journal of Economic History,* 6, 1 (1946) pp.1–23

Humphreys, R.A., *British Consular Reports on the Trade and Politics of Latin America 1824–1826,* Camden Third Series vol 63, Royal Historical Society (London, 1940)

Humphreys, R.A., *Liberation in South America 1806–1827. The Career of James Paroissien,* Athlone Press (London, 1952)

Humphreys, R.A. & John Lynch eds., *The Origins of the Latin American Revolutions 1808–1826,* Knopf (New York, 1965)

Luccock, John, *Notes on Rio de Janeiro and the southern parts of Brazil; taken during a residence of ten years in that country, from 1808 to 1818,* Samuel Leigh (London,1820)

Lynch, John, *Spanish Colonial Administration, 1782–1810,* Greenwood (New York, 1958)

Mathew, W.M., 'Anglo-Peruvian Commercial and Financial Relations 1820–1865' unpublished PhD (University of London, 1964)

Mathew, W.M., 'The First Anglo-Peruvian Debt and its Settlement', *Journal of Latin American Studies*, 2, 1 (1970) pp.81–98

Newitt, Malyn and Martin Robson eds., *Lord Beresford and British Intervention in Portugal 1807–1820*, ICS (Lisbon, 2004)

Núñez, Ignacio, *Noticias Históricas de la República Argentina* (Buenos Aires, 1857)

Platt, D.C.M., *Latin America and British Trade, 1806–1914*, A&C Black (London, 1972)

Randall, Robert, *Real del Monte: A British Mining Venture in Mexico*, Institute of Latin American Studies and University of Texas Press (Austin and London, 1972)

Robertson, W.S., 'The Juntas of 1808 and the Spanish Colonies', *English Historical Review*, 21, (1916) pp.573–585

Robson, Martin, 'British Intervention in Portugal, 1793–1808', *Historical Research*, 76 (2003) pp.93–107

Rock, David, *Argentina 1516–1982*, University of California Press (Berkeley, 1985)

Rodrigues, Paulo Miguel, *A política e as questões militares na Madeira no período das guerras Napoleónicas*, Centro de Estudos de História do Atlântico (Funchal, 1999)

Socolow, Susan Migden, *The Merchants of Buenos Aires 1778–1810*, Cambridge University Press (Cambridge, 1978)

Socolow, Susan Migden, *The Bureaucrats of Buenos Aires, 1769–1810: Amor al Real Servicio*, Duke University Press (Durham and London, 1987)

Strangford, Lord, *Poems, from the Portuguese of Luís* de Camões, *with remarks on his life and writings*, J. Carpenter (London, 1803)

Street, J., 'Lord Strangford and the Río de la Plata, 1808–1815', *The Hispanic American Historical Review*, 33, 4 (1953) pp.477–510

Szuchman, Mark and Jonathan Brown eds., *Revolution and Restoration. The Rearrangement of Power in Argentina, 1776–1860*, University of Nebraska Press (Lincoln and London, 1994)

Tenenbaum, Barbara, 'Merchants, Money and Mischief', *The Americas*, 35, 5, (1979) pp.317–339

Terragno, Rodolfo H., *Maitland & San Martín*, Universidad Nacional de Quilmes, (Buenos Aires, 1998)

Webster, Charles K., *Britain and the Independence of Latin America 1812–1830: select documents from the Foreign Office Archives*, 2 vols., Oxford University Press (Oxford, 1938)

Whitelocke, John, *Buenos Ayres. Truth and Reason versus Calumny and Folly: in which the leading circumstances of General Whitelocke's conduct in South America are explained*, D.N.Shury (London, 1807)

Whitaker, Allan, *Brewers in Hertfordshire*, University of Hertfordshire Press (Hatfield, 2006) pp.22–4

Index